Experiences of Community Care

EXPERIENCES

OF

COMMUNITY CARE

BRUCE LYNCH AND RICHARD PERRY

LONGMAN

Published by Longman Industry and Public Service Management,
Longman Group UK Limited, 6th Floor, Westgate House, The High,
Harlow, Essex CM20 1YR, England and Associated Companies
throughout the world.
Telephone: Harlow(0279) 442601
Fax: Harlow(0279)444501
Telex: 81491 Padlog

A catalogue record for this book is available from The British Library

ISBN 0 582-09599-9

Printed in Malaysia by PA

Contents

Foreword

I believe that I can bring to the recommendation of this publication a reasonably broad perspective since, in addition to work over the last 8 years in writing the reports on Management in the Health Service and on Community Care, I am increasingly involved with the voluntary sector, most particularly as President of Age Concern, England

I confess that the subject of community care is of very particular interest for me since it reflects the social changes which I have seen in my own lifetime. The old communities based on the villages or small urban areas have largely disappeared. The motor car enabling people to live away from their work and to travel extensively, smaller families, one-parent families and increasing divorce have all made the community and the families far less stable. In addition many of the old industries such as steel and coal, in which I was brought up, have shrunk, and the communities built up round these industries and welded together by hard times and hard, dangerous work, have undergone enormous change.

I confess that, when I started work on my report on Community Care in 1986, I had not realised 'the enormity and complexity of the problem. I equally admit at the same time that as managing director of a very large company I had not appreciated the extent to which employees were preoccupied with caring for relatives, elderly, disabled or ill. Finally, I had not been aware of the tremendous activity in the voluntary sector to handle the problems and opportunities with which they were confronted.

The terms of reference which Norman Fowler gave me were, 'To review the way in which public funds are used to support community care policy and to advise on the options for action that would improve the use of these funds as a contribution to more effective community care'. I quickly began to understand the complexity of the problem. The introduction to this book gives the results of my recommendations and the way in which the government translated those recommendations into legislation. Importantly, local authorities were confirmed in a central role for the provision of social care. The implementation needs sensitive handling, particularly in relationship to the voluntary sector. Local authorities have their statutory duties, and they need to be accountable for public funds, which means a degree of formality and professionalism in preparation of agreements with the voluntary sector. the latter, on the other hand, may not have the expertise or the time to handle protracted and detailed negotiations, particularly if it is dealing with a large number of public authorities. As always, there is a balance to be achieved — a clear understanding of the services which the local authorities require the voluntary sector to provide, and some certainty of funding over a period of years accompanied by a minimum of bureaucracy.

There is, equally, a balance to be achieved between the professionalism of the average social worker and the need to understand that one is always having to make decisions as to where effort is best expended and between compelling priorities.

The studies in this volume show the range of initiatives in community care with people telling of their experiences in their own words. It illustrates the enormous range of activity. It shows how essential it is for the authorities to understand the need to foster, facilitate and encourage the work at local level. It shows, moreover, that the work of the voluntary groups and volunteers at local level is not simply the icing on the cake but is a substantial part of the cake itself.

The authors of the book are to be congratulated on the work. It illustrates more than anything else the challenge, the opportunity, the frustration, the tension, the highways and the cul-de-sacs in the provision of care. It carries the warning that voluntary effort may be diverted and discouraged in the scramble and competition for resources. This can be overstated since authorities are being asked simply to think through priorities much more carefully and to use money and staff where the needs are greatest and the best results obtained. This should not compromise the values of the voluntary sector rooted in something much deeper — quite simply the concept of care for one's neighbour. The voluntary sector is growing — it needs continuing sustenance, and it demands greater awareness of the enormous need in our communities. For those who are already working in this field, or who wish to translate a recent awareness into action, this book provides excellent case studies and experiences.

Sir Roy Griffiths

Acknowledgements

More than many, this piece of work owes most to those workers and agencies whose work it describes. It is their efforts, to establish and maintain networks of services which are sensitive to the needs of users, which indicate how it is possible to make contributions of some substance to the well-being of people and the communities in which they live. The support, friendship and time they have committed in the preparation of the material contained in this book, has been a key stimulant in furthering our consideration of the demands, challenges and opportunities for the voluntary sector in the personal social services.

Special thanks go to Ms Akhtar, Shula Allan, Charles Anderson, Cathy Bryson, Trish Combe, Dr D C Das, Geraldine Duncan, Gilroy Ferguson, Kirsty Gillies, Helena Guldberg, Jean Hain, Joy Harris, Vicky Hobson, Rosemary Raine Howe, Preeya Lal, Sheila Lauchlan, Paul Lockley, Felix Lynch, Marion Malcolm, Mr Mamtora, Fiona Meikle, Angus Millar, Joan Millar, Be Morris, Lami Mulvey and Myra Owens, Angela Powell, Magda Praill, Rohina T Gafoor, Carol Watson and Joan Wilkinson.

We are grateful to Moray House Institute — Heriot-Watt University for its support and to Carole Jackson for setting out the material in its final form.

We are particularly grateful to Sir Roy Griffiths for his support and contribution.

In addition, we want to thank Longman for its help and advice in publishing the material.

We, however, have to accept final responsibility for the presentation of the material and for the interpretation and analysis it contains.

Bruce Lynch
Richard W. Perry

I Introduction

1 New worlds in community care

Bruce Lynch and Richard Perry

It was against the backcloth of the Government's intentions for community care, that we planned our journey of exploration into the provision of community care services by voluntary agencies. We recognised that the Government's plans for community care were changing the face of British welfare policy, and would continue to do so for some time to come. The effects were widespread. Many local authorities were reviewing and restructuring their patterns of organisation and management. Voluntary and independent agencies were also trying to grapple with the implications, and grasp the initiatives which this new era embodies. However, we all need to see the reality, as opposed to the dream, of better services for people in need, the overall aim of the Government's plan. *Caring for People*, the White Paper (DHSS, 1989) in which the Government's intentions for community care development were detailed, described the prospect for service development which would promote the independence of users, as well as securing for them greater control over their lives. A real test of this new initiative has to be the extent to which the empowerment of users, and the responsiveness of service providers, secure better services and promote new relationships between users and providers.

Originally, the Government seemed to be quite reluctant to give local authorities a central role in this new age. The delay in responding to Sir Roy Griffiths' original report on community care (Griffiths, 1988) is indicative of real reluctance on the part of the Government to give Local Authorities a central role in ensuring that its own objectives for community care were realised. As a consequence, those objectives which relate to the provision of services, the character of service delivery, the pattern of public and independent service provision, and the accountability of the service provided in relation to financial and quality control, presented a test for local authorities which they appeared ready to tackle. Indeed, the Association of Directors of Social Services and the Association of Directors of Social Work have readily urged the Government to implement the Griffiths report and the ensuing White Paper.

The achievements which the Government now wants to see are identified in *Caring for People*, namely:

    (a) to promote the development of domiciliary, day and respite services to enable people to live in their own homes wherever feasible and sensible;

(b) to ensure that service providers make practical support for carers a high priority;

(c) to make proper assessment of need and good case management the cornerstone of high quality care;

(d) to promote the development of a flourishing independent sector alongside good quality public services;

(e) to clarify the responsibilities of agencies and so make it easier to hold them to account for their performance; and

(f) to secure better value for tax-payers' money by introducing a new funding structure for social care.

Of course, objectives of this kind are statements of intent. What they mean in practice will become clearer as providers and users build up and test the network of services developed.

Communities and community care

Since community is at the very heart of community care, the meaning attached to the term has an important bearing on the conception of the services which community care is intended to promote. However, community is a term which has a variety of meanings and applications, most of which entail the identification of some pattern of relationships between individuals and groups of individuals. Furthermore, the term may also imply a high degree of intimate personal interaction between people, with the quality and substance of relationships being characterised by commitment and a sense of purpose sustained over a period of time.

Community can also be a convenient way of identifying a particular geographical location, defining its boundaries in ways which distinguish it from other communities. Communities defined in this way might include rural villages and particular localities in urban towns and cities.

While the definitions of community considered thus far assume some measure of common local interest amongst community members, the term community is sometimes used to identify groups which, while being scattered geographically, comprise people with shared interests which might be derived from their religious, political or personal commitments. For example, quite often the term community is applied to groups of people who have shared ethnic origins. Indeed, public bodies like the police have, in their efforts to improve their relationships with individuals from minority ethnic groups, tried to maintain contacts with representatives of West Indian, Asian, Chinese and other 'communities'. In a similar vein, communities are sometimes assumed to be evident amongst individuals with particular disabilities like hearing impairment.

Given the variety of meanings attached to the term community, it will become evident from this work that its authors, and those whose services are described within it, adopt a rather fluid view of the term. As a consequence, they recognise that there will be an interplay between communities which represent the interests of those who use community care services, those who carry responsibility for their care, the communities in which they live and communities which reflect people's sense of social identity, ethnic origin or disability.

The practicalities of community care suggest that it may be helpful to consider how certain roles and the expectations attached to them might help us to analyse current developments and planning for the future. However, before we explore those issues, we ought to consider further the context in which these roles are likely to be performed. In other words, to recognise that the delivery of community care, irrespective of the way in which community is defined, may incorporate a number of divergent intentions. It may imply care within communities, or care by communities. Nevertheless, while the distinction may be helpful in our analysis of community care, in practice, community care may be both of these, care by the community within the community. However, let us consider first what care within the community might imply.

Care within the community

Care within the community might assume the development of services which are intended to promote non-institutional care: the provision of services which help and support sick, disabled and disadvantaged people in their own homes. Not that the provision of residential care services ought to be abandoned entirely. Indeed, co-ordination, collaboration and co-operation between service providers and service users ought to be reflected in a comprehensive range of services which can be tailored to meet the individual needs of particular users. Within that comprehensive range of services, health and social care should provide for the shelter and treatment of individuals in settings which make maximum use of the resources available as well as addressing the special needs of those requiring care.

A further dimension of care within the community suggests an element of decentralisation by service providers; localised provision established by agencies, whatever their size. Many local authority departments have undertaken restructuring in order to promote such decentralisation, recognising that relationships between service managers at a local level, and the communities with which they work, offer a better climate for sensitive service development, as well as more effective financial and quality control.

For services to be truly within the community, they need to be readily accessible and well integrated into the wider network of services and community groups. While accessibility might be promoted through decentralised management, the integration of different services may require some element of centralised planning. Indeed, if health and social service agencies are to ensure effective service development and delivery they will require good operational relationships between local service workers and between senior staff responsible for strategic planning.

Of course, the model of care within the community which implies localised service developments in the context of larger centralised agencies, may well involve tensions between the local base and the centre. Communication between local managers and workers, and central planners and managers responsible for budgeting may not always operate effectively, or be sufficiently sensitive to local need. And, as events in the past have shown, some communities may find themselves alienated from some aspect of community care development, whether that be a provision of services for people with AIDS or the establishment of group homes for people discharged from long-stay psychiatric hospitals. In some cases decisions about service development and location may emerge from hostile and highly political debate and manoeuvring.

Services which emerge from planned development by agencies, including local authorities, may, however, suffer from a surfeit of professionalism; the provision of services being dependent exclusively on the paid services of professionals or aspiring professionals. Professionalisation of services may have a detrimental effect on the relationship between service providers and service users; heightening the alienation between those who are empowered to deliver and those who, by virtue of their dependency, find themselves in a subordinate role. Care within the community may well accentuate the weaknesses which can emerge from the overprofessionalisation of caring services.

Care by the community

By comparison, care by the community carries with it certain connotations. It suggests that it is the local community which, through spontaneous recognition of the needs within its midst and through informal, as well as formal, campaigns of action and through consumer-led activity, promotes the development of services which carry certain characteristics. They are highly localised, able to respond more flexibly to the immediate needs of local citizens, create a sense of partnership which larger-scale organisations and services may be unable to create, and provide an outlet for volunteer effort and commitment which might have otherwise be lost.

However, care by the community may not necessarily be the provision of sensitive services in idyllic community settings. It may involve carers, already heavily committed to the care of their own kith and kin, offering relief and support for others similarly placed. In that way the burden on carers is a recycled burden, missing out on the respite and supportive care which other services may be able to provide.

Communities may not be made up entirely of an ideal network of supportive relationships. Communities may find it hard to tolerate, let alone support, the deviant or the misfit. Indeed, the history of community life suggests that small communities can be as punitive and intolerant as any other social grouping.

Localised service developments may also be dependent on the leadership role of key figures, who, when they move or are no longer directly involved in the issues concerned, may leave organisations floundering and lacking in direction. Alternatively, individuals may be reluctant to release the reins of control over organisations they were instrumental in forming, constraining development and frustrating the learning and contribution of others. However, local developments of this kind may serve to deprofessionalise services in a way which can enhance the partnership between service providers and service users, promoting the direct involvement of users and contributing to the empowerment of those the services are designed to help.

Small, localised initiatives may well be more vulnerable to the crises which result from short-term funding arrangements, budgetary crises in local authorities and the whims of the public benefactor. Financial uncertainty serves to expose the vulnerability of projects with limited power and few friends, particularly where the services involve users whose case may be unglamorous and lacking in prestige.

Carers in community care

Much of the care which surrounds those in need is provided by carers whose association with the people they help is one of kinship or close social relationship. Amongst many tasks, they provide practical care through physical and emotional support, seeing to the day-to-day needs of their kin and friends (Pancoast & Collins, 1976). Indeed, as some writers argue, 'Carers therefore cannot be regarded simply as a background resource. . .' (Twigg, Atkin & Perring, 1990). They are a diverse group of people coping with a diverse set of demands, sometimes over a sustained period for people with long-term disabilities, or sometimes over shorter episodes where, for example, physical health or mental health difficulties fluctuate.

The interface between these carers, sometimes referred to as 'informal carers', those people who rely on their help and the service providers of whatever variety, statutory, professional, voluntary or self-help peers, could so easily become an interface of tension. The achievement of a harmonious care package will depend on the successful negotiation of clear boundaries. The skills of workers: their competence in taking on the tasks involved in negotiation, assessment, planning, monitoring and evaluation, will have a major impact on the quality of care provided for each individual. We hope training will serve these skills for the brokerage and keyworker roles which they have to perform (Beardshaw & Towell, 1990).

Funding

The White Paper *Caring for People* argues that, since 1979, gross current expenditure on what it describes as core community care services rose by 68% in real terms by 1987/88. The largest proportion of this expenditure, which totalled £3400 million by 1987/88, was attributed to local authorities. In addition, it was argued in the White Paper that, by 1987/88, just under 50% was devoted to community-based services, including home helps, day care centres and the like. In addition, expenditure by health authorities on community health services also grew.

However, the single most significant area of development in expenditure appears to have been that covered by social security payments to people in independent, residential and nursing homes. The Government's intentions for community care include a reform of these funding arrangements for residential and nursing home care. It intends to alter the unintended shift which had occurred over the recent past; so that greater priority can be given to developing services which enable people to be 'supported in their own homes', avoiding, as a consequence, concentrating support on people in residential care. To this end, resources, which would otherwise have been devoted to income support and housing benefit payable to new residents in residential care, is diverted to local authorities. The net result is an adjustment in the revenue support grant payable to local authorities, phased over a number of years. Health authorities continue to receive funding for community care developments, although the amount intended to take account of community care developments would not be specified; as a consequence, like the funding arrangements for local authorities, community care funding would not be ring-fenced. (In other words, the specific amount made available by central government would not be identifiable, except for that made available by the mental illness specific grant.)

Local authorities and health boards are expected to work together in developing community care plans. This planning includes specific planning agreements designed to clarify responsibilities and to ensure that there are common themes and intentions. It is not unusual for local authorities and health service agencies to be encouraged to participate in joint planning and joint funding of projects. Indeed, joint funding plans were introduced by Barbara Castle in the 1970s, although they seemed to make little real headway into the provision of better services for the mentally handicapped and mentally ill. The effect on the development of community-based services is difficult to quantify, suggesting that its significance may not have been particularly profound. None the less, local authorities are now required to prepare community care plans in conjunction with health boards, housing authorities, voluntary agencies, including housing associations, and the private sector. Within this context, the Government is committed to promoting opportunities for individuals to live in the community where ever possible. The White Paper refers to a study in Scotland, published in 1987, which suggested that more than 90% of residents in hospitals for the mentally handicapped could be capable of being accommodated in the community, should suitable accommodation and support be available. The Government's aim is to continue the steady decrease in the number of people in long-stay hospitals of this kind. Furthermore, the community care developments are also expected to provide services which promote opportunities for people suffering from mental ill health, including dementia, to continue to live in the community wherever possible. To that end, the mental illness specific grant is intended to 'stimulate new proposals and serve as a source of additional finance for programmes' in the field of mental illness.

The projects which this specific grant is intended to encourage include:

- programmes of day activities
- day centres
- domiciliary services
- staffing
- care-related costs for supported accommodation
- respite and practical support for carers
- crisis services
- self-help schemes (see Circular No. SW10/1990, Scottish Office)

Financial assistance for projects of this kind will be made through grant applications submitted by local authorities and will, according to government guidance, be related to the existing or proposed provision of services designed to achieve the objectives identified, namely, to reduce the numbers of mentally ill people requiring admission to hospital, and to enable more people to leave hospital and live with suitable support in the community.

Voluntary agencies, which have a long history of negotiating and sustaining financial support from local authorities and central government agencies, will be familiar with the difficulties such dependency generates. Indeed, the more open-ended financial arrangements which some funding agencies have been willing to offer in the past, may be less likely to be reproduced in the future. The emphasis placed on the monitoring of services and the value for money impetus behind much of the community care strategy, suggests that agencies receiving financial support will be subject to even closer scrutiny. Few, not-for-profit organisations involved in the personal social services can survive without some financial support from central and local government agencies. Unfortunately, agencies may be uneasy about the extent to which their own policy commitments may have to be adjusted in the light of financial dependency on local authorities and central government. Self-help groups, in particular, have a campaigning edge to their work, but may find this edge dulled by the imperatives of financial stability and maintenance of services. After all, he who pays the piper. . .!

Making the organisation work

Self-help organisations, in their efforts to develop not-for-profit services in the interests of their membership, may be prepared to tolerate financial uncertainty in order to preserve their independence and integrity. Unfortunately, in an era of economic astringency, they have to make sacrifices. Access to the corridors of power in which decisions about the allocation of local authority and health board finances (including those covered by joint funding arrangements) may require these very same self-help groups, who, at one time, were champing at the heels of officials and elected members, to seek increasingly the favour of those who control the budget. So, while local authorities are obliged to take into account the views of carers and voluntary organisations in devising their community care plans (CCP), who can say what might happen once the process of resource allocation and review begins.

II Case studies in community care

The main body of this work is made up of case study material derived from the experiences of a selected range of not-for-profit agencies. These agencies were visited by us at differing points over a 12-month period. It will be evident, then, that these agencies were at various stages of development, both in relation to the original purposes for which they were established, and in relation to the adjustments which changes in the pattern of community care require. In addition, the Government's own timetable for the implementation of its community care plans was governed by uncertainty and was, eventually, subject to change. As a consequence the full impact of the new era of community care continues to unfold. The case study material therefore provides some snapshots into the ways in which that impact was revealed in the life and work of a range of voluntary not-for-profit agency projects.

It will be evident, from the range of case study material, that we have tried to incorporate a selection of agencies which provide services for people with differing needs. Readers will see that, amongst others, learning difficulties, Alzheimer's disease, disability, elders and mental ill-health are represented, along with urban, rural, black and other community groups. Small-scale projects operating on shoestring budgets, and larger-scale projects dependent on central and local government funding arrangements, are also represented here.

The accounts and experiences of the projects, their workers and the users are not intended to represent ideal models of practice or management. Rather, they are intended to focus attention on the kinds of issues which workers and users in community care ought to consider when they are about to embark upon, or review, service developments and delivery. The experiences of these agencies have helped us to identify some key themes which highlight some of the opportunities and challenges in this new era of development for welfare services. Given the variety of the organisations involved, it is inevitable that their structures and organisational arrangements differ. None the less, other organisations may be better prepared for the future if they take into account the lessons learned and the messages conveyed in these case studies.

2 The community garden — Lochend, Edinburgh

Felix Lynch

Keypoints

The account is included because:
▲ *it highlights the importance of the values and beliefs of key activities in setting up voluntary initiatives;*
▲ *it is a project which received neither financial assistance nor professional support from social work, community education or the health service;*
▲ *it is an imaginative project;*
▲ *the project has created an important community resource for the physically handicapped and for elderly in the community.*

Background

The background to Felix's involvement with the community garden scheme is both interesting and relevant since, as with many other activists in voluntary work, the seeds of their commitment to particular causes and client groups were sewn in much earlier events. In the case of Felix, the garden project is part and parcel of a much broader vision of a community. Moreover, it is this which fuels much of his motivation and dedication to the work involved.

The disabled

My contact with the disabled goes back 10–12 years.

I've been a member of St Ninians parish church for the past 40 years. Then, I was like a lot of people in the area. If you were not asked to do something, you did not volunteer. I wasn't a joiner. However, Father Jock, the parish priest at the time collared me one day and talked me into standing for the parish council and I was later elected.

At that time the only real contact this parish had with the New Trinity Centre for the disabled was through Father Jock. He used to visit the place on occasion and it so happened that just then, the manager of the New Trinity Centre had written to Father Jock asking if we as a church could do something to help towards the cost of a £1000 electric wheelchair for one of the severely disabled users of the New Trinity Centre which is in the parish. The man had undergone an operation to make him more mobile which had not been a success. Both his parents were elderly, and the use of the push wheelchair was severely restricting his ability to get out into the community. An electric wheelchair would free him from the virtual imprisonment of the home and the Centre. An electric wheelchair would allow him to get around unaided and would offer him a better quality of life. The letter asked if we could help, even with a subscription.

At the parish council meeting Father Jock read the letter and asked for our comments. Of course there was a great silence at first and, needless to say, I opened my mouth and spoke about the parish opening our eyes to our responsibility for the disabled in the area. I must have been quite convincing, because, after some general discussion, Father Jock suggested that a small committee of three be set up to take responsibility for the fund-raising on behalf of the parish and that I should be on it.

The first thing we did was to approach all the groups within the parish to see what they were doing about the fund-raising so that there wouldn't be much duplication. One group held coffee mornings and the youth group did a sponsored bike run and various other things.

Within a month we had raised £1000, but we decided to carry on and after three months raised about £3000 and presented all the money to the New Trinity Centre.

The friends of the New Trinity Centre

The fund-raising episode was only the start of a developing relationship with the New Trinity Centre and a concern for the well-being of the disabled.

So, through that, I developed a friendship with Steve, the manager of the New Trinity Centre, and both during, and after, the fund-raising I would pop in and see how things were going. However, my conscience was pricking me because of some of the problems Steve was telling me about concerning the Centre, and that gave rise to the friends of the New Trinity Centre.

I formed the friends of the Trinity Centre as an organisation to raise money for the Centre but I also wanted to involve the other parishes in the area, and in that way help the local ecumenical movement.

The August charity fair

The August charity fair itself was really the brainwave of Steve 8–9 years ago and happened about 18 months after the letter which led to the first fund-raising for the Centre.

We had been having a chat and he was saying that, whilst the Centre had been located in the community for 13 years, there was little real contact between the community and the disabled users of the Trinity Centre. So we decided we had to bring people into the Centre.

Steve thought 'Let's have a fair day', not simply for the benefit of the Centre but also for the local hospital. If we could get the various organisations in the community interested in the idea of the fair day we would give a third of the proceeds to the hospital, a third to the Trinity Centre and a third would be held back for help to the various organisations for local community projects. I spoke with Father Jock and he was definitely for it when he knew what our aims were.

Money was secondary to us. We were trying to take the Disabled Centre into the community.

At the first fair we had quite a crowd. At the start, some young kids would maybe stop and stare at the disabled, but, if you come now, you'll see that the youngsters don't think of it as anything unusual. That is one of the victories.

Two of the handicapped from the Trinity Centre are on the management committee and are very much part of the fair as such.

Local community groups managed the stalls.

The first two fairs were held outside in Lochend Park. The next fairs were held in the grounds of Craigentinny primary school. However, last year we moved from open ground to Craigentinny Community Centre which is more compact and saves the hire of a marquee.

Through the fair we have tried to involve all the organisations in the area including the three local primary schools. We devised a scheme whereby each year one school would get to choose the charities queen, and her consort and the two other schools would provide the escorts. That kept their interest going. And through the kids we were getting the parents interested. To further that, we now have a parade of the charities queen with pipe band and majorettes. We ask the kids to get dressed-up and offer prizes. We also have had a 'personality' to open the fair over the years.

Local businesses make contributions. Sunblest Bakeries, the biggest local employer, is very much committed to the area and supplies us with free rolls, pies and what have you. We also approached the Hibernian Football club to have a collection taken at one of their matches, and that has since become an annual event.

This year, the fair as a whole raised £5000.

The idea of a therapeutic garden

I am always on the lookout for fresh objectives for disabled people to pursue. Before I spoke with anyone about the garden scheme, I was thinking about the kinds of things which disabled people could get involved in which were new, which had not been tried before, at least not here, and where they could learn to do new things. I was determined that the garden was going to be something to stretch the disabled, because I knew from my acquaintance with parents of disabled that they definitely cocoon them to a great extent. Steve, the manager of Trinity Centre and myself, thought that, if we could set up a garden scheme linked with the Centre and get the disabled involved and talking about it at home, their parents might think about getting someone to build a wee box in their garden for them to grow things in, once they knew something about plants, because I know a lot of the disabled have homes with gardens but they are never encouraged to work in their own gardens.

Finding the ground

What we were looking for was ground somewhere private; away from the prying of sympathetic eyes, away from 'Oh, look at these poor people there in the wheelchairs, or gardening on their knees'. We were also looking for ground that would not be easily vandalised. We had spoken to Father 'Mac' [the present parish priest for St Ninian's Catholic church] about the garden idea and subsequently the three of us had a meeting. He said that there was ground at the rear of the church house and asked if we could do anything with it. We went round and looked at it and thought it was beyond redemption. The ground had not been cultivated for the past few years. The weeds were at least 2 or 3 feet high and the ground itself was at different levels. We thought the first thing we would have to do was clear the ground.

Phase 1 — Progressing the idea

Finance

When we had the first discussions about the garden idea, we were naturally thinking of how we would finance it and get the labour for it. We thought at the time that the August charity fair might be interested. I went to the August charity fair who were always looking for community projects and sold them the idea that this would be the first project that they could have a direct link with, and asked if they would help it get started. I was given £500 initially and later another £500 for the project.

That gave me breathing space in which to write begging letters to different companies and various sources which was quite successful. One of the companies I wrote to, the charitable trust, sent £1000; Hewlett Packard sent £50; The Royal Bank of Scotland £50 and Christian Salveson donated £100. I also got hold of some of my friends who worked in companies for their support. I approached a friend in British Telecom and submitted an application through him and they came up with £100. Father 'Mac' also gave a donation.

I was also able to borrow £1500 from the Scottish Council for Spastics to buy tools, materials and equipment, although that loan may be written off by them.

Getting the workforce

Through his role as a director with a local printing firm which did publications for the Scottish Development Agency (SDA), Felix knew something of the SDA's involvement with the Community Programme scheme and initially he sought their advice and assistance with the garden project.

We had to think in terms of how we were going to pay for the labour to get the work started because there was no money as such.

At that time, two years ago, no one had any formal position in the project. I was investigating how we could get the project started on a voluntary basis, as I am now. I did it because I had more time than Steve.

I approached the SDA knowing that they paid a certain sum of money to groups doing community projects, but, they (SDA) put a damper on it as far as I was concerned. It took a year before there was any fruition. We were hitting snags all the time. Everyone does as soon as you hit a government department. They insisted we follow certain rules, whereas we were trying to take short cuts.

I was told by SDA that, if I wanted to do a community project of this nature, I would have to submit to them a programme of what I wanted to achieve; the cost and how long it would take. I would also have to finance the cost of an administrator and a site supervisor to take care of the project.

At that time I was working full-time in my own job, and so I initially thought about employing a retired builder or construction worker as site supervisor. However, when I realised what we would have to pay him, and the cost of materials for the garden project, I knew 'it was right out of the box' as far as we were concerned.

However, I kept plugging away.

I asked if they would accept my working as site supervisor on a voluntary basis. I would arrange to take time off from my job to do the site supervisor's job.

That was not good enough because they then said 'well you will still have to set up an office because you will have to provide time sheets for the workers and have to look after the welfare benefit aspect for any workers on the employment training programme' and such like.

And I thought, 'well that could be a full-time job' as far as the administration side of the project was concerned.

It took a whole year before we dug the first soil.

The community business in training

In spite of these setbacks with the SDA, Felix continued to explore other avenues to move the project forward and, after some 9 months, made a breakthrough.

However, I'm fairly well known in business circles and just by speaking to various friends and such like I heard about this organisation called Community in Business Training, so I went to their office in Albany Street. They said they might be able to do the administrative side of the project involving the employment trainees but before that could happen I would have to submit to them a plan of what I intended to do, which they in turn submitted to their management committee. I was assured that, if it received their blessing, it was fairly certain to get the blessing of the SDA. And that is what happened.

The employment trainees

Felix's involvement with employment training widened the scope of his concern with respect to the garden project. He was very conscious of the issues surrounding the use of employment trainees and took care to build their needs into the development of the project.

The Community in Business Training Group took on the responsibility for getting in touch with the Department of Employment, with recruitment of the employment trainees, and for the administration of their giro or dole money. What we had to do was to give the training group the scheme I had worked out for the training programme for those trainees who would be involved on the project. They provided some general guidelines which I then looked at from a gardening instruction angle.

Under the old community programme schemes, workers got paid between £65 and £80 a week. When the government changed to employment training, the pay was reduced to what they would get as dole money plus £10 for travel expenses. That is what these people working here are getting.

Motivating the Workforce

All of the trainees are long-term unemployed. We take whoever they send us but it has worked. We have 12 trainees altogether. One of the bonuses for them, and us, is that at least seven trainees have gone from the project into permanent jobs.

You have got to show the trainees that you are going to teach them something, so that a programme is laid out for them. On the garden project, they have had training in building breeze blocks, laying slab paths, laying turf and general gardening experience.

I try to consider the needs of the individual as well. For example, I had one lad with me for nearly a year who was very nice, very shy. He was not retarded mentally, but when he first came to me he was very inward looking and awkward. Part of my thing was to bring him out. He has since managed to get a job in a hotel.

I only work my lads the 30 hours which is the minimum laid down in their contract because I feel that the money they are paid is so cheapskate. Although it's surprising, because some of these lads will be given a job to do and will work on after the 3 o'clock knocking-off time just to finish the job.

I also saw it as very much part of my job to get the trainees interested in what they were doing.

One of the things we instigated with the trainees was a cup of tea or coffee down at the Trinity Centre before we came up here to work on the garden. Most of the disabled make for the canteen in the morning for a drink and a blether. I suggested the day started off at the Trinity Centre because I wanted to give them an opportunity to see who they were making the garden for, and it worked well.

The trainees are also encouraged to go down to the canteen at the Centre for lunch and they still do that. They mix with the disabled, and that gives them an incentive.

Developing the idea of a therapeutic garden

Whilst Felix was going about the business of negotiating for a workforce for the project there was also the task of deciding how the ground itself would be best developed.

We had the ground but we had to level it. We also knew that there was no use in simply taking the tops off the weeds, so it took some time to clear the area. We knew our first priority. We wanted to offer the best possible use of the garden to the disabled so we consulted with the occupational therapist at the Trinity Centre. Her advice was that we would have to build boxes for the people in wheelchairs in order to bring part of the 'garden' up to a level which they were able to work from. The ground would also have to be levelled because what we were trying to do was to encourage people to get out of their wheelchairs and work from kneeling pads. We wanted to stretch them and involve them in new things.

We heard about a group called the Association of Occupational Therapists garden scheme and wrote to them for advice. It so happened that we were fortunate in that one of their officials would be visiting Edinburgh and she visited the site. We took measurements and showed her the lines we wanted to follow and some guidelines of the type of garden we wanted to create. She went away and later they sent us a plan which was all done for free and which we used with some alterations.

Steve, Neil, the chief engineer of the Trinity Centre and myself started on the layout, deciding where we would place the boxes and where we would have the level ground. That was done by having plenty of pegs and plenty of string. We pegged out where we were having the brick boxes, and the shape of the boxes, and then started to make the paths. Once we finished them, we started on the edging.

We wanted a garden not only where disabled could work in, but also wander through. We wanted to have a mixture of plants not only for colour and season but also for smell and touch which we thought was very important for disabled blind visitors to the garden.

During the past year, Felix's vision of the garden had broadened both in terms of its design and function.

We have always had fresh ideas about what we could do with the Garden as we progressed.

When we first started, all we wanted was a garden with levelled ground and brick boxes for growing plants. Then I noticed two small outbuildings attached to the ground we had for the garden and found these were used by the church's own gardener for his tools. I spoke to him first about the use of the two buildings and arranged to exchange a new hut for his tools. I explained that I wanted to convert one of the stores into a small kitchen for the disabled and other visitors to the garden to get a cup of tea. The other store building I wanted as a wee shelter for the disabled or the elderly if it rained.

I then spoke with Father 'Mac' and he said it was OK if the gardener agreed.

One of the things I was also trying to do was to make the garden independent of St Ninians' Church.

We don't want the wider community to say that the garden belongs to the Catholic Church. We want it to be known as a community garden to be used by everyone. That has been done. St Ninians has donated the ground to us.

Phase 2

The first phase of the garden was only half what it is now. That phase is where all the boxes and plants have been laid out.

The second phase, the part we are working on now, has been laid out as a small bowling green for the disabled or perhaps elderly people. There is also an archery range for the disabled and we are finishing off a small pistol shooting range. All of that equipment is already down at the Trinity Centre and the disabled will have it brought up when they want to use it.

We have also managed to buy a caravan awning which can be fixed to the garden back wall and will provide a place for people to sit out in the summer and plan to have the area under the awning slabbed for wheelchair access.

There is very little left to be done now. We still have to finish the archery and the pistol shooting range and some edging to the paths. The bowling area is already done. However, the full facilities won't be fully used by the disabled and all the churches and outside organisations until all the work is completed and that should be by the spring of 1991.

Getting resources

Much of the materials used in the construction of the garden and the plants and garden furniture which now exist are the outcome of Felix's ability to sell the idea of the garden to others in the wider community.

A lot of my business contacts, both in donations and such like, have provided the wherewithal. For example, the sand and cement I scrounged away from a firm in Gorgie and they in turn got in touch with the slab people for me to get a cheaper deal. I put it to them that it was for the benefit of the disabled and the elderly, in the community: that it was a community garden. I think most of them have grannies or mothers who are elderly, and felt it was a worthwhile cause so they were helpful in supplying materials to me at cost.

Brown Brothers donated a lift which we have now converted into a portaloo which is wide enough to take a wheelchair and is in the garden. Again, we wanted the garden to be independent of the church and, before the portaloo, people had to use the toilet in the church house.

One of the other things I've scraped up for the garden is a 6 foot greenhouse, but rather than locate it at the garden, it is down at the Trinity Centre. The reason is that, if the weather is bad, the disabled can work down there.

Involving the community

For Felix, the garden has also become something of a symbol of the community as an 'ecumenical community' which can collectively contribute to the welfare and well-being of its more needy members. Their role is both that of resource providers and consumers.

I am always conscious that, as far as possible, this is a community garden. I know myself with my own wife, an active member of Restalrig parish church of Scotland, that this project has brought the ecumenical movement a bit forward in the area. Take the coffee mornings we held in support of the garden. It would have been easy to have had these at Trinity Centre, but, I wanted to put it under the community banner. I put it to the ecumenical group of which I am also a member and then approached the Rev. J. Dixon of Lochend parish church for the use of his hall for the coffee morning. That gives the ecumenical groups a boost; keeps the scheme under the community banner and also raises money for the community garden. Now we have a common aim and this is one way we can show how, as a community, we are doing something for the disabled, the elderly and the lonely.

I also put the word out to the members of the various churches in the area that we were looking for donations for rose bushes at £2.50 each and some people gave £2.50. We asked members of the congregations and people outside if they were interested in donating bench seats for the garden and said that we would be happy to put a memorial plaque on the bench giving the name of the benefactor. We got donations from all the churches and we now have seven bench seats in the garden.

The community garden

We started out wanting to provide a therapeutic garden for the disabled, but we are also very much concerned with the fact that, within this area, 32% of the population are elderly. The clubs are full to bursting and not everyone uses the clubs.

Last winter I went around all the pensioners' clubs in the district and said that the garden was not only for the disabled but also for them to come over and have a cup of tea or coffee and a blether with their friends or just come and read a book. The garden is open all day and tea and coffee is free. I told them it was a community garden; not a St Ninians' garden, or just for the disabled.

We have one old chap who comes over quite regularly who said 'You know, up till now my day was that I got up in the morning and tidied up, which didn't take long. Then I had a walk to the newsagent for my paper, came home and read it, and that was me till the next day. Now I can still take a wee walk for my paper. Come over here for a blether and sit as long as I like, or till dinner time and then go home and read my paper, or even come back to the garden in the afternoon' and he is delighted with that.

Senile dementia group

The dementia club which is based in the tenement next to the church also come in every day. There are about 10–12 members and about three carers. They come here with their ball or their dominoes. They have a cup of tea or coffee and a wee blether, then most of them take a walk along the garden and back. Last week when we had the barbecue with 30 of the disabled, they came over. So it means that it's another recreation for them and, consequently, they are meeting other people who are in the garden, and, if other members of the various churches want to use the barbecue, that would be OK.

The garden committee

Whilst local people were actively involved in supporting the garden by fund-raising events they were less actively involved in the general development of the garden.

> The August charity fair see it as their project, but, to be quite honest with you, they leave it up to me to get on with it. There are only three people who want to have anything to do with the management of the garden project. One is Father 'Mac', the second is Steve and the third is myself, so that primarily I run the thing. I say to them, I would like to do this or that and do it. But, I know how far I can go as far as that is concerned.

Felix, however, is conscious of the need for greater community participation in the day-to-day management of the garden and has gone some way in trying to ensure that becomes a reality.

> Once the garden is completed in 2–3 months' time, I would like to see a management committee set up for the garden with representatives from the Trinity Centre, the August charity fair and the pensioners' clubs. I have already met with the pensioners' clubs and arranged that they will take turns, one day a week, to service the kitchen and make the teas for people using the garden. That way I think we will also get more elderly people using the facility and having more of an interest in it, and having more of a say in the management.
>   The disabled people themselves will look after most of the garden once the employment trainees finish their contract here and they too will be represented on the management committee.

The wider community

Felix was also conscious throughout the development of the garden project of the need to establish links with the wider community of interests in the area. Part of that process involved a judicious use of councillors and the press.

> We knew that the August charity fair could not do all of the financing, so we wanted to publicise the garden. Phyllis Heriot, a local councillor connected with the Trinity Centre, broke the first official soil in September 1988. We got the *Evening News* and other papers to send a photographer and do a write-up in the paper.
>   In June 1989, we invited the Lord Provost of Edinburgh to open the first phase of the garden. We also asked other notables such as the local MP, officials from the SDA and the Scottish Council for Spastics as well as all the local councillors .
>   We thought that, if we wanted to get the approval of, or, help from the Edinburgh district council, it would be politic to involve them. But actually, we like to be independent.
>   We also had someone from the BBC Beechgrove Garden down 2 or 3 months ago to view the garden. The occupational therapist from the Trinity Centre, along with myself, met the programme reporters who were very impressed and said they wished to do a programme on the garden. They were to come in July, but it was postponed because of

programme changes. However, it will probably be done next year. In fact, that will suit us better as the garden should be finished by April 1991.

Personal motivation of the worker

I have spent nearly 3 years on this project. The first year, when I was still in business, and 2 more years of my retirement.

When I first spoke with Father 'Mac' about it and the time was going by, he was wondering if I had forgotten about the idea. But I hadn't. It just took time.

At the end of the day, I get as much pleasure from it as anyone else, because I feel a sense of being directed to the work. In a spiritual sense.

The future

The garden for the disabled has had a number of important spin-offs. Together with staff at the Trinity Centre, Felix is working on a tunnel greenhouse for the Centre which will allow all-year gardening to take place. There is also a scheme afoot to have the disabled record on to computer all the different varieties of plants, their colour, texture, scent and season in order that the disabled can plan ahead the best combination of plant life for all the garden users throughout the year. In this respect, the garden has broadened the curriculum and the learning experiences offered to the disabled which was the intention underpinning the initial idea for the garden project.

Another development of the project is that Felix has been asked by an Edinburgh school for disabled to assist them create something similar for their pupils within the grounds of their school. Caring for the disabled in the community is therefore an on-going commitment.

Points to ponder

▽   The chance nature of the initial involvement.

▽   The length of time leading up to the garden project.

▽   The tenacity of the key worker.

▽   The role of local churches.

▽   The critical importance of employment trainees in this particular scheme.

▽   The attention given by the worker to the needs of employment trainees.

▽   The recognition of wider local participation in the management of the garden project.

▽   The developments in the training and curriculum opportunities for the disabled.

3 Braid House day centre
Sheila Lauchlan

Braid House, as a voluntary agency and registered charity, was formally established for the benefit of the frail elderly of Livingston in March 1982. Our main objectives are to help frail elderly maintain a reasonable standard of life while remaining in their own homes. Many of the frail elderly attending Braid House day centre would be acceptable candidates for residential care in old People's Homes or something similar if there were adequate places available for them.

The account which follows charts the development of the day centre from its beginnings as a small part-time day care facility for the elderly staffed by volunteers to an organisation with some 14 members of staff and an annual revenue budget of around £150,000.

Keypoints

The account is interesting because of:
▲ *the increased specialisation of the target group as the project developed;*
▲ *the dramatic growth in the scope and scale of its development;*
▲ *the accompanying growth of responsibilities and issues associated with that development;*
▲ *the timescale involved;*
▲ *possible implication of moves towards 'contracting out' the service.*

Background

Back in 1980, Livingston old people's welfare committee which was running quite a number of lunch clubs and old peoples' clubs in the town felt that they wanted to do something a wee bit more than run a club in the afternoon and they came up with the idea of having some form of day centre. Money came from social work to fund two part-time organisers to run small centres, one in the north of the town and one in the south. The centres started up in January 1980 with one minibus between both places, which meant that, on the whole, old folk had to walk to each of the two day centres. The day centres were not for the disabled we have now, but they were both successful. Around that time, our chairperson, who was a lay preacher, was conducting a service in a local school and it so happened that there was a lady there from Help the Aged collecting money from the children. Our chairperson said 'You come to Scotland and collect all this money and we in Scotland do not see any of it'. The lady replied that it was the Scottish people's fault because they did not ask. Our chairperson then said 'We want a "bus" and she was told to 'ask for a "bus"'. So we did, and we were delighted when we were actually gifted with it in April 1981. That made quite a difference to us because the 'bus' had a tail lift which meant that we could consider bringing people in wheelchairs to the Day Centre, especially people who were housebound.

Referrals

Within a year, we were looking for bigger premises. Because of the demand, we started looking for premises which opened 5 days a week and, in 1982, we moved to a larger building near Lanmuir House in Livingston. When we moved there, we decided to have a referral system where people would have to be referred by doctors, GPs, social workers, ministers and people who are out in the community and who were coming across old people who were housebound. Initially, we got quite a number of referrals from the day hospital and the GPs, now it is mainly the district nurses who are attending the elderly in the community. We also get a bigger referral now from home care because we have close contact with social work.

Very soon, there was quite a number of people being referred and, to many professionals, this was a facility to fill the gap between day hospital and residential care. It is possibly due to our naivety that we accepted such a high number of very frail elderly but, in a sense, this has further highlighted the need for this type of provision. We started off catering for 25 a day and we were soon up to 40 a day, and again with a large waiting list.

The frail elderly

To begin with, probably half of our day centre users were really housebound. However, by the time we left to come up to our present day centre premises in 1987, the majority of our users were certainly housebound – what we would class as the frail elderly. We now have 50 frail elderly a day. We have recently compiled a fact sheet on the number who need assistance in walking, toileting and other things that they would be unable to do for themselves. On average, there are 18 people a day who must have assistance to move around. Most of them come in 2 days a week but, we are having to cut that down to 1 day a week. We also have a waiting list of 60. One reason there is such a demand is because one of the major problems for old people who go to day hospitals is that they can only attend for a certain length of time, 8 weeks or so. Even the social work day centres have a limited period when they can attend. However, when their time was finished, especially in the case of the day hospital elderly, they were placed back into the community, but there was nowhere for them to go. Many deteriorated, and within 6 weeks they were back in hospital because there was nothing to get them going, or make them feel the desire to get out.

Within the frail elderly group we also have two or three who suffer from senile dementia but we do not have a high number because the Craigshill network operates a dementia centre two days a week and what happens now is that most people who have dementia are referred via Craigshill. In our experience, we have found that those already attending the centre who develop dementia feel more relaxed and at home in Braid House. The upheaval of changing to a new centre can often be very distressing. I think that when they are in with other people you get a lot more out of them because they join in and do things, they watch other people doing something at a table and they try it, or join in. We have found when we have done the likes of quiz games in the sitting room that it is often the people who have dementia who come out pretty near the top in answering some of the questions. It can be quite amazing what comes forth.

Funding

The present Braid House day centre is funded essentially from public funds found by Lothian region social work department. Although we do not receive revenue funding from Lothian Health Board, we have received a grant of £48,000 to enable the purchase of furnishings, an 18-seater adapted bus, a new Parker bath and two wheelchairs for the opening of the new Centre. The grant from social work is about £150,000 for this financial year.

There is also a charitable financial element to our funding but that is peripheral. It provides a little jam on our workday bread.

Day care staff

There are three full-time care assistants who undertake the bulk of the work. The senior care assistant started through a manpower services scheme and eventually got a permanent job here. The other two girls we employed when we got the money to move into this building. One was an occupational therapist helper from Bangour Hospital and the other was a playgroup leader. They are all very good. We also make use of volunteers and have had students from colleges here on placements. We have two drivers who are driver/handymen but, to be quite honest, they are drivers/care assistants because we need to use them during the day to provide extra assistance for the handicapped members who use the day centre.

Volunteers

We get the majority of our volunteers by word of mouth. We have tried recruitment and we contacted all the churches prior to summer because we were very concerned about whether we would be able to cope during the summer period because of staff needing holidays. We got no response at all from any of the churches in Livingston. We have also had open days which we advertised in the press and asked people to come along to see the work which is done in the hope of encouraging someone as a volunteer.

At the moment we have a total of 11 volunteers spread out over the week. Some come 2 days a week and some just on the 1 day. It is difficult to get them, and we sometimes find that when they do come in they find the work we are doing is too heavy for them. Some volunteers feel the type of work which is done in here is difficult and, although we are inclined to say we do not want to use a volunteer to take an old person to the toilet or to wash someone down or change them, we cannot always guarantee that this will not happen. If there is an emergency or, we have an 'accident' then we might have to ask them to do that. Certainly, some volunteers find the work is quite hard going and the older volunteer particularly finds lifting or assisting too heavy.

We do not ask carers of the centre's users to volunteer, because I think, for carers who use the service, it is a relief for them to have their relative looked after. Obviously, they cannot come in on the day their relative is not attending the day centre and they use the day their relative is here as an opportunity for getting out or for going shopping. I think it would be unrealistic to ask a carer to come in as a volunteer.

Training

We combine our volunteers and staff to do a training programme. We normally do this at least once a year. Because we are short staffed, we do not have time during the day when we can take a group of people away to do training. We run training programmes 1 night a week for 4 to 6 weeks covering every aspect of the work. We have covered first aid (13 members of staff have first aid certificates by St. Andrews Ambulance ASS), lifting techniques, bereavement counselling, how to cope with pensioners disagreeing, fire procedures, complaint procedures and whatever aspects of the work we feel would be useful for our workers to have knowledge on.

Employment trainees

We have had employment trainees but have generally found that they are very unreliable. Some trainees have only lasted 2 days. They think the work is too hard considering they are not really being paid. We have only had one girl who was successful in training and she is now employed with us. She came here as a care assistant trainee but a job came up in the kitchen and she took it because she was quite happy working alongside the day centre team. However, we have not found the use of employment training at all successful. Even though I interview first to ensure that the person is going to fit in with the team, I would say there is not the commitment to the work from the people who are coming off employment training.

Activities

We have a programme of therapeutic activities which include dominoes, bingo, movement-to-music, quiz shows, sing-along, arts and crafts. There are also baking sessions where they will bake something that they can take home for tea. Computers and parties are also on the agenda to help stimulate their interest.

In addition to our main objective which is to work with the frail elderly, we have used the space within the centre to offer facilities to other fitter elderly members of the community, which includes such things as indoor bowling, tea dances, woodwork, keep fit, dressmaking and an art class. However, we take care that these activities do not detract from our main purpose, the care of the elderly. Our object in this regard is to provide social facilities for the elderly which are in short supply in a new town and perhaps delay the need for 'pension' status. As a consequence of their coming here, they also have the opportunity to ask our staff for assistance with problems, so counselling assistance is provided. These activities are popular and are still expanding. At the moment, around 150 people attend the various classes each week.

When we first started our 50+ activities for the active and fit older people, the idea was that, if any of our frail elderly wished to go along and join that group that would be fine, but the activity group are a very energetic group. The group dances from when they come in at 1.45 until they go out at 4.00 pm and they never sit down. However, they are a different clientele group. Whilst there were a few of the frail elderly who went along to watch, they did not feel included. Similarly, the people who come in to use the bowls are also very active and it is very difficult for them to stand back when somebody very slow would try to use the bowls, so we realised that it would be much better to have separate activities for our own group and concentrate solely upon them. We have an afternoon a week when the hall is free and we put the carpet down and we take along the ones in wheelchairs and they get a chance to bowl, but it certainly does not do to mix the two groups, there is too big a difference.

Concerns

The staff are a very close-knit group in the day centre because of the type of work we do. There is a dedication to their work and they are asked to do more than what I feel would be asked of them in other centres. I think the girls are so committed because there is such close teamwork within the building. If there is a problem with a member of staff, it affects us all and that is something we have discovered very much this year. We have had a lot of problems affecting staff this year. If there is illness in someone's family, or, if there is a death, it affects everyone and brings us together. However, it also places some additional stress on us all, and on myself as the one with overall responsibility

Management committee

The management committee consists of eight volunteers from the community with representatives from voluntary/statutory bodies who are there in an advisory (no vote) position. They include social work, Livingston Development Corporation, disabled information and advice line, voluntary organisation council, church council, and the good neighbour networks. The success of Braid House owes much to the grit and determination of the committee, in particular, to the previous chairperson who would not take no for an answer. Over the years, there has been changes in the management committee, and it takes time to 'orientate' new members into the day-to-day running of the Centre.

We cannot expand with the existing staff numbers we have. I think that the management committee must look seriously at the future, especially with the changes which are coming forward. There is talk about our being contracted out by social work, and the management committee must look at that and say 'right, we can only take X number of users or, we must have more staffing or more money coming in to cover the cost of care for the number of frail elderly using the day centre'. The staff cannot be expected to accept more and more people who need help without saying there has also got to be more input of money. It is not a case of saying that just because we are good natured, we will take this extra person or push the walls back a bit to accommodate more people.

I feel that voluntary bodies are expected to do a lot more for less money and with less staff than social work day centres. I have been in one where they had four staff on the management team and eight workers for 26 people. They also had their cooking done by a separate service. We have a total of 14 staff which includes part-time workers, bus drivers, cooks and kitchen assistants and yet we have 50 pensioners a day plus the activity group. That is quite a difference and, on top of that difference in numbers, we also cater for an average of ten wheelchairs a day not counting the people who have zimmers or tripods or sticks.

The numbers game

In terms of the actual service which we offer our day centre users, I do not think there would be any real change in policy. However, it could mean that the management committee would need to start looking at what we are doing in a more businesslike manner if we were to contract out to social work.

It is getting to the stage where we have to look seriously at the numbers of people we are bringing into the day centre and then decide what numbers we can cope with. We may need to go back to our management committee and the referrers and say 'right, we have to drop our numbers, we can only take 20 really frail elderly and 20 people who are fitter and can move around unaided, rather than taking almost 40 who need physical assistance.

There is also a possible difference of viewpoint about how the service should be offered. One of the day centre problems is that we have people who have been coming a long time. In fact, some older people have been coming longer than they went to school. One lady was in her 70s when she came — she is now 84. However, there has been quite a deterioration in recent years.

One suggestion is that we should look at our clientele and say, 'right, you have been coming here for a certain length of time. We have provided you with this service and we think now it is time you stopped coming along and made room for someone else coming in.' I do not agree with that view at all. That is the model that some day centres use. But when you put the old people out and do not provide an on-going support very quickly there will be a deterioration. That is what would happen again but we are a social provision. We cannot just say to these old people, 'go home'. We know the importance of the friendships that have been made over these 11 years or whatever length of time that these people have come here for their well-being. We know the benefits which attending the centre brings these old people. Our aim is to stimulate, to get people going, to make them feel uplifted, to come out for the day perhaps feeling down, but to return home on the bus in a fit of laughter since they have had such a good day and have enjoyed the care and the companionship which we offer.

Points to ponder

▽ The readiness of the original volunteers/activists to attempt something more demanding.

▽ The use made of chance opportunities (the 'bus').

▽ The need for formal referral procedures as the project developed and grew.

▽ Move from volunteers to paid staff.

▽ Importance of staff support.

▽ Comparison made with other 'fixed-term' day care provision.

▽ Role and functions of the management committee of a large community care project.

4   Muslim day centre – Bradford

Mr Akhtar

Keypoints

This account is interesting because:
▲ *it highlights a response to gaps in services available to the elderly Muslim community;*
▲ *it is an all male day centre;*
▲ *it illustrates something of the impact of the host society on the extended family structure of the Asian community.*

Background

The Council for Mosques

The Council for Mosques was actually first set up in 1981 by the leaders of all of the voluntary Muslim organisations in Bradford. It was set up to provide guidance to its member organisations and to co-ordinate their work in order to provide a more effective voice on behalf of Muslims within the Bradford community. At the beginning, there were only 29 organisations including Mosques, Madrisas which is a place used purely for Islamic educational purposes, and other voluntary groups. These 29 organisations formed the present Council for Mosques. Today there are 36 Muslim organisations and each organisation has two representatives on the Council which represents over 60,000 Muslims in the Bradford/Metropolitan area. The Council for Mosques has two elderly day centres in Bradford. These centres are very popular, for the work and services which they provide to the elderly in need. The executive committee of the Council for Mosques provide full support and guidance to the day centre staff and operate a regular monitoring system to ensure that the centre is run according to the aims and objectives set forward by the council and by the funding bodies for the day centres.

Ryan Street day centre

The Ryan Street day centre is a purpose-built centre. It was first opened in around 1986/7. It was the second of two Muslim day centres for the elderly opened by the Council for Mosques in Bradford. The centre was first opened during the days of the operation of the MSC scheme. There were two workers at this centre, one of which was working full-time, the other part-time. When the MSC was abolished by the government, the centre suffered long-term closure due to the lack of funding. A large number of elderly Muslim people from this area suffered as a result of the closure of the day centre, as they had nowhere to go. After a long battle, funding was approved for one full-time co-ordinator for each of the two day centres in the city. This centre was re-opened in November 1990. Since that time, it has been a victim of some vandalism and theft.

At the present time, there are around 30 elderly people who attend the centre which is open 6 days a week. The sort of people who use the centre live locally and make their own way to the centre. At the present time, we have no transport facilities which would allow us to pick up people from further away. If we had transport, I feel we could double the number of those attending.

We have certain rules at the day centre to ensure that it is run smoothly. The users are requested to sign a daily register which will be used as proof of use to social workers who fund the project. Members are also requested to stay for the full opening hours of the day centre in order to gain maximum benefit. The centre is open from midday to around 6pm in the evening. Users are also requested to pay 5p entry fee towards the services. These rules were made up jointly by the staff and by the centre users.

Centre members are also requested to attend user committee elections and meetings, since these meetings give everyone a chance to help shape the pattern of the centre and to assist in the decision-making. We also have a user committee for the centre where members can bring any problems or complaints regarding either the centre or its activities. At the moment, the complaints are regarding the state of the roof and the outside landscaping. At the moment, we have an application in to the urban programme for landscaping.

The co-ordinator

I have lived, worked and studied in Bradford for most of my life. I am 39 years old and, during my adult working life, I have held a variety of jobs involving working with members of the public of different age and ethnic groups. I am also trained in youth and community work. For the last 2–3 years I have been with the Council for Mosques mainly in the role of advice worker. Much of that time has been spent dealing with the elderly who have problems including immigration, DHSS, health and housing. Having that background experience I am also able to offer some of that advice work here to members of the centre.

As the keyworker/co-ordinator my main duties at the centre are to improve attendance, i.e. is to try and make sure that elderly members of the Muslim community in this area know about the centre and make full use of the services which the centre provides and also to organise additional activities alongside those which the centre presently offers at this time. Because I have lived in Ryan Street for 8–9 years, I only moved out in 1984, I know most of the local people who use the centre. I have respect for them, and they have respect for me, so I have had no problems in getting them to attend. As a Muslim myself, I know the languages spoken which are mainly Urdu or Punjabi, and I also understand the religion.

As a Muslim who also has parents who are old and who looks after them, I know the difficulties which they are experiencing as the result of their age, and that helps me understand the problems of elderly people who come here to the centre.

As part of my role, I also do occasional home visits to our clients if the clients don't turn up at the centre for a couple of days. I visit to check that they are all right.

The centre users

People who use the day centre live locally, and are quite active, and make their own way to the centre without assistance from staff or volunteers. They are relatively mobile and can take part in any of the activities which take place at the centre during the day. However, if we were looking to the future, I am sure there are a large number of Asian and Muslim people who are housebound or disabled who could benefit from being brought to this centre on a regular basis. We don't have facilities for disabled people at the centre, nor do we have transport to bring people here. So, at the moment, the centre is geared around the able-bodied elderly members of the community.

At the present time, all the members who attend the centre are men. It is very difficult in Islam to integrate male and female members. A female is not actually allowed to be with a stranger and that is a problem. Even if we had the use of a female worker, we would have to have a separate day for the women. I think that, in some centres, run by social services, there is some provision made for female Asian women. At some time in the future we may provide something for them. Presently, we are closed on a Friday, and so it is possible that we could arrange something for women to attend on that day. However, I have only been in the post since April and am already working 6 days a week and so it is very difficult to take on something new at this time. If we were to consider seriously providing services for Muslim women at this day centre, we would need to have a female worker. Because of the lack of funding for a female worker, that has not been possible.

Although all of our male members are active elderly, they are either living alone or are alone during the day. A traditional Asian family has changed a lot over the last 20 years because most of the young people have been brought up in this country and they are bound to have been affected in some way by others around them. One of the things which has happened is that, when the young people marry, they often move away, either to set up another home of their own or to seek work. This means that the daily contacts people would have with their elderly parents are now affected by these changes.

Activities

There are quite a number of activities which take place in the centre. We have newspapers and books for reading which are mainly on loan from the central library and have to go back for renewal every so often. We also have a number of activities which include indoor games, card games, TV and video. We have general discussion sessions, user committee meetings, and occasional parties and outings. We also have a prayers' room. Muslims are required to pray five times a day, once in the early morning and the rest beginning in the afternoon, although some members actually go to the nearby Mosque in Ryan Street and then return afterwards to the centre. We have a number of different sects in our religion, but that does not pose any difficulties for the people who come to this day centre. We also run a number of information and education activities. We invite members of the local authority and other organisations who may be of benefit to the centre users to come and speak on an issue. At the present time, we are running sessions with speakers from the Bradford action on health group and have had sessions on dieting and healthy eating.

Currently we are also holding a session to discuss occupational deafness. Anyone who suffers from occupational deafness will be examined by the doctor who attends the centre and, if necessary, will be advised to put in a claim to the DHSS for compensation. This is because we have discovered that a number of our elderly Asian factory workers had been operating in conditions which over the years have given rise to deafness in some individuals. This information session is then a service to those individuals who are affected but are unaware of their right to claim occupational compensation for their disability.

At the moment, I am also trying to arrange keep-fit classes, sponsored walks, raffles and prizes. But, as I said, I only took up the post four months ago.

We provide a meal twice a week, and we have a volunteer who is willing to prepare the meal for that day. On the other days, because the people live locally, they tend to go home for their meal and then come back to the centre.

We are unable to provide services for people who are disabled, because we have no toilets to cope with wheelchairs or zimmers for the disabled and also we have no person who is trained in caring for elderly people with these disabilities. At the moment, as co-ordinator, it is very hard for me to do all the jobs that I am doing at the moment.

Benefits

Our aim is to provide a safe environment in which the users are encouraged to become involved and to participate rather than sitting alone at home. The benefits are particularly for those who are lonely at home, and have no one they can talk with. Here, at the centre, they can talk with other people, take place in activities and, by doing these things, they feel less lonely and are less likely to suffer from depression and all the sorts of illnesses which begin to take place in your body as you become older.

There is a strong commitment to involving the users in a decision-making process within the centre. This is accomplished by the users' committee meetings where we operate a voting system. However, some elderly people can be quite childlike in their actions, and sometimes one is almost forced to cajole them into taking part in some of the activities. A few just want to come and sit down and watch TV but we have been asked by social services to have a range of activities and not just have people sitting around all the afternoon.

We also provide people with information on welfare rights, health and information on housing difficulties. Last week we had someone from the Manningham housing association which has only recently begun to build houses in the area, to be rented out. If any of our elderly users were interested in moving into these new homes, they would have to apply as soon as possible so we were able to provide them with that information and assistance. We also offer individual counselling on a short- or a long-term basis on any age-related problems they may have.

Another important benefit which the day centre offers is that it takes account of the Muslim way of life. The way of life, the culture and religion of the Muslim elderly is quite different from that of the Christian or of the Hindu. There are number of activities which are forbidden in our religion according to Islam. There are matters related to religion, prayers, diet, and so on. Because we are a Muslim day centre we know about these things. We would welcome someone from another community to our centre, we would not turn them away, but, at the moment, only Muslims use the centre.

Funding

Our only source of funding for the day centre is through the social services. They pay the money to the Council for Mosques who, in turn, pay the wages. The wages themselves are made up by the Council for Voluntary Organisations in Bradford (CVS Bradford), they make up the wage slips. The social services pay for the running costs of the centre as well as for my salary. However, obtaining money from the council is not an easy task. We have to prove to them that people will benefit from the funding, and which section of the community it is who will benefit. We have to provide reports on the running of the project, so I am keeping a record of everything.

One of the things we have been asked by the social services is to provide a set of performance measures. These measures include such things as the numbers attending, the number of activities on offer, at least four different activities, a membership involvement in the operation of the day centre. These performance measures would be used by ourselves in the future as evidence of our work in order to secure continued funding for the post of the co-ordinator and for the running of the day centre for the next 3 years.

Volunteers

All of the representatives on the Council for Mosques are volunteers, but the workers at the two day centres are both paid employees. However, the centre also makes use of local volunteers. We have one gentleman who prepares a meal one day a week for users at the centre, and there is also another gentleman who comes in as a volunteer who lives locally and fills in for me when I have to leave the building; it is not always possible to do everything over the phone. However, I brief him before I go out, on what to do when I am not here, and have guided him on what needs to be done on those occasions. I think it would be possible to get some more people from the area to act as volunteers at the day centre but I feel that we really need volunteers who have previous experience in some aspect of the care profession on how to look after the elderly.

Points to Ponder

▽ The day centre's location within an established Muslim enclave of the city.

▽ The numbers of male members attending the day centre.

▽ The needs of the Muslim elderly with respect to day centre provision — diet, religion, culture.

▽ The absence of facilities at the day centre for Muslim elderly disabled.

▽ The presence at the centre of religious facilities for centre users.

▽ The use of performance indicators for funding purposes for the project.

5 Ghandi Hall day centre — Manchester

Mr Mamtora, Secretary
Dr Das, Co-ordinator and President of the Indian Association, Manchester

Keypoints

This account, told entirely in the words of Mr Mamtora and Dr Das is interesting because it highlights:

▲ *the gaps in existing day centre provision for the Asian elderly in the area;*
▲ *The role of elderly volunteers in mounting and sustaining a project;*
▲ *The keyworker/co-ordinator's impact on the development of the project;*
▲ *The importance of effective networking to the success of the project.*

Background

The workers

Mr Mamtora

I have been acting as secretary right from when the centre, which was then a club, first started in 1983. The idea for the club first came from the Indian Association, through the advice and instruction from some government department, who then approached us and said 'why don't you try and do something for your own elderly people?' So the Indian Association called me and one other lady and said, 'come on — you start and we will give you backing' — the backing of words, because they had no money to give us. However, they offered us the use of Ghandi Hall for one afternoon each week so we said 'Okay'. In the beginning, representatives from the Indian Association attended the club and offered their formal presence, but not for doing anything, you know.

So then we started. We had some spirit of enthusiasm. We were all volunteers. We provided tea, we bought our own snacks, our own record players, and we used our own transport to bring people to and from the club. When we started, we had only ten people. We had no facilities, no transport — nothing whatsoever — but the people were very happy.

So from ten — at one stage the number of people went down to five because we had no facilities to provide for them, we worked very hard. From five our numbers went up to 10, 15, 20, but there was still nothing to offer. But, finally, luckily during 1988 we happened to have contact with Dr Das and, from then, things have flourished.

Dr Das was then executive member of the Indian Association and I happened to write a letter to the Indian Association executive committee and said 'Look, you are not giving us any help. You have put us in this position, but you are not doing anything. You are not even putting the name of our day centre in your circulars.' I wrote telling them that we could not bring more people to the club because there was no transport to bring people down here. I could only bring four people in my car and then take them back again. Everything that was being done was also being done at our own costs.

So luckily, by then Dr Das was there and they pushed him: 'Go and see what they are doing.'

The first time he came we didn't know him. He was a stranger. He didn't speak my language.

I said 'Who are you?'

He said 'I am Dr Das.'

and I said 'Do you speak this language?' (Gujurati)

and he said 'No'.

so I said 'Then why do you come here?'

He didn't tell me the facts on that very first day, but, gradually, I came to understand why he was here. So I gave him all of my files and information on the club, because I used to keep a record and minutes of every meeting which we held. I had four or five files which I gave to him and he took up from there. Later he said, 'Oh yes, we must do something,' and from there things have flourished.

When Dr Das joined us, he managed to get some help. He worked very hard, day and night. He contacted government departments. He created a lot of contacts with local government. He went down and attended meetings and tried to get some help for the centre. He is a very soft person, he never gets annoyed at whatever you say, but he persists and that is what made us get some help. So it started, things moved in a good way. That's why I say we are thankful to him. Since we started getting help — one by one promises of help started coming in — our facilities improved. Today, in our centre we have about 75–80 members and another 60–65 on the waiting list. We provide free transport, we provide a subsidised meal, we provide entertainments — we provide a lot of facilities and the people are very, very happy.

We still need more and more help and he is the man who has done a lot of miracles and we pray for his long life because, if he was not there — believe me it is not to flatter — we would not be in the position we are in at the moment. That is why I say we are thankful to him.

Dr Das

I first officially retired in 1985 for four months, then I took a locum job in Trafford General Hospital where I worked for two years. During the period of 1988 which coincided with my full retirement, I was on the executive committee of the Indian Association, Manchester and, because they knew that I was a retired medical practitioner, they asked me to follow up some of the letters they had received from Mr Mamtora about the work which was being done at the centre. I met with Mr Mamtora and learned from him that he was bringing people every Friday afternoon to the centre — 5, 10, 15 people something like that — and offering them some snacks, access to the temple and then taking them back home at the end of the day. He also gave me files which he had kept on the work and which I took away to read. I then took the information back to the executive committee where the matter was discussed very seriously in the Indian Association. It was unanimously agreed that more attention should be given to this development of a senior citizens' centre than had been given before and that it was a very vital project. It was a vital project because people still do not recognise that there are now a lot of Indian pensioners living in Manchester. In my 30 years of working in hospitals, I hardly ever saw one or two Indian people a year attending the day centre or the day hospital. When they did come, they would be left sitting in one corner of the room. No one would speak to them — no communication. Staff would sometimes ask me if I could ask the person what her needs were and all that sort of thing. Knowing this, I said the best thing would be to set up our own facility, and that I could see what I could do. I agreed to make contact with Mr Mamtora to find out what went on at the centre, why they didn't get any grants and why the centre work had not been developed. The executive committee then elected me as co-ordinator from the Indian Association to the senior citizens' centre and I said 'I will do my best'.

So then I came here and started working with Mr Mamtora. He had a lot of files, on everything relating to the centre. He was very meticulous. Every Friday he would write up a record of the activities which had taken place that afternoon. There were also copies of applications which the day centre had made to the city council but which had not been followed up by the previous secretary, so the council just kept quiet and nothing happened. Of course, having worked in a large organisation, I knew something of how the system worked and where to pinch. So anyhow, with Mr Mamtora's help, I took all the files, papers relating to the day centre and having read them I had a few long talks with Mr Mamtora. So I said 'All right, let us do something'. But, in my own mind, I said, let me first find out what the burden of the case load is likely to be. How many Indians are there in Manchester? How many elderly Indians are there in Manchester? What can be done, and what has not been done, and what do they need?

I went to the Manchester city statistics department and they were very helpful, but the statistics they had were not up to date. There was the 1981 census, plus an 1983 survey of the ethnic minorities in Manchester which had been carried out by the planning department of the city council and in 1987 another survey they had done on ethnic minorities in Manchester. From these surveys, I found out that there were around 12,000 Indians living in Manchester itself, and about 2000 of those were Indian pensioners. I was really shocked at this. Then I discovered that there were around 200 pensioners who were living on their own and who were in their 80s or 90s. So, after doing that research, I knew then the size of the caseload.

Although I say I was surprised, I also knew that many people must be living on their own because, whilst they were still being looked after by their children — many were being looked after by their sons and daughter-in-law or daughter and son-in-law — the adult children go to work — so the whole day they are on their own. Also, the Indian traditional family system is breaking down rapidly in western society. Adult children have moved to other regions owing to job mobility. So many more elderly parents are now living on their own.

These Indian people, who are now in their 80s and 90s, first came to this country in the 1940s and 1950s after the second world war when there was a lot of labour shortages and they worked very hard in the textile industries and transport and also in some professions like teaching, medicine and nursing. At that time, of course, the wages were very low. National contributions were also low, so they didn't have much of a pension and they are now living on their own.

I started by first visiting the people who were living on their own and visited 216 families over a two-month period — Saturday and Sunday evenings, because at that time I was still working part-time as a locum consultant at Trafford General Hospital. I was really shocked at the pathetic state they were living in. I found that some were very frail. Many had not been out of their council flats for more than a year because they have no car and they are too frail to go by bus. They can only travel by bus when some relative visits them or when they are accompanied by someone else. So anyhow, I had a discussion with Mr Matura and said 'There is a great burden — we have to do something.'

Developing the day centre

Then I identified my aims and objectives. I thought that first of all we should seek to make a day centre where the Indian old people could come and get together and socialise — have a chit chat and everything like that. A place where people could meet friends that they had not seen for a long time or make new friends. They would have to have a place to meet, and I had in my mind that we would ask the Indian Association to give us Ghandi Hall for one day a week — at least to start. They would also need community transport to take people to and from the centre.

Dr Das then began a round of meetings with a variety of organisations in an attempt to generate wider interest in the project, and to attract funding and resources.

So I went to the city council, to the social services department, to community development, to Age Concern, to the race unit, to the Manchester Council for Voluntary Services, to Manchester Action for Community Care and all the people I could think of, or had heard about, who might be able to offer assistance to the day centre.

I already knew of some of these agencies through my work in hospitals — social services of course, and others I gradually learned about through the discussions I was having with other people. I also visited some other voluntary organisations including the Afro-Caribbean project at Mosside. They had been struggling for the last 9 years to develop their work so I learned some lessons from them.

The city council said 'Of course, it is quite a good project — you start, we will try to help'. However, the first financial help we got was through a Pennington bequest which is like a Trust, and they gave £500 to start the project. So, with that, we would have some money to cover petrol expenses and money for hiring some community transport and that is how we started. Then gradually, the community division also gave some grants to help with religious festivals and for outside trips.

I also invited the director of social services of Manchester to come and see the day centre. He came and he sympathised, but he said that he had had a cut of £400,000 for this year (1989) and so there wasn't much money available. So I said 'Look we are doing your work. If these elderly were going to your day centres then you would be spending money.' He replied that he understood the situation and that the Indian elderly were welcome to use existing day centre provisions. But they can't go there. They don't understand English and it would be out of the frying pan into the fire. They would just sit there and nobody would talk to them. There are differences in diet, religion, culture — differences in everything.

In Leicester they have got about eight day centres. They have day hospitals for the Asian elderly, they have two residential homes for the Asians — so why in Manchester is there nothing? There is no centre or place for activities for the Indian elderly people.

So anyhow, he said 'Alright, we haven't got any money but we will consider applications for next year'.

Next year, next year and it went on like that. I was really fed up and frustrated. That was two years ago. They only gave us £800 for the whole year for petrol and transport expenses. Last week I got a letter from social services who have imposed a 5% cut across the board, so we will only get £700 for the whole of the coming year.

Transport

Apart from the initial difficulties the project had in attracting support funding for the development of the day centre, there was also the ongoing problem of providing transport to convey members to and from the project.

Over the last 3 months we have needed three minibuses because of the gradual increase in the number of people who come to the day centre. We are now bringing people from central, north and south Manchester, Stretford, Trafford, Stockport, Gatley , because there are no other Indian day centres for old people — so they are coming from all those areas. The three minibuses are all community transport. We approached the Minehead Social Services Centre which is a local group and they gave us the use of one minibus free, but we pay for the driver. Age Concern, Trafford also gave us a minibus and we supply the driver. However, the community transport is not reliable — at the last moment they cancel. The day before, they ring to say that the bus has broken down. During the last 3 weeks the Minehead social transport minibus has broken down and the old people are ringing, ringing There is no transport, and we are sitting waiting'. The Minehead social services has now stopped the minibus completely.

Our other problem is that the three drivers for the minibuses are not voluntary drivers. They are all unemployed and they charge £30 for their services which is £90 a day for the cost of the three drivers and we require them 2 days a week. However, we cannot afford the cost of hiring three minibuses at £90 a day for 2 days a week and now the people tell us that they want to come 3 days a week.

I was so fed up with the problem of transport that I approached Help the Aged, London and said 'We want to have our own minibuses.' If we had two minibuses, we would then be able to expand our activities to three days in the week. We could do shopping for the frail elderly, we could provide transport for hospital visiting for those who have a relative and also use the buses to take people outside for trips. Anyhow, I wrote to Help the Aged and they sent representatives from London and from Preston who visited the day centre and gave me an application form — so I applied. Fortunately, they said they would give £7,000 for the purchase of one minibus — of course, a minibus costs £17,000, but they have given £7,000. To raise the other £10,000 we had to apply to the city council. I applied to the city council for the £10,000 and the transport committee, and the policy resources committee have approved the application, and it is now going for approval to the finance committee which is being held next week.

New funding

The difficulties confronting the day centre, which apart from transport, included running costs, and the quality of provision on offer to the members attending the day centre have acted as continuing pressures on Dr Das and his management committee. Their attempts to secure a firmer basis for the project recently have met with some success.

Because of all of the difficulties which we were meeting, I was fed up. However, I am on the committee of MACHEM and also on the community health council executive committee and, from here and there, I got to know that there is a joint funding grant which the three health authorities and the local authority can offer. I approached Manchester Action for Community Care and Paul Barker who is attached to the Manchester Council for Voluntary Services (MCVS) and said 'look, I can't get any financial support from the social services for the running of a day centre at Ghandi hall and, without support, I think it will vanish'. So Paul came to the centre and saw the people and everything that we were offering and was very impressed. He said 'Oh yes, we must try for joint funding for this project'. Well, anyhow, I sent off an application and then later went to the city council and met with the official, Mr Eric Taylor who was dealing with these matters and explained everything to him. The application then went to the joint funding committee for their sanction last year for £12,000 for each year to meet running expenses. That gave me great relief. However, because this building is owned by the Indian religious and charitable trust and the Indian Association pays

£2000 rent to the trust, we will now have to make a contribution to our use of the premises. Until now, the trust have said that as we are under the umbrella of the Indian Association we did not have to pay any rent. But, now that we will be getting grants under the joint funding, the Indian Association say that we will have to pay £600 per year for the use of the hall and the services.

The Centre facilities

The location of the day centre within the premises occupied by the Indian Association at Ghandi Hall were not ideal and the limitations of these became apparent as the project developed and the numbers of people using the centre increased. These developments, in turn, posed further sets of problems for Dr Das and the management committee of the day centre. General facilities within the hall have been improved and further improvements are planned for the future.

When the Ghandi Hall was bought in 1969 it was probably just big enough for the number of Indians who were living here at the time, but, during the last 30 years, that number has increased rapidly — five times or more. Toilet facilities, for example, were not suitable for the elderly people. There was no disabled access and the toilet facilities themselves were in an awful condition. I went again to the city council, disability section, and brought the officer here and he agreed that improvements were necessary. So, last year, they gave £15,000 and the toilets were improved, and there were ramps made for access for disabled people, and toilets for disabled people installed.

The size of the facilities are also limited in terms of what we can offer within the space. I want to have more activities available to people who come to the day centre. I approached the regional sports council and they came here and they were very impressed and gave £863 and we bought table tennis, badminton, darts, and indoor bowling but there is not sufficient space here. However, the Indian Association have plans for an extension to the hall which will mean that we will be able to offer more activities in the future.

As the project expanded, both in terms of the numbers using its services and the types of facilities on offer, attention was given coincidently to the quality and the quantity of resources available for elderly people attending the day centre.

The original seating we had at the day centre was unsuitable. We have a number of small, hard chairs, but it is unfair to ask elderly people to sit on these hard chairs for perhaps 3 or 4 hours. At other day centres, they have proper high back chairs. So again I applied to the city council for a small grant for equipment. They gave us £1500 for the chairs and for the tables. The high back chairs cost £200 each and we bought 20 of these but we need 40–50 such chairs for the number of members that attend.

Our kitchen is also a very narrow one, so meals are not cooked there but in Trafford and are then brought here by taxi. The meals are just warmed up here. I went to Age Concern and invited the director to

come to the day centre to see what was on offer and to view our
kitchen facilities. The director from Age Concern who came here made
an application on our behalf to London, and they gave £1000 which we
used to buy the cooker which we now use to heat the meals.

Activities

Two days a week we collect our senior citizens and bring them to the
centre and because they are here for 3 and 4 hours we need to give them
a cooked meal.

While they are here, we provide a number of activities and entertainments for them also — bingo, of course, and exercise classes. We
offer them some entertainments as we now have a new TV and video
recorder. The city council gave us £1100 this year to make that purchase.
So they have TV and we hire Indian films in their language for them
to watch.

Also, when I visited old people in their homes, many people were
not aware of the facilities that are available from the social services. They
were not aware of the social security benefits they are entitled to, and
they were not getting these. So I went to the social security department
and asked if they could send someone every week to give information on
benefits to the elderly and to interview people at the day centre, because
our Indians are very shy — especially the ladies. They don't want to
discuss their circumstances publicly. So I asked them at the department
of social security and they were very kind. They send us an officer every
Thursday to give us welfare benefits advice. We have a retired teacher
who acts as interpreter on the se days because many of our clients only
speak Goujarati, they do not understand English, especially the ladies.

Then I thought, we could have some local Indian doctors visit the
day centre to talk to the elderly in their own language — many are
Goujarati and I myself don't speak Goujarati. I am from eastern India so
my language is different. So local Goujarati doctors will sometimes come;
Punjabi doctors will sometimes come and sometimes Bengali doctors
come and talk about illnesses that can affect the elderly and how to
prevent these. A health visitor with an interpreter will also come to talk
about hygiene and nutrition, and what makes for a proper balanced diet
and everything. We also get someone from the social services to visit the
day centre who can talk about the services that are available to elderly
people.

We also have a temple here at the day centre so that people can go
and pray. It is very important to them that they are able to keep up their
devotions, and we are able to offer that here at the centre.

Then we thought that we would have a coach trip out once a month
because many of our elderly people have not been out. So I applied to
the community development who give £90 towards the cost of each coach
trip and to help with the festival attached to the day centre. However,
we also collect £5–6, it depends on the distance of the coach trip, from
each person who wishes to make the outing. We usually are left with
a loss of about £30 on the cost of these outings, and that comes out of
the running expenses fund of the centre.

We charge £1 to cover the cost of a meal at the centre — it used to be 75p; but, we don't make any charge for transport or for attendance at the centre.

Coming here has improved the quality of life for so many of the elderly, especially those who are living on their own. When we increased the days we were open to two days a week we had between 70–80 members coming on these days. I thought that we would be best having 30–40 coming on one day and 30–40 coming on another day. So I discussed that with them and with the management committee and they said 'No, we want to come both days in the week' — in fact, they want to come three days in the week because they look forward so much to the time they can spend here with their friends.

Volunteers

The day centre is heavily dependent on the use of volunteers to provide the services for the senior citizens who attend, and some further assistance now seems necessary especially in the area of transport.

Because of the difficulties that we have had in the past of meeting the costs of paying for the three drivers to bring people to the centre on the days when we are open, I approached the Manchester Council for Voluntary Services for two voluntary drivers, but so far without success. When we get our own two minibuses, we will need drivers, and we would prefer to have volunteer drivers if that is possible.

All the other people who work at the centre do so without any payment. The cooking, collecting and serving of the meals and the cleaning is all done by volunteers. The ladies who prepare the meals came forward voluntarily. They also do the cleaning but later the management committee thought that that was unfair, so we now have one day a week where the males will do the cleaning and the second day the females will do the cleaning — after all, the centre is for males and females.

But it is all getting too much; they are not getting any younger, they are mostly old people. To help with the burden of the work we have got an industrial dishwasher. It was purchased from a grant from the business community. I went and begged the business community and got £2000 and bought a dishwasher because you see we have over a 100 steel plates now for the old people and washing was becoming too much.

Future plans

The considerable progress and development of the day centre for the Indian elderly has, in large part, been achieved through the concerted efforts of the management committee, particularly Dr Das. Dr Das has sought to secure the centre's operation by establishing a wide network of contacts and associations and by publicising his centre's activities through a variety of routes. However, the ability of Dr Das and his volunteer management group to continue this work indefinitely into the future is possibly now under question, and attention is being given by them to securing the centre's long-term future operations.

There is still a lot that I want for the senior citizens, for example, language classes. However, it has been a lot of hard work. I have worked nine in the morning until sometimes late at night. My wife says I am now working more than before retirement. There are applications, correspondence, meetings, everything. I am also the president, this year, of the Indian Association, co-ordinator of the senior citizens centre, I am on the MACHEM executive committee, community health council, Manchester Council for Community Relations and the race relations executive. So before 12.00, or 1.00 I never go to sleep and then there are the festivals. We celebrate all the local festivals with the senior citizens at the day centre. The High Commissioner for the Indian Association is coming in August and I have invited the Lord Mayor to attend and that all needs organising.

I have also spoken on radio and written in community newspapers and visited Blackburn, Preston and Bolton and said day centres for the Indian elderly should be in every district and that Manchester should have three. When we started in November 1988, this was the only day centre in the north west. Now Bolton has started a day centre for the Indian elderly on a Tuesday, Aston-under-Lyne has started offering 2 days a week.

Now I feel we need a paid worker. The treasurer is 75, Mr Mamtora is 74 and I am 72. We need some paid workers we could supervise and advise them on everything, and then the work would go smoothly. For, if something happens to us, then what will happen? It will vanish. We could do with a development worker and a clerical assistant — something. Someone should be here to answer questions and the telephone. I work at home. The general secretary works at home. There is nobody else and I have pointed that out to the social services Director when he has visited. He recognises the importance of the work, but the costs. He can't do anything. They always say that they have to maintain the old established organisations. We haven't got anything. That is it.

I wish that social services would seriously consider these facts.

Points to Ponder

▽ The gaps in the provision of the day care facilities for the Asian elderly in the area.
▽ The special needs associated with Asian elderly — language, culture, diet, religion.
▽ The sterotypes of the role of the extended Asian family in providing parent support.
▽ The difficulties of attracting mainstream funding to the project and the factors involved.
▽ The increase in the scale of the project of a period of 3 years.
▽ The efforts of the keyworker/co-ordinator.
▽ The absence of paid staff to the project.
▽ The benefits to the user groups.

6 Scottish Society for Mentally Handicapped — youth club, Livingston

Jean Hain, Cathy Bryson and Myra Owens

Keypoints

This account told entirely in the words of the key volunteers is interesting because:
▲ *it is a good example of a grass roots response to the needs of the mentally handicapped in the community;*
▲ *it is a purely voluntary provision;*
▲ *the age range and degree of handicap of the club's members is extensive;*
▲ *funding is limited;*
▲ *it again highlights the difficulties of recruiting volunteers.*

Background

I wasn't in at the beginning when the club was first formed. I got involved about 10 or 12 years ago, although I had previously set up a similar club in Oxford where I lived at that time. The club itself is affiliated to the Scottish Society for Mental Handicapped whose headquarters are based in Glasgow although all the local branches do their own thing. Glasgow has no jurisdiction over us. We make our own money and we are not funded by Glasgow. (Jean)

The club is basically run by the parents and is all voluntary. Some time ago, some members of the management committee suggested that we get someone paid to come and run the clubs but the committee, as a whole, decided against it. We felt that to do that would take the club away from us, it wouldn't be our club. I don't think it would work the same way if someone was paid to do the job. They wouldn't have the same feelings for the club as we've got. We enjoy what we do here, once you start getting paid, it becomes a job. (Cathy)

There are always at least the three of us here every day whether it's running the clubs or just plain administration work which there is a lot of, or, attending meetings connected with the club. There is also another voluntary worker but he is not here at the moment. (Jean)

I was roped in by Jean to help do a video on some of the club's
activities. There were originally to be three or four mums involved, but
it ended up that there was just Jean and myself. We did the video and
that was it. One thing leads to another here. Once you say you will help,
you will not be given much option of getting back out again. I have been
here six years. Myra, our driver/secretary, got involved in much the same
way. She came in to give a hand one day and has been here ever since.
(Cathy)

Premises

Our original premises were two flats in a block owned by Livingston
Development Corporation. However, the LDC sold the block of flats
to Barratt Developments and I refused to move the club out of the flats
until we were given somewhere else. The LDC previously had suggested
that we locate our club at a local centre but there was not facilities there
which would have allowed us to store the equipment which we need for
our club's activities. What we wanted was somewhere that belonged to
the club and which was theirs. I was then asked by LDC if we would
like these present premises which was a five-apartment house. I went
and had a look and said, 'Yes please'.

LDC did a lot of alterations to the property before we moved in
including small structural changes to the kitchen, to cupboards and to
doors. That is how we came to be here and we have been based here
now for 8 years, although even these premises aren't entirely suitable.
The fire regulations put a limit on the number of members which we
can take and we are already at that maximum number. There are also
problems about wheelchair access. We just can't get them in. We don't
have a ramp, although we are going to try and have one built. However,
the social work department is unable to help with the cost of that because
they say that is not within their remit. You see, these premises are not a
private house but a club, and the social work funding only covers private
dwellings. However, we have written to Anneka Rice to ask if she would
accept the challenge of building us a new centre for our members.

We also have a problem of parking the minibus. The house is in a
cul-de-sac and parking problems often cause us difficulty in getting the
kids into the club. The local neighbours are generally quite good, but we
have been getting problems with kids from outside making fun of our
kids coming in, and that really upsets us. (Jean)

Funding

The club's main source of funding comes from a £2,000 grant from
the social work department which is augmented occasionally by small
amenities grants from West Lothian District Council as well as by
fund-raising events which we do ourselves.

We have a jumble sale every Thursday. We also go through the
Yellow Pages with the telephone book and write begging letters to
people. We apply to the district council, although they seem to be
giving grants to certain groups and we seem to be one of the groups

that aren't very lucky or well known. I think it's also about us just being volunteers, we are not professionals, we just do it.

Transport

We have a minibus ambulance which is 3 years old and which we got free from Lothian Region Council. It is used exclusively by us, although it is sometimes hired out to the Down's syndrome group in the area. We also have access to two buses from the Social Work Department for the clubs so that there are three buses in all coming here. Two social work drivers drive the social work buses and Myra drives our own bus. The social work department covers the hiring costs of their buses. Buses begin to pick up our club members at about 6 o'clock in the evening and start dropping them off again around 9 o'clock. We cover the district of Livingston which includes Livingston itself, Uphall and Broxburn.

However, there is the possibility that we may be going to lose some of the social work transport which we get every week. We were told that we might be cut back to having transport for the club from social work once a fortnight instead of every week, as happens at the moment. There was also some suggestion that we may have difficulty in getting transport for our Christmas party.

Users

We have an age range of 5–76 years, and the club meets on three nights of the week; Monday, Tuesday, Wednesday and also on Saturday morning. The Monday night clubs were for the severely disabled and, when we started off, there were ten members.

Now there are 30 members who come on this night but, not all are severely handicapped. Tuesday night is for the younger members, 5–16 year-olds, and there are anything from 18 to 30 members every week on the Tuesday night. Wednesday night is a club for over 16s and, in fact, we have one member who is 75 or 76.

The club members who come here have a range of disability and, before they come, we ask their parents or a relative to complete a form which gives us information on whether the person has any walking difficulties, requires help with their food or has an allergy to anything, whether they require drugs whilst they are at the club and, if they are epileptic, what is the best way of dealing with them.

Activities

Some of our members just like to sit and talk with their friends, some play pool, some computer games, some paint, some do dancing downstairs. They just mainly do their own thing. We are not here to teach them, we are here to let them enjoy themselves. It is basically a case of letting them choose what they want to do themselves. They have the choice of dancing, or using the painting room upstairs. These paintings on the walls were done by the club members. Also, we take the children away on holiday and on days out. There are also Hallowe'en parties and Christmas parties which we put on for club members.

On the Monday and Wednesday evenings, we do toasties for the club members and they can also buy tuck. On Tuesday night, we just do tuck. At the Saturday morning club which is from 9.45 am to 11.45 am and is for the 5–16 year olds, again, we just do tuck. However, our microwave which we used for the hamburgers, together with our answering machine, computer and word processor and money from the tuck cupboard were stolen in the break-in to the premises which occurred 3 weeks ago. Hopefully, the insurance will cover the cost of replacements.

The kids pay 30 pence admission and what they spend on the tuck, which is also a source of income. However, all the kids get a Christmas gift together with the parties which we run for them during the year.

Training

Basically, we just get on with it. We carry on the way we would do with our own.

Most of the adult volunteers here have a handicapped child themselves, and so, have some broad experience of working with people with mental handicaps. However, some of our volunteers have first aid experience and we have had St John Ambulance come to the club to give us an input on first aid. Dr Fichbacker from Gogarburn Hospital has also visited the club and spoken with the volunteers about the nature of 'fits' and what to do in such situations. But, in fact, although we have a great many subject to 'fits', few actually have them at the club.

Volunteers

When people first come here, we interview them and tell them what we would expect them to be able to do if they wanted to be a volunteer. We explain to them about the problem of someone having a 'fit' because that is a possibility.

We also tell them that we would expect them to be able to wipe the dirty noses of some of the smaller children, but that is just the wee ones. You find that with a number of young Down's children. But we would not expect volunteers to be asked to do any of that straight away. (Cathy)

There are two club members who use nappies and, although it is very rare that they need to be changed, Jean has been the one who gets the job of changing the dirty nappies. There was also a problem we had a few weeks ago with one man in a wheelchair who required the toilet but there was no way we could get him and the chair into the toilet, so we just had to get a urine bottle for him. We just have to get on with it as best we can.

Most of our volunteers are also committee members. We have a total of 20–22 volunteers. We got some of our volunteers through a school project and, after that had finished, they stayed on with us and introduced some of their friends. Mainly, it is a case of sisters, fathers, mothers who are volunteers. They range in age from 16 upwards. On average, we have about six volunteers attending the evening clubs and between two and three attending the Saturday morning club. If it happens that enough volunteers don't turn up, we just do it ourselves.

Occasionally, someone will come along, but that doesn't happen very often.

Parental Support

We do a playscheme at Easter and in summer. This was the first playscheme we have done in 2 years because we decided that we were not getting the help and support we needed from the parents. We sent a newssheet round to all the parents letting them know what was going on and inviting them to attend, even for a couple of hours, one day in the week that the playscheme ran. In fact, it is only for the playscheme that we have asked the parents to come in one day a week. We felt that if we were going to provide a full day out, we wanted a parent or a responsible adult to accompany the child, but there was not a lot of response to that at all.

Only two or three turned up. We don't get a lot of support from the parents. However, if we forgot to turn up one night in the bus to pick up one of their children, they would be on the phone straight away. We sometimes feel we get used as a babysitter service by many of the parents and, if it was not for the children getting so much out of the clubs and the playschemes, we would not do it. But, it's for the children. It really gives the children something to do and occupies their minds. The playscheme is for 5–16 year olds and they had a great time this summer. We went all over. As far as Dunoon, to Portobello, the Safari Park, North Berwick, the fire station, the bus station, we went swimming, to the airport — we had them all over and they had a fantastic time. The volunteers enjoyed it as much as the weans did.

There are also fund-raising events. We write to all the parents inviting them to contribute or support the event and if we get one or two turning up, we are lucky. We had the break-in and there was a fund-raising event for that. We had it advertised on the local radio and had the event opened by a well-known celebrity. All the parents got a leaflet and only five actually turned up on the day. A few parents hand in boxes of biscuits for auction, and one or two parents will save pennies in a jar for the club and we are very grateful for that, but again, it is always the same few parents who will provide that support.

Even the Christmas shopping, where we buy a Christmas present for all the club members is getting to the stage where we feel we cannot afford the time any more, and feel that parents could be doing a bit of the gift choosing as well.

The management committee

There is a management committee of about 22 members, but you never get all 22 members attending. In fact, I think there are several members who could be scrubbed from the books. They have never attended a meeting this year.

Network and professional support

Schools

Because of the problems we have been having with the local school children, we had written to all the schools in the area asking if we could come and talk to the pupils about mental handicap. Only three replied and none of these schools invited us to meet with the children.

Social work

We have a liaison officer at the social work department who is responsible for the handicapped and who comes by every so often. But, everything we do is on our own back. We have also been told that, because the social worker is not paid overtime, she would no longer be able to attend evening management committee meetings.

Community development

A community development worker from Livingston Development Corporation has been very good in helping us sort out any problems we have had, such as repairs to the club premises or recently, helping us with doing posters and publicity work for the auction, as we are not very good at doing posters ourselves.

Contact with other similar groups

We don't really have much contact with other handicapped groups except the Scottish Down's Syndrome Group. We go to their disco every month, and we also loan them the use of our bus on occasion and they, in turn, share some of their equipment with ourselves. (Jean)

Long-term prospects

What we really need is larger premises. The Livingston Development Corporation have offered us the top of the Howden Health Centre, but for us to use that, a lift is required to be put in which would cost £53,000. However, even if we could raise that money, over 20 of our members are not fully ambulant, so there would be difficulty in getting out of the building in the event of any fire. So, we are having to turn away from considering these as possible future premises for our club.

The long-term prospects are not too good as far as we can see. I don't know what would happen if all three of us were to say 'Right, that's it, we have had enough'. I don't think the club could continue. But there is a limit to what we can do. There is a lot of work involved. We are all here 5 days a week doing office work plus the clubs at night or attending meetings and there is the problem of fitting in our own social lives as well. (Cathy)

Motivation

Basically, the club is run by ourselves. It is all voluntary and we get a great deal of pleasure. Otherwise, we wouldn't be doing it. We are in here every day and we all pitch in to help. Sometimes, we even cry on one another's shoulders. All of us have a handicapped child of our own and know what the club means to the kids. Without the club, the kids would be sitting at home watching TV. But this is their club, they like it here, they are at ease here. They come here and they are able to do their own thing and we think the service we offer the mentally handicapped in this area is tremendous.

Points to ponder

∇ The length of time some volunteers have been associated with the club.

∇ The sheer commitment of the volunteers.

∇ The difficulties associated with the accommodation which houses the club.

∇ The sense in which the volunteers relate to the whole person and not simply the handicap.

∇ The importance of transport.

∇ The limited parental support.

∇ The limited professional support.

7　Oasis: the mental health in the community project
Shula Allan: August 1984 – October 1986
Be Morris: October 1986 – present

Keypoints

This account is included because:
▲ *the Oasis model has been taken up by other voluntary and statutory agencies in Scotland;*
▲ *a professional worker plays a key role as both catalyst and support worker in developing the project;*
▲ *the process involved in setting up the project is clearly worked out;*
▲ *there is a sense of real participation and ownership of aspects of the project among the women involved in the self-help support groups.*

Introduction

A number of mothers of young children experience problems with their mental health. Some suffer from depression (including post-natal depression), others phobic or anxiety problems, many others feel extremely isolated and lonely, all situations associated with a high degree of stress and low self-esteem. Family and friendship networks, when they exist, are often inadequate in supporting these situations and are themselves put under strain. Often alone in their homes, these women may feel guilty and ashamed of being seen as being unable to cope. Professional help, if it is sought, is often unavoidably unable to provide the on-going support necessary to sustain progress to recovery and integration back into the community. Yet, within these same communities are women who are enduring the same situations or who have come through similar experiences, who understand the fears and feelings, and are willing to share and use them as a tool to help both themselves and others. This is an account of a project undertaken by the Edinburgh Association for Mental Health which responds to these situations.

Background

The focus of the project was, and continues to be, the development and
support of 'Oasis', a women's self-help group in Gilmerton which aims
to be both accessible and acceptable to women, particularly mothers of
young children, who may be experiencing a wide range of problems
which could be threatening their mental health and well-being. These
range from mild distress or isolation to anxiety and depression or more
serious conditions.

Initial research into the project's possible location was conducted
in three areas of Edinburgh, Oxgangs, Broomhouse and Gilmerton to
ascertain in each:

- *if* there was a predominant sector of the population whose specific
  mental health needs were not being adequately met by existing
  provision;
- *if* when identified, these needs could be met in practical terms
  within the community, as an adjunct to existing facilities, reflecting
  the communities perceptions of an appropriate response;
- *if* local residents, and professionals working in the area would be
  willing to encourage, participate and support such a project.

EAMH chose to focus on women because, when we looked at the
statistics of admission into the Royal Edinburgh Hospitals, we discovered that the highest intake was for women between the ages of
25 and 64 years of age and that these women came from three main
sectors of the city, Gilmerton, Oxgangs and Broomhouse.

EAMH decided to site the project at Gilmerton for the following
reasons:

- Gilmerton has a large and varied housing stock, including high-
  rise accommodation, containing pockets of deprivation, sited as a
  considerable distance from any existing mental health facilities, for
  example, drop-in centres.
- Professionals and local activists in the area had themselves identified
  the lack of appropriate response to mental health needs of mothers
  of young children living in the area.
- And, importantly, Gilmerton had two major growth points at that
  time, a social work children's centre which aimed to encourage the
  growth of local initiatives, and a community centre about to be
  opened, staffed by volunteers, who wished to develop a 'social
  welfare' element within the centre.
- Because this was intended to be a pilot project, we felt we couldn't
  go into an area which had little resources. We wanted to go into an
  area which had some sort of established network, however small,
  and Gilmerton was the area we chose.

Setting up the project

The worker at that time was Shula Allan. Her role was to discuss with
local people the issue of mental health and find out what were the local

mental health needs of women in the area. Her time was spent sitting around in cafés meeting and talking with women, getting in touch with local activists to discuss the issue of mental health and, again through discussion, raising the level of consciousness in the community that mental health was something to do with them and not just to do with institutions like the hospital. She also went around the different professional workers in the area discussing the idea with them. At the time, I think there was a mixed response coming from the different professions. Some workers were very interested whilst others were unsure because they were uncertain of what they would be referring people to. At that time, we didn't know what the project would be since we felt that it would depend very much on the group members' needs and what they themselves wanted from the project. It was anticipated that members would be fully participating members in the process of building up the resources. It took a long time to build up trust with some members of the medical profession.

As a result of these discussions a planning group, made up of professionals and local residents was formed aimed at both building up links between them and gaining local credibility. This group worked closely with Shula in planning entry into the community centre.

However, initially there were some reservations within the community centre about the setting up of a mental health project within it. There were fears that women would present disturbing behaviour, or be labelled by other users. Lengthy discussions aimed at exploring the myths of mental stress and illness and focusing on the realities of mental illness, however, helped those who were unsure to realise that stress and mental illness was something which can affect everyone and that mental health is as an important factor in well-being as is physical health.

The planning group were also responsible for recruiting volunteers, and for launching a local publicity campaign, through the local community newspaper, local schools, in children's centres and nurseries. Contact was made with all local health visitors who reacted positively to the project and from whom the majority of referrals were initially made. Contact was also made with the area social work department, and other agencies in the city. The planning group has since developed into a management group for the project and meets monthly together with members, to discuss development and plan future progress.

The Oasis group

The 'Oasis' group was formed in October 1984, initially with some eight women, some of whom who were among the women originally contacted by Shula and based at Gilmerton Community Centre. It was never a case of offering anything to the group. It has always been responding to what the women themselves wanted. What they wanted actually fitted in with our own objectives for the project. The main thing the women wanted was a chance to talk, in a close confidential way, with other women who had experienced similar situations, to talk through their own problems, receiving and giving support to other women and really be beginning to work on their own self-esteem.

Aims and objectives of Oasis as defined by the members are:

- to provide support for women during or recovering from mental illness;
- to build a network of mutual self-help, using personal experience;
- to promote exploration of mental health issues within Gilmerton.

The drop-in facility

Oasis initially offered three drop-in sessions weekly. Members in the group rose from 8 to 13 women who attended regularly, joining in discussions and activities. A number of other women attended more spasmodically. These sessions were structured in such a way as to provide an environment for confidential discussion of both personal situations and wider issues as well as activity sessions which provided a basis for developing potential and enhancing personal self-esteem. There was also a regular craft skills exchange, as well as speakers from other agencies who were invited to join the group for discussion on issues such as mental health, personal experience, relationships, child management, primary health care, tranquilliser addiction and stress. By December 1990, the group was meeting four times per week with an average of 36 attendances per week at these group sessions. However, over and above the attendances at the group sessions is the voluntary involvement by a number of the members' in the home visiting scheme.

The home visiting scheme

30% of women have become involved with Oasis through local publicity and recommendations. The majority, however, are referred by health visitors, GPs, children's centre staff, hospital social workers, Women's Aid and the Royal Edinburgh Hospital.

Many of the women were unable to join the group situation immediately, due to the lack of confidence or the nature of their problems. These women were visited in their homes in liaison with the referring agency, by the worker at the time or by a volunteer from the project who discussed with the woman the ideas behind Oasis and how she could possibly benefit from it. Arrangements would then be made for another member of the Oasis group to accompany her to the centre. In some cases, however, long-term support in the home was necessary and a number of women were visited regularly by Oasis volunteers, and/or the worker, many of whom were themselves initially contacted whilst in similar circumstances.

Today, the home visiting service is co-ordinated by the group members themselves who meet monthly with myself to discuss any problems encountered and to deal with the recruitment and training of new members as volunteers. Again it was a case of recognising the women's expertise. They themselves had had the visit and knew what it felt like to have a stranger come to the door with knowledge that you had, or were having, difficulties. The women knew what had been helpful to them and what wasn't in that situation. I would have meetings with the women to discuss who should go on what visit. Initially, the idea was that the visitor would be someone who had shared a similar experience as the person being visited. For example, if someone being referred had experience of post-natal depression or a drug problem, we would send someone who had been in that situation to make the home visit. However, after trying that for a while the group themselves felt strongly that they didn't want to be labelled as being a person who had experienced a particular kind of difficulty. Now it is very much a case of matching the visitor with the referee. Depending on how much information we have, we then decide which volunteer will make the visit. In addition, members in crisis situations are visited by fellow members. An immediate response by Oasis on return home from hospital, together with understanding of the problem of coping again with home management and family relationships, is recognised by the group members as an effective way of sustaining the recovery.

Training and support of volunteers

As women use Oasis to move back into their community, support needs differ. Initially, there is a high degree of support from other members and the workers are aware of the ease of moving into a situation of dependency. Volunteers from the group can use group sessions to discuss the difficulties which they encounter in sustaining support, and the worker provides individual support which focuses on the women's own personal development and progression.

A training programme on counselling has also been prepared by the Oasis group which was designed specifically to develop counselling skills in a self-help group, relating to mental health issues, and was produced as a resource to be used in future training programmes.

Early difficulties

The project encountered several difficulties during its first 8 months. The first of these was the difficulty in developing a *drop-in facility* within the community centre. As one of many centre user groups, Oasis had no permanent use of a room and could only operate within the centre's opening hours. A local councillor was approached to ascertain the viability of an application to the Edinburgh District Council for tenure of a flat or house in Gilmerton, but whilst she offered support in principle, indicated a number of difficulties in securing a tenure. The second difficulty was the *creche* facilities available to the group.

> The fact that we only had one room for Oasis meant that both the children and the women were in the same room, which was quite distracting. Initially, the women themselves were doing the creche on a voluntary basis at one end of the room while the group worked at the other. We started to recruit volunteers for the creche and by 1986

obtained another room in the community centre which allowed Oasis and the creche to meet separately.

We got our volunteers through advertising in the local paper and through the Volunteers' Exchange. Our experience of volunteers with the creche was mixed. Some of the children who attend the creche have behavioural problems of withdrawal, or have experienced a degree of vulnerability as they had been exposed to stressful situations in the past. Whilst we only took volunteers who had some training, we nevertheless had a high turnover of voluntary staff which meant we had to find money for a paid creche worker.

By 1987 the creche was operating on all four sessions and was run by a paid worker funded at that time through the Small Projects' Fund. This facility was invaluable to the group in providing stability within the creche and thus enabling the mothers to use and develop Oasis to its full potential. However, that funding was only to March 1988. On average, there are 30 attendances in the creche each week. Some previously isolated children now enjoy play with other children, while their mothers can fully participate in the group activities, knowing that the children's activities are supervised with continuity and by people they can rely on. Oasis make no charge for the creche or for the women attending the group.

The third area of difficulty for Oasis was *funding*. The funding for the pilot project worker was through the Unemployed Voluntary Action fund. However, that grant, which was for 2 years, expired at the end of November 1986 after Oasis had been granted a 3-month extension. The project was then taken over by joint funding between the Lothian region social work department and Lothian Health Board, initially until the end of March 1987. The social work department funding package for 1987–88 was continued although the mental health unit allocation was temporarily delayed.

Today the Oasis project has changed significantly in that it is now mainstream funded through joint funding for a 3-year period which is great in that we know the project is secure and that we can plan ahead. However, we are also locked into what we are required to do on the basis of last year's grant, which means that there is no room for further growth.

The health board have continued to fund their side though there are rumours around that the Region's health board's financial straits might mean that future contributions will be limited to staffing rather than staffing and finance. At the moment the community psychiatric nurse works with us which is in addition to health board funding.

The fourth difficulty was the early *expectations* of the efficacy of Oasis in meeting a wide of range of needs within the group which were often initially unrealistic. The nature of mental health problems can often involve a long journey to recovery. However, becoming involved with other women, who have endured or are still enduring a similar situation, enabled the women to see that things could and would get better.

Change of worker

When the project decided to go for mainstream funding, I was asked to hold the position as worker from October 1986 to March 1987 as there was not going to be a decision made on funding until March, which meant there was a gap from October to March 1987. There was doubt at this time about whether Oasis would still be able to run. Fortunately for the group, I had spent a student placement with Oasis and, whilst there were difficulties for some of the group members letting go of Shula, there was also a degree of confidence in the group in that they knew myself and had worked with me in the past.

The numbers game

By the end of 1988, Oasis had become very big, possibly too large with between 14–15 members coming to our meetings. Too large for any successful outcome in terms of everyone having a chance to speak or in terms of the support they could be offered.

About 30% of the people who come now have stayed for 1–3 years although by now we had gone through the process of building up their own self-esteem and they are taking on more supporting roles with other members. They have done this by telling their story and letting new members of Oasis learn what can be achieved within the group before finally leaving and moving on. However, the majority stay for 2–6 months.

Unlike the hospital setting, we don't discharge a case. Women can come and go in Oasis — it's open ended. Some women come all 4 days when Oasis is open, some only 1 day of the week. Oasis has always been a quality service and we have always resisted saying to women, you can only come on a Wednesday or a Thursday or whenever. There are no restrictions yet. Possibly in the future, funders might be encouraging or may wish to see a different group of people each day the group meets. In theory it could be the same eight to ten women who are coming on each of the four days of the week. It has never happened in practice. It tends to be the few who are more committed to the project who tend to come more frequently to offer support rather than coming for support.

However, at this time there are no restrictions placed on the project by the various funders in terms of referrals or who would be accepted into Oasis.

Inter-agency support

The way in which the project has been encouraged and welcomed by the community centre's management and volunteers has contributed greatly to the viability of the project. Oasis is now seen as an integral part of the centre's activities and enables members of Oasis to feel that they are not isolated because they are enduring difficulties in their personal lives. Consequently, Oasis members mix freely and happily with other centre users and volunteers and make extensive use of the community care as well as taking part in joint centre activities. Centre volunteers themselves now refer women to Oasis and also encourage the use of other centre facilities. A further indication of the centre's commitment to the integration of Oasis into the community centre was the provision of a place on to the management committee for Oasis members.

In supporting and making referrals to Oasis, other professionals are recognising that Oasis can help women to begin to take control over their lives and mental health. Interest is being shown by psychiatrists and psychologists working with Oasis members, and they have indicated an interest in meeting with the group offering any expertise and back-up needed. However, it may be that Oasis has become a victim of its own success.

I think there may have been a tendency to refer women to Oasis, knowing how stretched resources were and wanting to offer the women something and that could result in a referral to Oasis. That is an ongoing piece of negotiation work being undertaken mutually between Oasis and the referring agency in deciding which individuals would be suitable and which person would not be suitable for Oasis. When a referral is perhaps questionable, in that the person has a lot of problems, and the referring agency is not intending to keep in touch with the individual, we would suggest somewhere else. Basically, we are concerned that the referees do not regard Oasis as purely a place for people with severe mental health problems. A large number of women who come to Oasis do have emotional problems, but Oasis is also there for people who are new to the area, and for women who feel isolated within it.

Success

The project is benefiting women by providing support, sustaining and aiding recovery from crisis and relieving situations of extreme loneliness and isolation. It is allowing women to convert what has been a negative experience in their lives into a tool which they can use to help others. The volunteer experience is also used by women as preparation to return to the work environment. The project is providing a resource in a community of minimal resources, seeking out and developing group and individual potential for growth which had previously no way of manifesting itself. Oasis continues to flourish in the community centre and is establishing a higher profile with statutory and voluntary agencies, both within Gilmerton and in Edinburgh as a whole. The Oasis model is also seen to be one which meets a variety of needs, and, although the model was originally developed by the Edinburgh Association of Mental Health, it has been taken up by other statutory and voluntary agencies and has been extended throughout the city and other regions with Oasis having been used on a consultative basis.

Conclusions

The initial idea was to go into an area and set up a mental health resource in that area and help it to become self-sufficient and move on to another area. However, after the first two years of Oasis being established, it became apparent that this was not possible. The nature of mental health is such that groups will always have a high level of vulnerability. Care must be taken not to pass too much responsibility to the key activists to the detriment of their own mental health or to the detriment of the group. Such a group needs a worker attached to it.

Over 100 women have been in contact with and supported by Oasis. Of these women 70% have been referred by statutory and voluntary agencies and the remainder by personal recommendation of Oasis members and as the result of local publicity.

As the project has developed, it has become obvious that there are many other individuals in the Gilmerton area whose needs are not being met. As the project is gaining in credibility, approaches have been made to Oasis by local residents, social workers and by the community psychiatric nurse, asking the Oasis group to consider widening their support systems to include these other vulnerable individuals. As the Oasis group has been endeavouring to provide effective support for mothers with young children, it has not felt able to provide the resources to widen the model. Moreover, in the view of the financial limitations to the existing project there appears little room for further expansion and growth.

Points to Ponder

▽ The factors affecting the worker's judgement in siting the project at Gilmerton.

▽ The factors influencing the setting up of a planning group.

▽ The importance of separate creche facilities for women with young children.

▽ The importance of interagency contact and support.

▽ The development of the home visiting service and its significance for those taking part in the initiative.

▽ The constraints on further development.

▽ The existence of unmet need.

▽ The limitations on the worker's total withdrawal from such projects.

8 Out-of-the-house project

Lami Mulvey and Vicky Hobson

Keypoints

Craigentinny health project

This account of the 'out-of-the-house' course is interesting because:
▲ *an adult education course was used as the method for addressing specific needs of a targetted group of vulnerable women in the community;*
▲ *the course itself is part of a much larger collaborative initiative involving social work, community education and health board professionals and departments;*
▲ *community development was the overriding strategy adopted for the project as a whole;*
▲ *the planning, organisation, implementation and evaluation of the actual project is so detailed;*
▲ *there were direct spin-offs for both those participants on the course(s) and for the community as a whole.*

Background

The Craigentinny health project is the product of a number of initiatives which were brought together collaboratively by locally based staff in social work and community education, the Lothian Health Board and the Regional Joint Working Party for Mental Health.

The joint working party on mental health services, in its first report of March 1986, had considered the value of a *community development* approach, whereby local users, residents and staff could develop resources and establish what was needed prior to any major initiatives being undertaken. However, support finance was the catalyst which brought these elements together. Discussions involving locally-based social work and community education staff and those in the joint working party shaped up the two departments' support finance applications into a coherent project which addressed the opportunities and needs identified by the local area teams. The joint working party recognised the opportunity to test out its objectives and recommended that Craigentinny be given top priority for support finance.

The Craigentinny health project was set up in 1987 with initial funding provided, for a period of three years, by Lothian Health Board and managed by Lothian Regional Council's departments of social work and education. The project employs two full-time workers and one part-time clerical assistant. Its primary aim is to provide a network of resources within the community, addressing issues concerned with well-being — the resources being locally based, easily accessible and responsive to the community's self-defined needs. After a period of time which the workers spent talking to people in the area — residents and those working in the area — they recognised the need for resources addressing, amongst other things, the well-being of women in the community.

Since it was set up in 1987, a number of initiatives have been established. What follows is an account of the development of one specific initiative which reflected an important element of the work undertaken, both in terms of the commitment of one worker's time and resources to the project, i.e. one full day per week, and in terms of positive outcomes achieved for the participants in that initiative.

Out-of-the-house-project

We were going visiting and writing to various projects around the country for ideas and although some of these made use of community education models in their work there did not seem to be any direct employment of community education staff and that was interesting. However, it also meant that I found it a bit more difficult to try to define my role. There seemed to be a designated role for social work but not such a clearly defined role for the community education worker.

The initial idea for this project came from a report I had read of an out-of-the-house course run in Birmingham. The course had been designed to raise self-confidence through assembling new skills, to widen the opportunities of local women and to learn about new opportunities for training and education. That course operated on an art-based curriculum. We thought that elements of the course might be suitably adapted for use by the Craigentinny health project, and that the target group should reflect the aims of the health project. The target groups we identified for this initiative were:

- women with low self-esteem;
- women who are isolated and lack support;
- women who have little success in education;
- women who have little experience of paid work.

The aims of this course were to provide an educational opportunity for women who are isolated and have little successful experience in work or education to reflect on their situation and re-assess their potential. The course itself was designed to provide a variety of arts-linked activities for one day (4 hours) per week, for example, photography, clay work, drama, dance, short story reading, writing; where women can develop listening skills, study skills and confidence. A creche worker was also employed to enable women to be confident and feel free to leave their children and take time for themselves.

Funding

The Craigentinny health project agreed to pay the fees of the part-time professional tutor/organiser who was appointed and the Adult Basic education unit of Lothian Regional Council agreed to meet the cost of any additional tutors employed during the 10 weeks of the course. Lami Mulvey, a full-time project worker at Craigentinny health project worked alongside Vicky Hobson, the tutor organiser for the course.

In addition to the full-time worker involved, costs were as follows:

Tutor/Organiser	£1242.00
Visiting Tutors	£ 160.00
Creche Worker	£ 120.00
Transport	£ 50.00
Total	£1572.00

Stages of the pilot project

Recruitment

The women we targetted for the out-of-the-house project, were likely, in addition to being traditional non-participants in education, to be lacking both in confidence and self-esteem, some perhaps experienced feelings of isolation and depression. Because they might be hesitant and easily discouraged, it was decided from the outset that sufficient time and funds would be allocated for the tutor/organiser to meet potential members at least twice before the course began.

The course dates were fixed: 17 April–14 June 1989, and in January 1989 the tutor/organiser began contacting possible sources of referral.

Craigentinny health project was, by that time, well established with a strong network of contacts in social work, community education, local health practices, the Royal Edinburgh Hospital, and with community psychiatric nurses, health visitors, etc. Through the regular team and management committee meetings, and other activities run by the project, I was able to alert other professionals to the course, whilst Vicky, the tutor/organiser made contact with and visited local health practices, Leith Home Start, the Andrew Duncan Day Unit, Lochend Children's Centre (a social work day nursery), the nursing officer for the area, Leith Drugs Project, community education area teams and workers leading a variety of women's groups, and attended the social work department's team meeting to provide information about the project and invite referrals.

A publicity leaflet which contained a separate returns slip was mailed to the organisations and the professional workers previously contacted and others within the defined geographical area.

Initial meetings

All those returning slips were contacted by Vicky, the tutor/organiser, by telephone whenever possible, otherwise by letter with a stamped addressed envelope, to arrange a meeting. Sometimes the meetings took place in the women's homes and Vicky spent as much time as necessary at these meetings talking to each potential group member to explain the aims and possible content of the course and to ascertain:

- whether it was the sort of course they wanted;
- what they felt they would like out of the course;
- whether any domestic or personal difficulties might affect attendance or commitment;
- how they might respond to a wide variety of arts activities;
- whether they had any previous experience of being in groups;
- whether their expectations of the course were realistic.

All the women interviewed were either referrals from, or had been given course information by, professionals, either doctors, social workers, charge nurses or occupational therapists at the Andrew Duncan day clinic, the adult basic education unit or by health visitors.

Course information had deliberately not been made freely available in libraries and community centres as we did not wish to attract additional course users.

If, after meeting the tutor/organiser, individuals were interested in joining the course, and it was felt that they would benefit from it and make the commitment to attend regularly, they were invited to come into Craigentinny Castle, see the premises, meet myself as the project worker, and have coffee with one or two other potential members. In this way, we felt able to dispel as many of the external barriers to attendance as possible, everyone would have met the two workers who were organising and running the course and they would have met at least one other person intending to join the course as well as having found their way to Craigentinny and become familiar with the centre.

Educational guidance and counselling

It is important to stress here that, whilst women presenting themselves were carefully interviewed to ascertain whether they would benefit from the course, Vicky also used her considerable experience of adult education and guidance to refer women to other providers if, on either side, it was considered that this was not the most suitable course. Women were referred, and sometimes personally introduced to, the adult education tutor.

The applicants

Out of 31 women returning forms requesting further information, all were invited for interview. Of these, ten either did not respond to invitations for an interview, or did not turn up, or were out when visited. Further attempts were made to contact these people without success. Firm places were offered to 12 women, and all others were provided with alternative suggestions, or put on the waiting list.

The participants

The age range of the 12 women accepting places (between 23 and 61 years) was quite an even spread. Two were attending the Andrew Duncan day clinic, three had children attending the Lochend social work children's centre (one a single parent living in bed and breakfast accommodation) two were attending a women's group/drop-in centre in Portobello, one was a member of the women's café, a project run by the Craigentinny health project and she, and one other, referred by her GP, had become isolated and withdrawn as a result of caring for dementing relatives for some years, and were now alone. The remaining three were referred by their social workers, having been identified as being in need of confidence building, friendship, support and encouragement, and a free daytime activity to get them out of their domestic settings.

Half of the group were experiencing or had, at some time previously, suffered severe depression. Three were taking medication for this. One was suffering from multiple sclerosis and was consequently not very mobile and also had visual problems. Several had money problems or rather were experiencing poverty for a variety of reasons. One woman was subject to severe asthmatic attacks. The group members were all experiencing personal, domestic or physical difficulties in varying degrees.

Previous education experience

The original target group had been women with little success in education although, in the event, none of the group had any literacy problems. Their previous experience of education, which, in nearly every case, had ceased on leaving secondary school at the minimum permissible age, had been mixed. However, one or two members at the initial interview had expressed a desire to go on to further study.

Previous or current employment

Out of the 12, two women were employed in low paid domestic work. Two had been hairdressers, two had done clerical work and two had been unskilled workers in a factory and a shop. One woman had some work experience on a YTS scheme.

Several women expressed an interest in gaining enough confidence to return to work of some sort. Others expressed an interest in gaining work of a more skilled nature than they had previously held.

The two single parent members were entirely dependent on social security payments, as were three of the younger married members. One other member lived on her old age pension, and two others were receiving either disability or sickness payment.

Child care

Both workers were aware of the importance of good child care, and the creche worker appointed was seen very much as part of the group, and was included in as many activities as possible. There was only one pre-school child in the creche in the morning. The other pre-school children either attended the social work nursery, or attended the local primary school in the morning and were collected at lunch time, joining the creche in the afternoon.

The setting

Craigentinny health project has its own attractive premises in Craigentinny castle.

Extensive refurbishment had taken place and was completed the day before the start of the out-of-the-house course. The setting itself is comfortable, welcoming and accessible and the importance of this must not be overlooked. The women were able to come early and leave late, and to call in or phone either Vicky or myself. This factor is vital for women who are feeling vulnerable in any way. Having premises for their exclusive use, together with the learning and commitment to a group, of being able to relax, in familiar non-threatening surroundings — these were all vital in building up confidence and self-esteem. This would not have been possible had the course operated from premises booked only for the hours of the course, and employing only part-time sessional workers.

The course programme

Having established child care needs, we were able to plan a course fitting in with domestic and other commitments of the women. The course ran between 10.00 am and 2.00 pm and included lunch as part of the course to enable the group members to have time together informally and build relationships. Although the course was to be art based, offering a variety of tastes and activities, nevertheless we felt it important to include communication skills and to build study skills into many of the sessions. Vicky and myself planned the initial sessions, and the remainder of the programme was subsequently negotiated with the group.

Discussion and evaluation were timetabled after each new activity or exercise and this proved invaluable in reinforcing the cohesion, allowing negative or uncomfortable feelings to be expressed and eliminating any potentially unsuccessful activities.

Each session was led jointly and followed a highly structured and timed programme. Because group work was new to the majority of the members, activities were organised in pairs, trios, small groups and the larger group. Those women who were members of therapeutic groups at the Andrew Duncan day unit acted as catalysts within the group, their openness inspiring confidence and involvement from the quieter members.

The Activities

Possible topics which had been mentioned by members prior to joining the course included writing, drama, play reading, clay modelling, music workshops, paint, photography, video work, visits to art galleries and museums, crafts, dance and movement, discussions on women's health, depression and images of women.

From this list, Vicky and myself planned the outline of the first few sessions:

Session 1   Introduction: communication and learning games
Session 2   Visit to the history of education centre: discussion of school
            experiences.
Session 3   Women and well-being: stress and relaxation, aromatherapy.
Session 4   Visit to theatre workshop: drama workshop.
Session 5   Images of Women: group collage, group poem, video on
            women and fear, self-defence session.

The remaining five sessions were negotiated with course participants
during the first few meetings.

Over the period of the course, skills discussed and practised included:

- setting goals and objectives for the course;
- communications skills: giving instructions; the importance of giving
  and receiving feedback, both verbal and non-verbal;
- understanding learning: various ways and methods of learning: what
  helps, what hinders;
- making and agreeing ground rules for the smooth running of the
  group;
- listening skills: what makes a good listener; empathic listening;
  mirroring, reflecting, observing and recording; listening for facts,
  feelings and intentions;
- using case studies for the purpose of identifying with feelings,
  identifying possible solutions, predicting;
- note taking; recording; reporting back;
- discussion of an activity within a group: agreeing on what to include
  in a presentation and making a verbal report to another group;
- writing: creative writing, writing to express feelings or record events;
  group writing;
- assertiveness skills; role play;
- relaxation;
- visualisation;
- planning and organisation of an autonomous follow-on group.

The skills were practised alongside the programmed activities. Evaluation
played a vital part in each session. With regular feedback, the women
were able to see what they had learned or achieved, and to build on
this in the following session. None of the study skills were practised in
isolation. There was constant reinforcement of what had been learned,
how it might be useful in the future, what made it difficult, what was
the next step, etc. Once the women began to feel at home in the group
they were able to join in the planned activities. They gained confidence
and strengths from practising some of these skills in a safe and supported
environment.

    As group leaders, we thought that much of the success of the course
lay in its highly structured programmes. The women were able to involve
themselves in a wide variety of activities, often giving them a release from
the tensions of their personal, domestic or health problems.

    The activities which the group themselves decided upon for the
second half of the course were:

Session 6   Visit to Museum of Childhood

Session 7   Craft taster day: choice of creative writing, water colour
             painting, jewellery making, mosaic making or calligraphy
Session 8   Voice workshop
Session 9   Music workshop
Session 10   Communal cooking
Evaluation of course
Relaxation/Visualisation
Future plans for the groups.

The exact shape and timing of each session was finalised the day before
by Vicky and myself. However, given the composition of the pilot group,
flexibility was all important. We were able to write case studies which
were directly relevant to the women's lives or very recent experiences, or
to introduce situations in assertiveness sessions which had been raised at
other times. On more than one occasion, the timetabled programme was
altered, and in one case abandoned, when an important issue concerning
commitment to the group arose which we felt should be pursued without
delay. That responsiveness on our part increased the women's sense of
importance and value, and encouraged them to volunteer more critical
feedback about activities and issues within the group.

Attendance/Commitment

Twelve women had been offered places on the course, and by means of
regular contact with them up to the commencement of the course, we
were able to ensure that group members were able to take the first step
and attend the first meeting, often the most difficult. All 12 attended
the first session: transport was arranged weekly for the member suffering
from multiple sclerosis and for one other member of the group.

By the fourth week, it had become obvious that one member had
personal problems which prevented her making a full commitment to
the course. Another reported that she thought that she just could not
return. A particular woman had been caring for a dementing father for
some years and had become isolated and withdrawn. She found the
group too large and had difficulty talking about her problems. She was
counselled and encouraged to return or talk about her future plans, but
was firm in her belief that the course was not what she wanted.

For the remainder of the course the group consisted of ten members.
Attendance was interrupted by a variety of crises. An emergency admission
for acute appendicitis in one case, serious chest infections in another, and
two hospital appointments.

After any absence, group members were contacted by telephone or by
letter, and every effort made to reassure them of the group's concern.
This was very important, particularly for one woman who found being
in a group difficult. Regular telephone contact was maintained and she
did return to the group. 'I was becoming a hermit. I had to get out for
my own sanity.' She is now taking a leading part in the new you group
which has been formed.

Towards the end of the course, another group member found part-time employment. This was both a source of great disappointment to her having to leave the group, but also a delight in that she felt that being a part of the group had given her sufficient confidence to apply for work. She was still very much part of the group and returned for part of the session and the evaluation session which followed.

We feel that the successful retention rate on this course was due to the generous allocation of time to each individual during the recruitment stage, to the careful familiarisation with the worker and the setting and to the follow-up and contact work under taken between sessions. We also feel that several important points are worth reaffirming in relation to commitment.

1. Group members' expectations of the course must be realistic.
2. They need considerable amount of individual time and support before the commencement of the course.
3. Group workers must be accessible, at least by telephone, but preferably in person, between sessions, and be prepared to visit and support members in a variety of ways.
4. Regular support and follow-up is necessary of those who miss sessions or express doubts about their ability to attend.
5. Accessible and permanent premises, and full-time workers, are invaluable in imparting a sense of worth and belonging to group members.

Outcome and benefits derived from the course

In the final session on the course evaluation, we devised an exercise which included the skills of listening, speaking and recording, to allow each group member to assess what she and the group as a whole had achieved. This was a set of questions, each one to be discussed with a different group member, to elicit the maximum response. This provided us with important feedback which was most favourable, and confirmed the value and benefit of this type of course.

Two women who had been attending the Andrew Duncan day unit twice a week were discharged during the course. They reported back favourably to the unit, who readily supported a course which enabled people to get out and take time for themselves in a supportive atmosphere. Another group member with a long history of depression related the fact that, when she had been discharged from a psychiatric hospital years ago, there had been no groups of this type, and she had felt bereft and without support.

The assistant co-ordinator at Lochend children's centre also wished to put on record how invaluable she had perceived the course to be for those women with children attending the centre.

One woman with a long history of depressive illness, who had been in a variety of educational and therapeutic groups before, and according to a previous worker 'had never become part of any group', emerged as a driving force in forming the new you group.

Other changes which were gradual but noticeable were domestic relationships. Three women reported that they felt more confident in here and in getting their point across at home.

Writing

Vicky and I had planned to encourage writing wherever possible. The original stimulus for writing was the visit by the group to the history of education centre, from which we hoped that various memories would be triggered. When we returned to the centre after the visit, we tried a decoding session using a photograph of a primary school class and looked at pieces of writing about school and other photographs in the hope that everyone would write something, however, short. Vicky and myself had made contingency plans for those who felt they could not write or remember anything, but these proved unnecessary. The group members set to with a will, and each member produced something which was taken away and typed up. This elicited the response from several members who were keen to do more writing, and we encouraged them to bring in and share anything they wrote. We also included creative writing as an option on the taster day, week 7.

Pieces of writing came in steadily over the weeks; some creative, some reminiscent, some poetry, some about the group itself, and such was the quality of it that, at the end of the course, several members of the group collected and edited the writings and produced a booklet entitled *Branching Out*.

Future plans

The participants

One of the broad aims of the course had been to alert women to educational possibilities. At the conclusion of the course, three women expressed an interest in joining a creative writing group, another intended to join a two-day second chance to learn course, and two others intended to return to study for more qualifications with the eventual aim of seeking employment. One member of the group had already found part-time work during the course and most of the other women would continue to attend a women's café or drop-in centre in Portobello.

However, what became apparent from quite early on in the course was the group were anxious about what would happen to them when the course was over. The out-of-the-house course had never been intended as an end in itself. In view of the careful selection and counselling before the course began, and the beneficial effects achieved through attendance, it was vital to ensure that group members were offered further opportunities to build on their newly acquired confidence and sense of achievement. Discussion of future plans was timetabled in several sessions. In the final session, various options and ideas were examined. All of the group wished to continue meeting. Craigentinny health project was prepared to assign a small budget to this group, and to make space available for them, and the project offered some group skills training to three of the members who had volunteered to run the new group. It was agreed that they would plan activities in periods of 6 weeks. A name was quickly suggested by them: the new you group. The group decided that it would start initially as a closed group. They were anxious not to lose the momentum and commitment they had achieved so far and were quite aware of the pitfalls of lack of organisation and commitment. Future members from subsequent out-of-the-house courses would also be welcome to the new group should they choose to join at some future date.

Evaluation of the first out-of-the-house course by ABE organiser

This course benefited from having external evaluation of the course at three stages of its development. This evaluation focused on two aspects of the course. The first, the experience of the participants, and second the design, organisation and implementation of the course itself by the professional markers.

That evaluation confirmed the positive assessment made by the workers and their judgement of the women's experience of the course. It also reaffirmed the importance of planning, organisation and the time required to ensure such standards were attained.

> The success of the pilot course lay largely in the skills and good organisation of the workers but it would not have been satisfying or stimulating had it only run for 2 hours a day for 10 weeks.
>
> This course was qualitatively different from other women's groups essentially because there was time to reflect on their learning and develop into a support group, sharing their fears, anxieties and enjoyment. I would argue that the additional input of tutor hours and organiser time make a course like this a much more valuable education experience as students have the time to explore new skills and knowledge, as well as to develop confidence in themselves and in their abilities to learn in a supportive group. (ABE organiser.)

Out-of-the-house course Mark II, III, IV

Since the conclusion of the first successful out-of-the-house course, there have been three subsequent out-of-the-house courses which have met with equal success. However, for the last two of these the education tutor/ organiser has changed and whilst Lami, the original project worker continues to remain in post, she will increasingly adopt a less up-front role in this particular initiative which to date has occupied about one fifth of her working week. By the fourth course, Lami was also able to reflect on the developments which had taken place and on some of the issues encountered.

Issues

One of the issues which was around and still continues to be around is the whole nature of joint work involving in this case the three different bureaucracies of the health board, education department and social work, each with its own financial arrangements and each with its own ways of managing its budgets, and somehow our management committee has to marry these together. There is also the issue of just dealing with these three different bureaucracies in an administrative way as well as dealing with their different expectations and priorities. For example, sometimes it seems that there is less emphasis placed on preventing people in the community from having to go through the whole mental health spiral. Sometimes it seems that the health board would prefer us to work with people who they considered to be sick. In the case of community education a number of community workers don't feel they have the time or the skills or the resources to become involved in community care, that community care is sometimes regarded as peripheral within community education and that is a debate which is going on. Social work services too have their expectations of us and somehow we have got to balance all these different expectations of the different agencies. I suppose we try to resolve this through constant communication, with GPs on the ground, staff at the Royal Edinburgh Hospital and staff of the social work and community education sub-teams for this area.

Developments

We have got a lot of interest from the hospitals as more and more from the first out-of-the-house courses returned to the day units and fed back how well they had done on the course. What has happened is that, on the third out-of-the-house course, referrals were coming from both the wards and the day unit and they too returned with tales of the support which they had got from the course.

More and more people are beginning to acknowledge that this kind of community provision with its integration of people referred from wards, day units, GPs or from the social work department is really helpful rather than separating and stigmatising these individuals. All of the women have been through one kind of hell or another. The majority have been very depressed, and it is usually that which has taken them to hospital. Here they support each other. They can look at someone who is incredibly low and think, 'I was there last month' or 'I could be there next month'.

Within the group, the women are able to share their experiences and draw support from one another. One significant thing which everyone says from all of the groups is the fact that, within the group, they don't have to put up a front. That itself acts to relieve stress.

Over the period of the three courses, Lami and her co-workers have come to recognise the importance of this mutual sharing of experience and have built that into their programme.

The issue of well-being is now an important element of the course. The group has begun to discuss things like depression or the kinds of things they are going through. However, we are trying to use these experiences as constructively as possible. Rather than people getting stuck talking about their own individual problem with depression or assertiveness, they are actually trying to use that discussion constructively and relating it to the rest of the course. They do that by our encouraging the women to

explore through their writing or their painting their feelings on the issues
that they have discussed and explored during the day. Our objective at
the end of any session is to improve the person's self-confidence and
to help them recognise that they have learned something from their
experience and to feel they have achieved something at the end of it.

The new you group

A significant outcome of the original out-of-the-house course was a development of the new you group which has continued to flourish. The original
women who still constitute the core planning group of the new you group
have learned the importance of structure and organisation in the planning
of their work, and that is demonstrated in the way in which they have
proceeded to structure their own activities. Although not directly involved
in mounting any of these programmed sessions, Lami continued to offer
advice and support to the planning group.

> I used to meet with the women on a regular basis and we would
> plan for 6-week blocks for the new you group. They were very
> diligent in the structured way in which they dealt with the issues
> being raised for discussion by the group. The women also made use
> of the learning techniques from the first out-of-the-house course like
> brainstorming, pairing, case studies and so on. Not only did they hold
> their original membership but also attracted people from the second and
> third out-of-the-house courses.
>   What also happened was that places like the hospital day unit had
> positive feedback about the new you group and started to refer women
> directly to the new you group — by-passing professionals like myself
> which is absolutely brilliant and which is a real credit to the women
> who are involved. That is still continuing to the point where the new
> you group has now exceeded a comfortable size, and they are going to
> have to step back and take a look at their numbers. For example, last
> week there were 17 people in the group and there are also a couple of
> dozen on the mailing list and it may be that we will have to talk to
> our referees about that.
>   We are having a meeting to discuss whether it would be useful to
> divide the group into two smaller groups and bring them together at the
> end of the day as they get so much support from one another.

The role of the worker

> To some extent, they have benefited from not having a professional
> worker there all the time. Part of my role is to help co-ordinate the
> planning group to shoulder the responsibility. However, I think if the
> composition of the planning group changed, and we lost a number of the
> original core members, it would require some group work input which I
> would organise.
>   I also take care of all the administrative stuff connected to the group
> and helped the original planning group write to the inland revenue
> regarding their charitable status. I also act as a safety net for the group.

If there is a crisis, they can come to me and I will help them with it. For example, if there was a lot of distress in the group, I would be able to step in and remove a couple of people until they were able to rejoin the group.

Also what has happened is that the woman who is the pivot of the new you group has been taken on by this project as a sessional tutor. Because she has been given the additional responsibility, I supervise her regularly and she also has the support of colleagues from another group who assist her so that she doesn't have to take a session solely by herself. However, that key worker is getting a lot out of the experience.

Lessons learned

One of the things I learned from the out-of-the-house course was that a structured programme of 10 weeks was a benefit rather than a hindrance to the participants. We had organised and planned the programme well, and had also demanded things from the participants in terms of their own learning which really helped.

The women came out of the sessions feeling they had achieved something — that it wasn't just a discussion or some vague notion of let's get round and support each other. Our learning group had a curriculum which was negotiated with the women, and then carried out to quite a fixed timetable.

We also learned the importance of being sensitive to the dynamics of the group because, often, people in the group were on medication, depressed, whatever, and their attention spans were limited. That meant we continually had to inject some excitement and challenge to the group. You couldn't let things slide. There had to be a lot going on so that the women's concentration didn't flag. We also think there is a very definite role for community education in working with people whose confidence is at rock bottom for whatever reason.

Evaluation

The original aim of this pilot course was 'to provide an educational opportunity for women who are isolated and have had little successful experience in work or education and to reflect on their situation and re-assess their potential'.

That course achieved this aim; in fact, exceeded our expectations in terms of successful outcomes and benefits. The group took full advantage of the opportunities provided by the course. Commitment was high, and the drop-out rate was low. Communication between members of the group developed from the outset. Initially, many of the women had expressed doubts about their own abilities and potential: at the conclusion of the course they felt delighted — with the fact that they had stayed the course, with their achievement and new skills which they had learned, with increased confidence in self-esteem, with their relationships with other members, and with their growing awareness of themselves in relation to others outside the group.

The course also proved to be a stepping-off point for the members.

When it began, if they had voiced any need at all, it was merely a desire to get out of the house and take time for themselves. As the course progressed, they began to articulate their needs more clearly, set goals for themselves, and to become more aware of how they could influence their own lives and relationships.

Whether these goals were short term or long term, educational, emotional or vocational, the group as a whole was able to use the pilot course as a step towards achieving these objectives.

The choice of an arts-based activity proved a sound one, whilst many of the activities were new to most of the group, they are the sort of activities which provided immediate feedback and the sense of achievement and, frequently, spontaneous laughter. For many, a valuable release from their preoccupations.

Although the course has been of great value to these women, it has reached only a small proportion of those people for whom it would prove beneficial. Valuable referral networks do exist and are well used, but finance and funding are lacking for this type of innovative course.

Points to ponder

▽ How the worker came to choose an educational course as the method to be used to respond to the needs of such women.

▽ The availability of resources and staff for the course.

▽ How recruits to the course were enlisted.

▽ The use of a fixed timescale for the course.

▽ The advantages of a negotiated curriculum.

▽ The achievements of the course for those taking part.

▽ The competing interests of different professional bodies participating in the initiative.

▽ The transferability of skills and experiences in setting-up the self-help 'new you group'.

▽ The direct referral to the new you group.

▽ The changing developmental role of the key worker as the project developed.

9 Handsworth Community Care Centre

Angela Powell

Keypoints

This account is interesting because:
▲ it indicates how the disadvantage and sense of alienation experienced by members of ethnic minorities can be addressed;
▲ it explores the impact of policy changes in the health service on local community care services;
▲ it indicates how cultural factors impinge on definitions of mental ill-health;
▲ it illustrates how one agency engages with the families of users and the community within which it is set.

Background

Handsworth is a district of Birmingham, approximately 4 miles from the city centre. Its population is culturally diverse, including people who are of West Indian and Asian origin. As the account of the work of the centre reveals, its emergence reflects a commitment to provide a community care service which is particularly sensitive to the experiences and difficulties of black people.

> What we try to do is provide some sort of recreation, a social atmosphere to the wider community. The centre was set up mainly for people suffering from mental health problems or ill health. We found that the majority of people that we cater for were coming from the hospitals and then being taken back to the hospitals by the police — not having anything to do when they were released from the pyschiatric hospitals — walking the streets. Maybe, if they were hungry they would go to the shop and take something and then they would end up with a charge. So a lot of our clients have criminal charges, as well as having mental health problems. We decided in 1983 — the community, church and local people decided, well, nothing is happening — and we asked what would they like to do. They wanted a centre that would cater for the food that they eat, which is mainly an Afro-Caribbean diet. A centre where they could come and not be forced into it. We have got

a timetable, but it is not rigidly enforced. We lay out the timetable and if you want to do it, then you do it. If you want to sit down all day and talk with someone, that is what you do. Also we have got a welfare officer. She goes out and visits the clients wherever they may live, hostels, prisons, hospital. The craft officer helps motivate the client into doing activities — providing something to do. A training officer deals with the clients and also the trainees that we have from employment training (ET). That is just basically getting a taste before we refer them on to colleges or whatever is there for them.

Since the new community care development, we are getting something like 45 clients a day. They don't always stop on the premises, they pass through the centre. It used to be regularly 25–30 per day, but, since the wards are closing down, we tend to have got more clients coming in.

From year one I was here and then I left. I was working part-time and, in 1984, I came back, I was full-time and I have been here ever since.

Initial funding

The first lot of funding was through the Manpower Services Commission — it was a project under the old community programme. Since 1987 that changed to employment training where the emphasis is more on the trainees than the project. The community programme was more for the community. So the funding was cut dramatically. Now, coming to 1990, funding has been cut from June 30th because ET has ended and the new TECs introduced. Officially we have trainees here until August from ET, after which all funding will be completely stopped from ET.

We also get inner city partnership (ICP) funding for four staff. We had one-off small grants like slippage grants from social services, which run out this year — actually we have had it for 2 years. So we have lost one member of staff who was paid out of those funds. I am hoping that we can continue on ICP funding and also some mainstream social services funding.

All we have received this year, so far, is some of the specific mental health grant. What we hope is that we can move from the present building to new premises. It is the planning permission which is holding it up. It is 200 yards from here. So we have got some funding, and that is for 3 years. Otherwise, we are not sure what funding we will get, and we will have to put in for what ever grants are going and hope that we get some. We ought to get some since we are the only organisation providing these sorts of services for black people. There are other day centres, but black people feel more free with this centre and the activities we provide. They can come in here and shout and nobody will arrest them because of the old stereotype that black people are aggressive, they talk loud and play music loud. They can actually do that here and not feel that someone is watching them. Language and culture and ideas can be expressed — they feel safer here.

It is provided mainly for Afro-Caribbean people, but we won't turn anybody away. We have got, as you can see, Asian women and we

have got white people. We don't stop anyone coming because mental
health problems affect everybody. We tend to get more male clients.
On the books, we have 98 clients, of which 70% are probably male. I
don't know why. The young ladies do use the centre but we do have a
women's support group — the majority of them are on a home training
course at the moment. They prefer to come in and take activities and
go, more than sit down in the centre. We have a regular group of at
least five women who use the centre. The majority use us when they
need us, whether it be with DSS or housing problems.

Workers' roles

We have got Emerald who is the welfare officer. She does most of the
visiting and she helps with the support groups, that is one of her roles,
putting on parent support groups, women's groups, organising visits
for the trainees to other day centres, working with the community
psychiatric nurse (CPN), social workers, attending case conferences,
case reviews, key worker situations. She tries to organise most things.

Then we have got Eleen who is our craft instructor and she deputises
for me. Her job is one of the hardest; she has got skills in knitting,
sewing. She also does weaving, she organises activities, educational
visits, day trips, the annual holiday we have, any sort of fund-raising
and getting sponsors for the centre.

With our new proposals, we have identified the need for two people
to take on this area of work. With the new emphases on community care
and closing hospitals, we have got more people coming in. We find that
we are doing more for the people who leave the hospitals without social
workers or a keyworker. We have to go out and find the right agencies
for them, even places for them to live.

We have got a part-time cook. She provides the menu, shopping
and discussion with the clients. We have coffee afternoons — she will
cook the food and all that, the menus for the community lunch at
Christmas.

The training officer at the moment does training basically for the
12 ETs. Also, he is arranging a trainee package, more like a taster for
the clients who use the centre. It would be in computer studies and
basic office skills at the moment, that is what we are working on.

I am the co-ordinator, project manager. I co-ordinate the project
and its activities and the staff. I go to a lot of meetings, liaise with other
agencies. In fact, because I have been the worker here the longest, I
go to a lot of case reviews on request by the clients. If they could
get me to do everything they would, although we have other staff
here to take on that role, and I have got to let go of some of the
clients because of the work involved. Because of community care, we
are talking about preparing business plans, running care as business,
and I don't intend, if I can help it, to lose out on the quality of care
that we give the clients. My own background — I started off as a youth
and community worker. I have been doing management. I have always
been working with people, including children with special needs and
now mental health.

Project management

While the project owes its inception to initiatives taken within the local community, including the local Methodist church adjacent to its premises, it has developed into a distinct independent agency.

It's independent of the church. It's a voluntary organisation. We need to move because there is no privacy. We have only got the big hall and two small rooms. Since 1983, the project has expanded. What it started as originally was a drop-in centre, but we have outgrown that and become more a day social service. We plan, when we move, to open in the evenings and some weekends. This is what the clients have actually asked for. At evenings and bank holidays, that is the time when they feel lonely and bored. We are not allowed to do it at the church, as the hall is rented out in the evenings.

The management committee includes a social services representative because they give us funding, also someone from Birmingham City Council's economic development unit (EDU).We have got an occupational therapist from All Saints Hospital, a training officer from social services, two parents from amongst the clients' families, two clients and a few people in the community who are just local. In all, there are 12 members on the management committee.

The project co-ordinator is, therefore, accountable to the management committee and the other staff employed by the project are, themselves, accountable to the project co-ordinator.

A new centre and new plans

While the move to a new building would free the centre from some of the constraints of the existing premises — including hours of opening — the building, to which project staff hope to move in the near future, offers other opportunities for change.

Well, first I need to tell you that the building has nine rooms, compared to the two rooms we have here. We intend to start some new projects. These include a prison visiting service, which we had started but we haven't been able to continue. We will have things like a quiet room, a non-smoking room, we will be doing music, weight training and keep fit. There will be a computer room and there will be an advice room. At the moment, we do have an advice club, as we call it, on Wednesdays, but there is not really any privacy, my office has to, for example, double up if a person wants to talk to the CPN in private. So we intend to have a quiet room where you can discuss matters. So those are the main things that we intend to do, along with the clients. We will also have a laundry room and a kitchen for them to cook in where we can do training. We hope to get them more independent, because that is what we are supposed to be doing, to help them live within the community.

Users and their families

It will be evident from what has been said already that the centre maintains some contact with users' families. They have an opportunity to be represented on the management committee, and the pattern of home visiting extends some support to others within the community who have some responsibility for the care of users. However, contact with each user's family takes into account the views of the users concerned.

> We keep in touch with the users' families if they want us to. They know that they can come in at any time. Any reviews that we are told about clients, we always invite the family and neighbours. We are known in the community. We actually get people coming to us asking for help or information about other agencies they could use or approach, even the local police station. Some of our clients do get arrested, and the local police do know us, and that they can ask us to come and see to a client.

Referral system

We do have a referral system. For the community it is usually verbal. They come in, phone or ask us to visit. With social services or the health authority, we have got a referral form for them, because basically we need to know why a person was diagnosed, or what sort of behaviour patterns they have, who is their nearest doctor — because we can't always get that from some of them when they come in. There is also self-referral.

> We are an open door at the moment, and I don't think that we are going to change that policy. The main reason that the centre did start in 1983 was for people who got turned away from the usual day centres; those were the ones that we take in. They were usually people who had behavioural problems — we seek to be more understanding. So we try not to turn away people. I could only think of one person where we had to do that. We would do that if somebody was particularly disruptive and was upsetting other clients who use the centre, but so far, as I said, there has only been one in the 7 years that I have been here.

Relationships with other professionals

The work of the centre brings its staff into contact with a range of other professionals, including, doctors, nurses, social workers, and the police. The quality of relationships between the centre and these other professionals is, therefore, important.

> It has got better. It is something that I, personally, worked on, because you know, voluntary organisations always seem to be seen as second from the statutory side. We are often seen as volunteer do-gooders, but they don't look at you as a professional. I, myself, have gone out to make links because I want a good service for the clients who use the centre. Things like home helps and support in the families weren't known to a lot of the families, and so, because of some of the work that has been

done, we have been able to get a resource book published by the social services this year. Families need to know information about where they can get help. I mean, like respite care, a lot of people thought that that was just for elderly when in fact you can get it for mentally ill people. So I have gone out of my way to help the parents and families of the clients.

We have some good working relationships. I sit on a few committees like the joint care planning group, it's a sort of joint funding planning group, which is funded part by health and by social services and you have a representatives of the voluntary organisations, users, community, health council and planning sitting on these groups.

The two main hospitals that we have contact with are All Saints and Highcroft. We take clients from anywhere in Birmingham. But working with the doctors and social services you have to stop in this catchment area. Like we would be in area 2/3 social services, for the health authority we are in north west district. We do sometimes get in dispute. You see, I believe that when someone is sick they need some help. Last week, for example, we had somebody breaking down, but because he was in Rubery Hospital under a consultant, no-one in west district would see him, because he is still under south district. This is where I find community care is going to get into a lot of problems, when consultants discharge their responsibilities. If you get a client who, after discharge, stopped his medication, the consultants don't usually like working with that person and we tend to have that with a lot of younger people. But if someone responds by taking their medication then we don't have any trouble. We usually work with people who are giving society trouble.

The day centre itself does not have a psychiatrist acting in a consultancy or advisory role to the project as a whole. However, some consultants do visit the centre to see their patients. Neither is a social worker linked with the project, although project staff know the areas worked by local social workers.

The challenge of community care

The biggest difficulty I am having at the moment is actually getting the community to accept that mental health is going to be operating in the community. It is not that the community does not want to accept them — the people suffering from mental health problems — it is just that they don't understand the problem. I believe that we have got to educate the community, especially in an area such as Handsworth where they see it as a drop-in area – where so many people who live in Handsworth appear to have mental health problems; where they are opening all these bed and breakfast hostels. So the community is actually getting tired. You can't actually say to a shopkeeper 'a person with a mental health problem is hungry and that is why he is stealing'. He doesn't want to hear that: they have got a mental health problem — he is losing business. We need to educate the community which is something we are planning now, ourselves, with the health promotion team and social services. We are going to put on a workshop in Handsworth using libraries, shopkeepers, leisure centres, recreation centres — so they understand when they see all these people coming in.

The hospitals aren't supposed to be closed yet, but we are actually getting a lot of people coming out of the hospital, walking around, nothing to do. Some of the clients, I don't think, will be able to live in the community, they have been locked in the hospital for 20–25 years. Everything has changed, so it is going to be very hard. It is going to be difficult for the community which wants to have an open heart but doesn't understand their problems.

Our problem at the centre is to make sure we have the staff to cope with the number of people we have coming out (of hospitals). There is a pilot community mental health team in Ladywood, made up of professionals like social worker, psychiatric nurse, occupational therapist, keyworkers, and they try and treat the patient out in the community. At the moment it seems to be working — that is the pilot. The Handsworth team should be taking off later this year. So even if we get support from those sorts of teams, then I am still not sure that it is all going to work if I tell you the truth. They have been saying for the last 15 years that All Saints Hospital will close. Now, actually seeing them knocking down bits of it, making changes, it is quite frightening. Some of the clients are saying 'but where will I go if I have a relapse?'. 'What if I start hearing the voices that tell me to set fire, where do I go?'. 'If I go to the police they will beat me up.' So it is actually putting fear into some of the clients. We are trying to say to them that we hope that we will be able to have a telephone line going, but I don't think that will start for 2 years at least.

The city's community care plan

It looks very nice — what is written up — it is just that I have a feeling when we write or suggest lovely plans that we are always under funding. If the government will give us the resources, I think it could work. That is one of our main problems. Even though Roy Griffiths said community care could work, he didn't actually imply that you would need resources. As if, volunteers will be doing it free over a long time. You don't have to put a lot in, because they are looking to voluntary organisations to provide a lot of these services. They find that we have been doing it so cheaply.

The administration of community care

At the moment they haven't got it finalised what the forms will be, Social services are looking for a kind of service level agreement, but the health authority want tenders, to find out if it is needed, who is the provider.

One of the main things with voluntary organisations is that we are always having to put in bids. I won't say that I am a professional at doing it, but I can get help. I have been on courses to do business plans and so I have actually got ideas from there. What I might have done is underfund myself. I have got my proposal together and I think will they give me the money. In some parts, voluntary organisations are providing services at a third less than the statutory services. I was on a social services management course and one of the people responsible for a residential home was talking about a budget of £23,000 a year. I was saying to them that I am working on £8000 a year for a day centre, that is the running cost.

What I gathered this year from all the talks which had been going on, was that social services wasn't monitoring our service, wasn't evaluating, wasn't looking at the performance. We have always had to do it because we have been putting in for grants. It is not affecting us but it seems to be affecting the statutory organisations. When we are putting in for bids, like the inner city partnership, we have to tell them how much we want for that year and forecast how much we want for the next 2 years. We have to monitor, it is something that we have always had to do, evaluate and review. Every 6 months the staff get together and we close the centre for half a day and review how we should be doing things, whether we should be doing it, whether we can do it.

Users' complaints

At the moment with us, our complaints procedure is simple. However, for a service level agreement, social services want to see a form. We usually ask the client if they have got a problem and, if it is against some of the staff, they come to me. Then I will ask for it in writing, bring it to the management and see what I can do. If I can deal with it, I will. If it is against me, they can then give their letter in writing to a member of staff who will forward it to the chairman where it will be discussed. The client can come to the management meeting to discuss the complaint. So the users have always had that procedure. But the only thing we haven't done yet, we need to get a form now because of this service level agreement and we need to make sure that all of the clients know about it.

We have users' meetings every Thursday where usually they discuss what they don't like. I mean, last week one of the problems was that we have this scheme, 40p a day for five cups of tea. Usually it had been 15p a cup of tea. One of the clients decided he doesn't want to drink five cups a day but he would like to drink three today and two tomorrow. Well, he was out-voted.

There are some problems that we have with the clients. Some of them have been in hospital for a long time, and have become used to a reward system. I don't like it. In the real world, you don't get rewards for making your bed or keep putting on clean clothing for the week. Some clients will come in and sweep up and then say that you have got to give them 20p, or a cigarette. We are not into that. We tell them it is the real world.

Client reviews

Some of the clients are not really known to anybody except us. For them, we will discuss what is the plan when they get better, if they accept that they are sick. If they don't accept that, they have got a problem, we try and have a talk with them every 3 – 6 months.

Some clients, who are known to other agencies, are often subject to review procedures organised by the other agencies. In those circumstances, the project staff will participate in the review discussions.

I refuse to have a referral from the health authority or social services without a worker. If you are in the hospital and know your social worker, you feel safer. If you are just given a bus fare to come to the centre, it is not nice.

If the main users don't come for a few days, we quickly go out to visit; for the simple reason that it may be a relapse or they have had an accident like the young lady that we didn't see for 2 days and she had burned herself. She ended up in hospital for nearly a year. She was living in a warden hostel. I have never forgotten about it. I thought, how could the warden in the hostel not have noticed. It happened at the weekend and we didn't see her for 2 days.

Community care in action

Part of our care and planning is to go and visit the home that the clients are in, see what it is like and if it is suitable. We can refer them to the right agency. There are a few hostels to work with and we can usually get clients somewhere within 6 weeks.

One of the best outcomes that I have seen so far is clients, not fully recovered, but recovered so that they can actually work and live in the community where some people don't even know that they have had an illness. That to me is a great pleasure and we have had a few from here. Four have actually gone in to full-time work, living as normally as can be expected.

Black people and mental illness

Black people do suffer a lot from mental health problems. Some of them are very hard to diagnose, they all tend to get diagnosed as schizophrenic until they have been more fully assessed.

Hostel life

With so many hostels in the locality, and many of the centre users living in them, it is inevitable that the staff are aware of some of the benefits and disadvantages of hostel life. One hostel, known to the project co-ordinator, operated a particularly rigid regime.

They have to be out of the hostel by 8.00 am in the morning, after they have had their breakfast, and they are not really allowed to go back until 5.00 pm, especially at weekends, it is horrible. I see them Sunday mornings when I come to buy my paper, they are sitting on the benches, it could be raining or freezing.

Also the food and diet are a problem. They tend to get cold food. Hot water was one of the problems as well. Just for washing your face in the morning, there would be no hot water. Sometimes the heating would be turned off if residents decided to stay in the hostel.

One of our clients who was very dissatisfied asked me to get in touch with the social services, which I did. When he went out and visited, the landlady said I was interfering. She telephoned social services to get me sacked, but I don't work for social services. In fact, they investigated this woman. They have been investigating her for years before I came here to work, and they are still investigating her.

For many of the black people, their dietary needs are not being met. Simple things like rice and peas and chicken, which are a tradition to most West Indians, and rice and chapati for Asians, they couldn't even get that. They were told to buy it out of their own money. Now, when you live in a hostel you get about £9.00 and that is to last you the week and has to buy you everything.

There is one private hostel that I work with, and I wish all the private hostels would do this, give their clients a choice of what they eat. A sort of two-choice menu each day. But for special evenings they have the residents cook a meal for everyone. They have got a board for a menu and they say 'put down the things that you would like'.

That is just one hostel, I wish all the rest were like that. You know, actually give the people a choice. Well, from this new community care plan, they are going to have to do all these things because, even private homes are going to have social services coming in to inspect and monitor.

Part of my job is to liaise. We have a landlady and landlords' meeting, where we, as day centres, will meet with them to tell them what we expect. If the clients, for example, didn't want to go home at dinner time, then the hostels could get a reduced fee. So we do try things. If we are having outings or a community event, we invite them to let them see what is going on. We are not against them for being private.

Training

I am going to do the CQSW next year. I am also trying to get together, for myself and staff, a training package. We feel our needs, we can get the academic side by going to college, but work experience is what we need.

Some of these clients when they are on a high, they can really be on a high. You have got to be emotionally stable to take the abuse. So it is for things like that that we want on-site training. We are trying to work a programme together with the help of the training officer from social services.

Points to ponder

▽ Racism and discrimination in mainstream mental health services.

▽ The importance of monitoring attendance and ensuring follow-up users.

▽ Procedures for illiciting and responding to user complaints.

▽ Training opportunities in specialist agencies.

▽ The boundaries between the rights and responsibilities of users, carers and project staff.

10 Ark housing — Musselburgh

Marion Malcolm

Keypoints

This account is included because:
▲ *it illustrates how larger organisations can initiate locally based projects;*
▲ *it identifies some ways in which an organisation can respond to change in-service expectations;*
▲ *it considers how central government policy in relation to financial support of users can frustrate the legitimate aims of agencies.*

The project was established over 5 years ago and is one of a number set up by Ark Housing; a voluntary organisation which aims to provide housing for adults with learning difficulties. The organisation itself has been in existence for over 7 years concentrating its efforts in the east of Scotland.

Originally established with a staff of three, it now employs 4.5 full-time staff and provides accommodation for ten residents.

Staff background

Staff involved in projects of this kind have varied backgrounds and come from different professions. The project co-ordinator, for example, is a teacher.

I was a teacher and then I was in business. The business was being sold and I actually came to a point in my life where I could choose what I wanted to do. The obvious thing was to go back into teaching and do supply; and then go on to do full-time. However, for a long time I had been interested in the field of mental handicap — for no particular reason. I just felt that people shouldn't just be put into institutions and left there, and everybody has potential. Since I was able to choose what I was going into, I made enquiries to see if I could get training. Unfortunately, I couldn't because I had been trained as a teacher and I couldn't get any help financially. It so happened that this job was advertised and I put in for it. I have really been trained by being on the job and I love it.

The organisation's background

The main organisation acts as a facilitator for local initiatives.

> Ark itself really will only build a project if the local community has
> actually shown that there is a need for it. It's not Ark going out, going
> to a town and saying there's somewhere where we can build; rather,
> somebody in the community approaches Ark. This certainly happened
> in Musselburgh. Two people in particular plus, of course, some local
> residents, thought there was a need for a base here and they got together
> with Ark. The local people fund-raised to furnish the house, and Ark
> itself got money from central government for the bricks and mortar.
> Once the project was up and people were living in it, then its funding
> is through DSS paying the board and lodging of residents.

The project

The project provides a home for ten people. That number seems to reflect
a view that it provides a viable population financially and socially.

> It was really trying to get a balance of as few as possible that was viable
> financially between financial viability and as small a number of people
> as possible. All community houses in Ark tend, at the moment, to have
> ten people living in them. Some have extra people living locally with
> whom a link is maintained without them actually living in the house.

Management of the project

> For the overseeing of the house there are four staff. My manager is
> actually chairperson of our local committee. But also I am employed
> by Ark and therefore responsible to them myself. It's actually a
> double-edged thing. There's a voluntary local group who are still
> functioning and Ark have always given them a fair part of running
> their houses. Head office itself has a structure, a personnel officer,
> director, administrative staff and a residential services department
> who also oversee what is going on. There may be a change in the
> near future with Ark. There have been consultations with all the people
> involved and it may well be that line management will go to Ark, rather
> than to the local committee. However, the local committee will still have
> an overview of the house, seeing that things are running smoothly.
>
> It is also double work because you actually have to make sure that
> you inform the two separate sides. If there's an issue that has to be
> dealt with, I have either to deal with it myself and then make sure I
> inform all the correct people or check out with people first. That causes
> a great problem because it is actually contacting people. It would be
> much easier if there was one line management.

Organisation of work in the project

With several members of staff working in the project, it is necessary for each
to have a clear idea of their roles and responsibilities. However, it would

appear that there is a fair degree of common responsibility shared amongst the staff members — agreement about and what these entail.

> Basically we divide the work up among us. We all do the work that is necessary among us. I would say the other assistant co-ordinators should do more than me. I should have more of an oversight, rather than working directly with the residents. I'll be working today with people in the house, but the way we work it, each staff member has a particular responsibility for certain residents. Not that they do all the work, but they pull all the things together and maybe do the planning with the resident. I have an oversight of that, rather than having direct responsibility for a particular resident. It also means that the residents don't think that they are special because I am the manager and I am working with them.

Project aims

> We are really aiming to make people as independent as possible within this setting. We are not aiming to teach people skills, either living skills or social skills, with a view to the residents leaving. If someone wants to leave here, this has to be their choice, not our choice. This in my opinion, distinguishes Ark from other organisations providing hostels. Ark actually has the philosophy — a community home is a home for life for each resident, or until that resident says that they want to leave. We are really looking to make people more independent within this setting, really realising their potential. Like we've had people coming whom we were told would never be able to handle money. Yet one person has been decorating her own room, goes out and buys records, goes to the post office, buys clothes and yet has only been here a year and a half. She gets a great deal out of it, having her own money which she is able to spend on herself, rather than someone taking her to the shops and handing over the money.
>
> Even if we felt that somebody wasn't ready to move, but was saying I want to move, we would help to check all that out and help with the actual move itself, obviously in co-operation with the social work department or whatever.
>
> There are quite a few residents saying they would like to move sometime. It might be anything from a year to 10 years, but they don't see themselves being here until the day they die. That's fine, it's just a sort of general aim at the back of their mind. Some may be able to move into more independent settings with three or four other people. However, some of our residents have actually said that they would feel uncomfortable living with two or three other people in a shared house, whereas living with ten you don't have to have special relationships with anybody and everybody has their own space, their own bedroom. It's not much, but at least it is their own. They can be independent, they don't have to sit down at the table at night to have their meal. If they want to eat on their own that's fine.

Resident responsibilities

The staff generally see themselves providing the support which will allow
the residents to run the house themselves. In this respect, it offers an
environment which is primarily supportive rather than controlling.

> How we work is actually helping residents to take responsibility for
> the house. That might mean working alongside the residents, helping
> residents to do it properly or, helping residents to organise themselves
> to do it. For example, this morning there are just three people in the
> house. They will see that what needs to be done is done. I haven't
> time this morning to be working with them, so they organise it amongst
> them. But obviously, if things were being missed or somebody isn't able
> to manage properly — they maybe know the beginning and the end but
> not the middle part — then that is our job to see that they are shown
> how to. So it is basically rolling up your sleeves and living together,
> rather than staff standing there and saying this is what you must do.

The user population

> The residents come from two main areas. Either people who have been
> in care for most if not all of their life; like children moving on to a new
> home. Or, people who come from their families straight to here; usually
> because there has been a crisis in the family, like either parent has died,
> or has become extremely ill.
>
> When we have a vacancy, it is advertised, particularly through social
> work departments. Mostly residents have come here because somebody
> else has recognised that they needed to come here. The individual would
> come and see the house and would have the ultimate choice to come in or
> not. Once people are in, we then try to impress on them that the choice to
> stay is theirs. Everyone has the front door key and can virtually walk out
> the door and not come back. It is unlike other homes in the past — doors
> aren't locked. People aren't told when they can come in and go out.

One element in the development of community care over recent years has
been the relocation of residents from former long-stay psychiatric units,
particularly those catering for individuals with learning difficulties. Ark
housing projects form part of that trend.

> A few of our residents have been at Gogarburn, (a local hospital for
> people with learning difficulties) although I don't think anybody has
> actually come from Gogarburn direct. Quite a few of our residents
> have met other residents earlier in their lives, some when they were
> at Gogarburn or Gogarburn School.

The changing population

Since all the residents have an opportunity to move on, if they so choose,
there does tend to be some movement amongst the resident population. In
fact, over the period of the project's life approximately half of the residents
have moved on.

Other Ark houses are more stable than ours. Our turnover is quite high for Ark housing, I believe. Two of our residents died, so that affects our turnover rate.

Three of those who moved actually identified that they wanted to move on. They wanted to be more independent. Some because they reached the stage when they didn't like living with another nine people.

Two others felt that it was becoming too overwhelming. Even so, staff would have preferred to have worked with them for another few months; that it would be very difficult for them and that they would come across problems. Perhaps a little bit more time in here would have made things a little easier for them. But, at the end of the day, that was their choice and we went along with it. Both of them have a council tenancy.

Satellite homes

Given that some of the residents have moved, and probably will in the future move on to more independent living environments, is there a possibility that projects of this kind could offer, in a more systematic way, support of single or multitenancy homes?

There is a possibility that, at some point in the future, we may have satellite houses. We would still be responsible for the people in them. They wouldn't come in here, they wouldn't share the house because of that support, but we would go out to them and help. That's a possibility, it's not that we are doing anything at the moment, but other Ark houses have done it.

Funding and residents

Some of the changes taking place in the funding of residents in hostel accommodation do seem to have an impact on the independence and self-esteem of the people concerned.

The money is paid by DSS to the resident who, in turn, pays it to Ark to stay here. It might be stopped going to residents and it might just be paid in bulk to Ark. This we would very much see as a backward step. We certainly work here but residents hire and fire us. Their money pays our wages and it gives them some self-worth. They actually see that they are handing over money, it's a transaction.

We try to give them the feeling that it is them running the house, their choosing, them saying what they are eating, what television programme. The food in the fridge, for example, they don't have to come and ask. If it is 7 o'clock at night, and they want to, they can go and help themselves, because it is their house.

I think finance is the main problem. The residents have a great lack in their personal allowances. If they don't have families to give them extras, their personal allowance gives very little, particularly if you are trying to help people to go out and about and buy reasonable clothes for themselves. Holidays are just not on unless you actually fund-raise locally, but that's like asking for charity from people.

Relationships with other organisations

Some of the success of the project does hinge on its relationship with local authority services, including social work and housing departments.

> I think, hopefully, we have a very good relationship with the local authority. Mostly, we deal with the one locally in Musselburgh but it depends where people have come from. Sometimes they keep their social workers, say, if they have come from Edinburgh.
>
> It is important that we are not vying with each other, we are not trying to score points. At the end of the day we are trying to provide as good a service as possible to the client. It is important that we get on, and that we liaise together. I am also aware that, I think, social workers take a back seat when people come in. However, having said that, we could pick up the phone and say that we want somebody involved, or help with something.
>
> One or two residents don't have social workers, but most people have.
>
> We do work closely with local doctors. We have built up a relationship, and most people know us and will give us advice.
>
> Because of the people who were moving out, we were liaising with the local housing department, they were extremely helpful. And really, unofficially, have said, if we wanted to use them more in the future, they would co-operate as best they can. That's with individuals, it's not policy as such. Just if somebody was wanting to move out, I am sure they would listen. In fact, people are very willing to co-operate if you are prepared to ask them.

Relationships with the community education service seem to be particularly strong, reflecting the background in community education work of one of the workers.

> It so happens that Jackie knows the contacts to go to and we have used them for advice, and also in helping people to have a day placement. Not all our residents go to adult training centres and community education staff are helpful in that respect.

Future prospects

> I am aware that, when I first started here, everybody kept saying really our aim is to get much smaller community houses. Ten is far too big. Then Ark did a survey asking residents and six out of ten of our residents said they liked the size and smaller wouldn't be better. So I actually see a place for the community house as well as other options like living alone or sharing with another person. I also see a help in people having 24-hour staff back-up, helping people to make their own decisions. I wish, however, that there were more options for people. More choices, also, in work. Quite a few of our residents have identified the fact that they would like to work, full- or part-time for payment. Unfortunately, if somebody here actually got a job, they might lose their place because they wouldn't be able to earn enough right away to pay for the board and lodgings.

Still, some are doing work experience, but don't get paid, other than a very small allowance. They don't see themselves as proper workers, and therefore think they are devalued as people. I would like them to see that they were part of society, making a contribution.

Someone who is about to come here is helping with a lunch club in another part of Edinburgh. I would have thought that some people involved in that would be being paid, not all would be voluntary workers.

One of our residents was working with children and there was a special thing on one day. She was asked by the people she was helping out, if she would come along that day and help with the creche facility for which the people using it were paying. She got paid for her work for that one day. It wasn't much, but she got paid by cheque. She really wanted them to frame it. It wasn't the actual money that was important, it was the fact that she was paid by cheque, that she was worth that. She really felt 10 feet tall.

Points to ponder

▽   The Ark philosophy.

▽   The importance given to the support of client choices.

▽   The constraints of funding.

▽   The relationships with voluntary and statutory agencies.

▽   The potential for personal client growth within the project.

11 Edinburgh Association for Mental Health — supported accommodation project

Fiona Meikle

Keypoints

This account is included because:
▲ *it emphasises the variety of skills and professional backgrounds which successful voluntary social service organisations have to draw on.*
▲ *it is an illustration of the ways in which a voluntary body can accommodate and develop initiatives established by statutory agencies.*
▲ *reveals that the notion of contact and 'care packages' were an established part of social service provision before the current era of community care.*
▲ *it emphasises the significance of partnership and collaboration between different service providers in promoting the well-being of service users.*

Introduction

The major purpose of the project is to provide housing in the community for people who have mental health problems. The project aims to provide support, but not intensive support for people who have experienced mental ill health. It is intended to support people who can manage their daily lives, but need generalised support from the housing project team, support which might include assistance with budgeting.

The project is part of a range of activities undertaken by a team of EAMH workers who include administrative staff. This project uses volunteer befrienders as well as the three project's housing team members, two of whom are part-time support workers and one a part-time housing manager. Befrienders are drawn from those volunteers recruited, trained and supported through the befriending scheme operated by Edinburgh Association for Mental Health.

Background to the project

The project started in 1981 when the team took over some 12 flats in the community which were run by the Royal Edinburgh Hospital and were part of its housing in the community. Those flats were managed from the hospital and were then transferred to Edinburgh Association for Mental Health in 1981. Some of the tenants who were in the flats originally are still with us today.

I think the switch happened because the Royal Edinburgh felt it inappropriate to be looking after flats in the community and it would be more appropriate for the Association to deal with those. As far as I know, it was a straight transfer of management. The property was always rented from the district council so the flats used by the hospital were rented. The project rents from other landlords and then sub-lets the flats.

Workers' background

One of the support workers had been involved in the provision of supported accommodation for 12 years, working as a housing manager, and latterly as a manager for supported accommodation. That accommodation had provided mainly care for the elderly, although latterly had included shared houses for mentally ill people. The other support worker had previously worked in a hostel for women.

The present staff of the team are relatively new to this particular project. Fiona has been with the project since June 1988 while Frances joined in April 1989 and Annie in October 1989. One of the team is moving to work with a federation of housing associations in the near future.

One of the team members, who is a member of the Institute of Housing, is a housing manager and has had quite varied housing management experience. It is a very practical job which requires a good understanding of tenant groups. I am fortunate to have that too so that I can deputise on that side. Annie has come from a background of being a support worker in a hostel, where many residents had mental health problems.

The support workers are funded by the social work department. That allows us to keep our rents at a reasonable rate. The housing manager's post and the administrative posts are funded by the District Council housing Department.

Managing the project

The project workers try to work together collectively rather than operating a managerial hierarchy.

We do not have an hierarchy, we all work together. EAMH have a co-ordinator/development officer who is ostensibly at the top, but we run things as a collective. The housing team are accountable as a group to a sub-committee which is accountable in turn to the executive committee. The housing management's sub-committee is chaired by a person from the executive, then we have one other executive member; the rest are co-opted members who have specialist knowledge. I think in the last few years we have got more policy together and approved by the housing management sub-committee and executive. We have been able to work in a freer style within the remit we have been given, so we are basically taking our own decisions on day-to-day matters.

Project development

The project has been able to achieve some expansion since its inception.

We have a few more flats now than we had in 1981 and in the last 2 years we have done quite a lot of work swapping some of the flats we had and getting flats in better districts. We have also obtained a few single flats for people ready to move into their own accommodation, and a few of our tenants are, technically speaking, not our tenants, but tenants in their own right with housing associations. I think it is something like 14 flats, 12 of which are shared and three or four are single. In all, there are 22 tenants, so each worker has about 11 tenants to work with. We have expanded housing management a lot and give a better service to the tenants seeing the flats are regularly decorated, maintained and improved. We get furnishing grants for new flats. Renovation, and replacement furnishings come from the service charge.

User population

There is some turnover in the tenants who use EAMH supported accommodation, although some tenants stay a long time. Turnover in tenants tends to vary and can be difficult to predict. Tenants are of varied ages.

Some people prove to need too much support and we are not really able to give them that. More appropriate housing is then sought, if the tenant is agreeable to this.

Generally, with the younger tenants who are coming to us from hospitals and those who refer themselves, there is a higher turnover than there used to be. We would like to grow to meet new demand, but it is difficult to get funding. There is a need for more flats, and we gauge that by the number of applications we receive. Our applications are received through a small accommodation agency. This agency, Routes, accepts applications from a range of sources and has a co-ordinator who accepts and processes the applications. This service allows some element of applicant choice, and time for applications to be discussed and supporting references collated. It acts rather like a clearing house which passes applications to the constituent organisation which is considered most likely to meet the needs of the referred person.

It is extremely hard to say what the level of demand is. However, I can say that in the first 9 months of Routes being open, there was something like 300 applications. Of those, something like 250 applicants were interviewed and of these, 56 were actually housed. That indicates the level of shortfall in the provision of housing for people in need.

I think it is a pity that Routes is not able to represent all providers of housing for the mentally ill in the locality. Some housing associations do not feel that they have enough accommodation to warrant their being a member of Routes and the social work department is not actually represented there. In addition, while Routes feels that its funding is insecure, it is not really in a position to expand.

Many, although not all, of the people who are provided with accommodation have been attending hospital, although not necessarily as in-patients.

A lot of people have had periods in hospital some time ago. Some people come to us from agencies that provide more intensive support and people who have managed to cope with that are now considered suitable for accommodation which provides a lesser degree of support. Some people are self-referred and most people have had contact with psychiatric services at some time. There is also a bigger and growing group with a wide range of mental health problems. These include depressive problems or behavioural problems or people who have experienced deprived backgrounds. Some people have just never learned how to live with people and this has manifested itself in general mental health problems. We operate with quite a wide remit and, as a consequence, work with people with a wide range of difficulties.

A user's support contract

Part of the support worker's role is to put together a package of support for each tenant and set that out in the form of a contract. This represents a relatively recent development in the way the project's staff manage their work and engage with the users of the service.

This is a new idea which only started two years ago. When I came here there was no formalised support and no contract established with clients. We think it is important that support is formalised. As a consequence, support workers know what to do and what is expected of them. It is also important that tenants know what they can expect and I think formalising the arrangement encourages that. Generally, when we are interviewing someone, we get a good idea of what is needed. When they sign up the tenancy, we sit down with the tenant and discuss what kind of support would be most suitable. Basically, tenants are encouraged to say what they need. They are getting a new home and require the support which is going to make the very best of that facility for them. So the support is designed around the help which they have been using in the past and the support which will be available in the future. That is the starting point, so the first support contract is really to formalise this. A hospital worker could be involved in helping a tenant to set up in a flat, and there will be perhaps a new GP to be involved. There may be daytime activities involving workers, ourselves, the housing manager and possibly a befriender. All these will be party to the support provided and the contract established.

The tenant starts with this new contract, which is signed, and which is given a date for first review. That usually takes place about 6 weeks after they have moved in. We then go over the contract again and firm up on some of the things and discuss how relevant parts of the support contact are. Tenants are free to say what they would like and who they would like to have within the support contract. Our job is to try and keep it together and keep the community support going, and we work with an enormous variety of people including home helps, workers from day hospitals, community psychiatric nurses, etc.

Relationships with other agencies

The day-to-day work of the project, including the devising and maintenance of support services set out in each user's contract, means that relationships between the housing team and other agencies need to be strong.

Our relationships with other agencies are generally good and open. I think it is important that different agencies get feedback. For example, we take minutes of each review, and while some agencies are busy and it is difficult to get workers to come to review meetings, they are kept informed. Participation of some agencies can be improved by assuring that the timing and location of review meetings are suitable. I think in a way what we are doing is getting the best out of the community services that are around by harnessing them in this way and demonstrating that they have a part to play. They know that there is a named worker from the project linked with each particular tenant..

It also had spin-off in another way. It has made some agencies who do not generally work in people's homes, much more aware of what does actually happen with somebody who is living in the community. This is particularly true for people who have worked with the health board. It is interesting for them to be aware of what is involved in the preventative work set out in the contract.

The social work department are involved in different ways. Sometimes it is an area team member, other times a hospital social worker. Often, they are just involved in the outset, and if things are going all right, they withdraw.

We certainly have contact with community education and quite a few of our tenants take courses at colleges. Some people do training, ET training at SAMH.

We also have contact with the sheltered employment team from Albany Street who may help tenants to find employment or, if they have been out of work because of their illness, can get them back into sheltered employment.

Health projects in Edinburgh have a great deal to offer: these are the health projects in Craigentinny, Wester Hailes and Granton. Services provided by these projects could well form part of the support contract agreed for particular tenants.

Someone from the District Council housing department sits on our housing management sub-committee, since that department is a key funder of the supported housing. This helps us in identifying how problems might be tackled and which departments might be most appropriate to approach. We benefit enormously from that knowledge and help.

Relationships between the housing team and other agencies seem to be good.

> The people who are on our housing management sub-committee are carefully chosen because they have got special expertise and we use it. We use it as a regular contact and source of help, knowledge and support.

Key problems

It may be that the project's current managerial arrangement, based on collective responsibility, requires review.

> I think that you could say that there is often discussion about what kind of supervision and line management we really need. It is quite difficult to arrange for supervision. We all have a choice, we can either choose someone from the executive to be our personal supervisor, or we can ask somebody from outside of the organisation to do it. It's clumsier than having, say, a head of department who carries responsibility and the can. It is also time consuming.

The funding of the project and its possible expansion is, inevitably, another key area of current concern.

> Our other problem is funding, of course. Although the social work department, I think, are putting the workers on to a 3-year programme of funding, we were on a yearly basis. That meant that jobs were not certain from one year to the next, and quite a lot of time was spent filling in funding applications each year. It would be good to be rid of the funding problem, although it does sharpen the mind to think about where every stick of furniture is coming from or replaced from. You are very careful with your money.
>
> The other thing is that, in order to keep supported accommodation within a reasonable cost to our tenants, ours are not registered. We like to leave tenants a little bit of leeway about becoming employed and some tenants definitely do want to go on to employment. It is nice to be able to provide supported accommodation to people who are to be employed. So, we have taken the decision to keep the accommodation unregistered. I think there is a gap in the market for non-registered supported accommodation. By registered, I mean registered with the social work department. That would mean that our tenants would have to be paying something like £150 per week for their accommodation. At present, for many of our tenants, their housing costs are met with the help of housing benefit. If they are working, and not entitled to benefit, then at least £38.00 per week is not out of the question. We do have two tenants working who pay their own rent, but all the rest are on housing benefit. Housing Benefit is sent directly to ourselves, but what 'top up' the tenants have to pay they pay direct to us. We offer budget support and our book-keeper has a very flexible budgeting scheme into which some tenants pay household bills contributions. All our tenants have to take responsibility for their share of the household bills, including electricity.

We have a policy on rent arrears, although we do everything to avoid having to evict a tenant. So we work towards supporting, helping, reminding, discussing with our tenants to avoid them falling into arrears. We do have a pretty liberal policy on repayment which we try and keep to, but it is a constant battle not to let people fall into arrears of either rent, or household bills.

Continuity of care

Since the work of the project is devoted to people who have past or continuing mental health difficulties, some of them do require periodic in-patient treatment and care. The project tries to provide some continuity for tenants in this position.

Usually we can hold a tenancy for a period of time while tenants are in hospital. We don't put a limit on that tenancy because it depends on the illness, it depends on the likelihood of their coming back, it depends on the tenant's wishes about coming back. It also depends on housing benefit making an exception to the rule to pay their rent and service charge whilst they are away.

New initiatives in supported accommodation

That's really the development side of the job and it is something we have a meeting about every 3 months or so in the team. In addition, it is discussed in the housing management sub-committee from time to time. At the present moment, not only do we want a few more flats, but there are some people and some groups of people in the community who are not well represented in the supported accommodation field. We feel that some minority ethnic groups are not really very well represented and have not been able to state any particular need for supported accommodation. We feel that young mothers have not been particularly well served either. So those are the two fields, if our application for a grant to expand in the spring is successful, that we would like to look into.

There are other needs. I think there is a gap where houses are placed and, especially in East and Mid Lothian. I think there is a bigger need for care houses in the community, with perhaps resident staff, but I don't see us getting into it just now.

Training

There is always something new coming round. There are always new statutory regulations to think about, benefit changes and welfare needs. There is a lot of training that the support workers can benefit from. Counselling, stress management, dealing with your own anxiety, etc, and we find it where we can and, if we can't find it, we do a bit of in-house training. We don't have massively big training budgets, but we can utilise it quite well. However, if you are working part-time it is hard to make sufficient time available for training, but I think there is always a need for training.

User involvement

The project staff have been involved in new developments which are designed to encourage greater participation by tenants in the organisation and development of the service.

> One aspect of development that we have been working on this year is to encourage the users of our service to participate in the service that we are giving. This is quite slow to get going, and some of our tenants do not like the idea. But this year we have managed to get started a tenants' group. They have called themselves mind over matter and have been going now since last May. They had a social work student on placement who took this on as a project to work on for about 6 months. Tenants meet every few weeks and talk about social issues and business issues. The newssheet they edit themselves and they now have a chairperson. When the support worker finished her 6-month placement, we got a small grant to employ someone for the next six months and we were able to employ the same student as a worker. That has really gone from strength to strength. Although it only started with three or four tenants coming, they now have sometimes as many as nine, not often, but sometimes, which out of 22 is not bad. It has been beneficial for some of the tenants who have become active members, who have organised meetings, outings and writing the newssheet.
>
> I think our hope is that they will want some kind of representation on the housing management sub-committee, but they have not asked for that just yet.
>
> Of course, the tenant's contract is another way in which we are able to harness the participation of the tenants in planning for their own future.

Points to ponder

▽   The value of user/agency contracts.
▽   The implications of contract negotiations.
▽   What are the essential requirements for partnership in 'care packages'?

12 Association for Mental Welfare — East Lothian

Joy Harris

Keypoints

This account is included because:

▲ it indicates how, in the relatively neglected field of mental ill-health, voluntary organisations demonstrate sensitivity to the needs of carers and users.

▲ it features some of the tensions between established services, and those being promoted under the specific grant arrangements incorporated into the community care plan of central government.

▲ it suggests that, in providing funding for initiatives of this kind, central and local government agencies may leave voluntary organisations with the impression that the continued participation by their own workers is an unnecessary duplication of support.

Background to the Project

It was set up a number of years ago by a group of people who felt that there was a total lack of facilities. Originally it was parents who were coming together with older children, who had become adults, who were having mental health problems and they found that they had no support. It started off with some research being done which established that social isolation seemed to be the biggest problem. I think there were some people who were interviewed who were attending day hospital, and contacts were made around those kinds of areas.

I think being in a rural area, the difficulty was deciding whether to go for a central point and to offer to say, 'Whatever your problem, come here and we will help you with that' or whether to say, 'We will try and bring something to you'. So, the original aim was the groups would be set up in each area. Originally it was thought that they would be self-help groups, so that wherever you live, there should be a self-help group near you that you can link into. Five years on from, and funding from the unemployed voluntary action fund, that hasn't happened: this self-help bit hasn't materialised. What we were finding was that people who were coming forward needed more help and weren't at the stage where they could put something back in or support others.

People quite often expressed the fact that they didn't want to go anywhere near where they lived, they didn't want people to know that there was a problem, they wanted to come somewhere where they wouldn't be known and discuss it with people they wouldn't need to see unless they chose. Originally, the project had one worker, the funding funded one worker, and when she left two people came to job share and they had been sharing the job for about 18 months when I came. So I am doing a half post.

At the point at which I came in, all my hours were spent running groups. This was because the self-help bit didn't materialise. At some point, a ground rule had been established that there had to be two people working with each group. Some of the problems were heavy going and it was felt that co-working was necessary. Although sometimes there were volunteers around with the skills to work with one of the workers, several of the groups Margaret and I were running together. So that 18 hours just is soon taken up. From there, there has been a evolution to thinking that we have to get out of this hole that we have dug, we couldn't develop anything. Margaret and Alison, before I arrived, tried to start new things but had to stop some thing in order to start something else because of their hours. What we are aiming at now is offering a choice to people.

The aims of the organisation haven't changed in that we are still trying to promote the concept of mental health and to get a higher profile for mental health, more choice of things in the community for people who have had problems. At the same time, we try to work on the preventative side as well. We see ourselves as filling that enormous gap between somebody who is maybe anxious about something and reaching the point where they can't cope, and the person who is hospitalised with either a mental illness or a problem that has become too big for them to cope with in the community. But that is a huge area.

The funding of the project

Funding came from the unemployed voluntary action fund. Wherever our funding has come from influences how the project is worked and because that was the first place to offer funding for the project, the use of volunteers had to be emphasised and that was where the self-help bit came in. It was felt that people would be able to help other people so that, for a couple of years, that was the emphasis.

Now, our funding has changed. For the last — this is our third year and we are jointly funded by the Lothian Region health committee and by the health board — we get money from an endowment fund from Edenhall Hospital and we do that through the unit general manager of the east unit.

Management of the project

I have a line manager who is on both our planning committee and our executive committee and so that's my line of management. The executive committee is a mixture of advisors from health, social work, community

education and it has user representation — we have a volunteer on
it — we have somebody from the RSSPCC. So, quite a mixture of
people. The planning group has people, I suppose, more locally involved
as well as volunteers.

Workers: their backgrounds

One of the workers' backgrounds is in social work although she has had
some experience of community education. The other worker in the project
used to be a psychiatric social worker.

Yes, her background is in social work. She was in psychiatric social
work across in the Southern in Glasgow before she took the job over
here. So, her background is in social work too, although that was not
a stipulation of the job description. The girl that she was working with
before I came did not have a social work background. Originally, the
research worker had come from personnel and after she had done the
research, she applied for the full-time post so she got the whole thing
off the ground from having done research to setting up the project.

The user population

I think there are about 40 involved in groups at the moment. The
numbers have fluctuated and we hit problems last year with the publicity
budget which had run out after 6 months, so we've found that our main
source of referrals are people referring themselves. There are several
areas that we have targetted for work in this coming year, one is to try
to get more direct contact with GPs who we feel would be absolutely
key to this.

To what do you attribute your difficulty in relationships with GPs?

Well, I think that we find that they are so busy doing the work, they
are too busy to listen to things that might actually help the people they
are spending their time with. The kinds of people that we have time
to spend with are people who come to them in their 5 minute slot but
they need a lot more time to talk.

It would appear that most people now tend to be referring themselves as a
result of seeing posters.

I know from the statistics for last year that most people referred
themselves. A lot through the advert in the local paper. When that
stopped, the level of referrals went down. We now have a fund-raising
committee who have agreed to fund half the advertising costs and we
are funding the other half. The other thing is posters — trying to keep
them up to date. Having said that, most of the referrals are self-referrals.
However, we do get referrals from GPs and from health visitors, I think
it was as a result of requests from health visitors, that we established
a group for women in Tranent and they have been the main source of
referrals to that.

There has been a slight increase in the proportion of women referred in the current year.

> More than half of the users this year are women because there is a specific women's group and there is about eight in that and that's a fairly strong group. In the past it's been more men.

Managing a job-share

Margaret and I felt we had had to work together for a certain length of time to establish our own relationship, ways of working together, and sorting out our individual strengths and weaknesses. Then we would reach the point where we thought we need to cut down on the overlap and work out how we can work differently so that we can reach more people and get some things developed. At about that point, we were working out the division of labour, Margaret discovered she was pregnant so we were then not looking at how we would work together but how we could incorporate a locum for 6 months. That became the ideal opportunity to advertise for a Group Worker and I came off groups altogether with the exception of the development of the Springboard project. So I have not been working directly with groups since about March.

Project activities

Margaret's back now so we are in the process of renegotiating how we all work together, but I can just tell you what goes on in any given week. On a Monday evening, there is a mixed group which meets with my co-worker and with a volunteer who has a psychology degree and has worked as a full-time counsellor. She is jobhunting in this area at the moment but she is working with us as a volunteer and also as a sessional worker. She is starting up some groups for us and will be paid for that.

We are working with a mixed group and that's a younger age group; when I say younger, I mean it's younger than some of the people we work with. It's, I suppose, up to about 40 but starting 20s. We are not dealing usually with people under 20. They are sometimes referred from GPs and sometimes self-referrals. The way we operate is that, if somebody is referred, we offer them a personal interview with one of our personnel, Margaret or myself. We can either go out to the house or they can come here, whichever suits. At that point, we discuss with them what the problem is and what their options are — whether there is something that we can offer directly which is appropriate for their needs, or whether we need to refer them onto something else. If they are in that kind of age bracket, and are wanting to work on a specific problem, which is identified at that initial interview, and areas for change are earmarked, then some sort of contract or target is worked out.

On a Thursday morning is the woman's group in Tranent which has a creche. That is a group of people who have been mainly referred by health visitors, and most of them have had a specific mental health problem for which they have received treatment. I think all of them at the moment would be seeing a psychiatrist, not on a particularly regular basis, but they would have had contact with a day hospital.

They are doing a lot of targetted work within the group. They would have space to talk about, maybe, something that has happened within the last week that has distressed them, and that they need to talk about. If it's appropriate, the groups stay with that but there is also a programme of targetted work around building up their confidence. They have worked on relaxation techniques, on positive thinking and being more assertive. The problems aren't specifically to do with children; it's not a mothers' group in that sense. It's for them to work on particular problems. They seem to enjoy that kind of structure — there have been quite a lot of positive changes that we have seen with people in that group.

On Thursday evenings there is a group run in Dunbar which is run by two volunteers, one of whom is a psychiatric nurse at Herdmanflat which is the local hospital and the other is the person who did the original research, setting up the project and the full-time job. She still works with us as a volunteer and also does sessional work for us sometimes. That group — Dunbar — is very much out on a limb. It's one of the most extreme points of East Lothian. That tends to have a less clear remit in that it suits people who live out that way. It tends to be older women who are using the group. Once you get down to one man in a group, he tends to feel so isolated that he will move out into something else. You really need to have two men coming in at once for it to become a mixed group, so that's been just women for a while and the man who was attending that group is now using the springboard group here, which has a higher proportion of men.

We had a group which was for older people who needed long-term support. For people with mental health problems, it's not always a case of feeling better, it's a case of needing long-term support. So, we needed to find a way of working that wasn't putting pressure on people and saying, 'You're not getting any better and we need to get new people in this group so that we can tell our funders that we are doing a good job'. In order to avoid playing that game, what we wanted to offer was a drop-in group where there wasn't pressure on people, where people joined the groups where they are working on the problems. We ask for commitment to come to that group but when they want to leave it, that is something that's worked on with the group.

With the drop-in group, the idea is that they don't have to commit themselves to coming every week and that they can come if they feel like it. There wouldn't be pressure on them not to come if they want to come over a long period of time. It's much more a social group and that works much better. We had a core of people who were needing that but within the group there were people also wanting to work on something specific, so we separated out the needs basically. We were offering an unpressured social drop-in but the other thing we were offering is short-term targetted groups with specific topics so that, if anybody in any of our groups wants to do 4 weeks, 6 weeks on relaxation techniques, they then opt in. You have the enthusiasm there whatever the topic is, rather than saying 'We think you would all benefit from doing some relaxation', when you might get two keen people and six who just sit and chat.

We got some sessional budget last year which we are using to pay sessional workers, but we have also linked in with community education and they have funded one of the workers with the women's group and also funded a sessional worker to work with the targetted groups we are running as an off-shoot of Springboard. We have done relaxation techniques. We are also just about to start with funding through the adult basic education unit who have a positive discrimination budget, an activity called 'speak up for yourself'. It's really about communication skills and confidence building skills. It's generally about assertiveness, but we are not calling it assertiveness because there is more to it than that. We will be able to take up to ten in that and I think that's starting with an introductory session next week and this is the one where ABE have funded a creche. We are needing to lift it out of this building and take a community based building. We will be starting up 'look after yourself' which is a sort of health-based topic group as soon as this one finishes.

The springboard project approached other agencies in the community as soon as we had that idea, so that the planning of it has been multidisciplinary. That has its problems — different statutory agencies have various opinions about voluntary agencies and vice versa. So, for us, we felt very keen, we thought we had hit on the answer and wanted to get on with it, but we had had to do a lot of talking and getting people to the level that we are at, of thinking about planning for Springboard. The idea is that the Springboard project, which meets here and the planning group for it has representatives from social work, community education and the health board, as well as ourselves. The idea is that, when the planning is being done, we would not plan to expand here and say 'come any day, it'll be on every day of the week', but that we can say 'yes, there's a lunchtime session in Haddington and there's an evening session. . .' The expansion will be to get sessions going in Musselburgh, Prestonpans and Tranent. That will become the local focus but then the planning group for that will be the local community education worker, the local CPN (community psychiatric nurse) and somebody from the local social work department. So, that's the bit that the work's going into at the moment. In Musselburgh, we were already having discussions about setting something up there and originally, we were meeting about setting up a befriending scheme but it became obvious that that wasn't the gap, the gap was some community-based project, so that there's now a steering group established to set up Springboard in Musselburgh.

The Springboard project represents a new development. It seems to provide group support, using the services of staff from different agencies, but on a rota basis. It aims to strengthen the self-help element of the work by avoiding the development of member dependency on one or more permanent group leader.

Well, what we've planned for it. The compromise on the leadership thing is that the group isn't led in the sense that a topic-based group has somebody who is leading it who is paid to lead that specific group. What we have said is that, when we advertise a Springboard session, there will be an experienced worker here but it won't be the same person each week. This was to get away from people becoming dependent on seeing the same person every week. We are tapping into them becoming more self-sufficient. There will be an experienced worker but that worker isn't particularly controlling what's going on in the group but is there to offer guidance.

We offer a phone line at the same time, so that workers would be able to take any phone calls that come in where people want to refer themselves or explore what's going on here. The people at the moment on the planning group will take sessions, so we have a community psychiatric nurse who will come and be here once a month at the evening session or whatever. He can use that time maybe to introduce someone who has been referred to him. He can use that time to say, 'Well, if you come along on such and such, I will be there and I can introduce you to the group'. He can use his sessions as a kind of link between him going out to somebody's house and helping somebody come out from their house into a community group.

It's been happening here since, well September, which was the key launching time. We have launched it at the same time as developing it because, as its remit is quite low key we felt we could cope with having things on-going as well as developing the planning side of it at the same time. Otherwise, we would have had a 2-year gap while everybody planned what to do with nothing actually happening. In a sense, that was what put us off the befriending scheme. We heard the Midlothian experience had been a year of a group meeting to discuss it and then a year after that. We didn't feel they had reached many people. There were only half a dozen people who had been befriended as a result of those hours and hours of work. We felt there had to be some other way of reaching more people, and befriending might happen within the group itself. So that we wanted something that we could get on with quite quickly.

Evaluation of the new development, after only 3 months, is difficult.

Well, I think, for a start, we need to view it as early days. The core of the group here is the people for whom we had been running a group. That was quite a traumatic time because we actually decided to be totally honest about it and say 'This group is finishing, because we don't consider it's working' and having a sort of planned finish. The impetus to start an evening session came very much from that group, so there was a lot of negotiation around the fact that it wasn't their old group coming back. So, to evaluate it, we feel there's been response to the short-term targetted groups. Some people are saying 'Yes, I am interested in that' and other people are saying 'No, I won't be coming to that because that doesn't interest me at all' or they are saying 'I am interested, but I can't come at lunchtime. Let me know when you are going to put that one on at night'. So there has been a lot of response to that.

We feel the drop-in is working in that, although we have a core group of people, that's working quite well too because they are the people who will say 'Look, let's organise a theatre trip', whereas somebody coming in for their first time might not have the confidence to do that. They have organised their own social events. Some of them are involved in the fund-raising so there are links there, but we are also getting people who have left one of the other groups for whatever reason. There was somebody, for instance, coming on a Monday evening who got a job which meant he couldn't come regularly and decided that as he knew he had been asked for commitment to that group, he would rather use the Springboard group on days when he could manage it.

We are getting people leaving groups. The other thing is we have had people who have not felt ready to go into other groups which they realised would be a more intensive experience than Springboard. They have said 'Well, I'm not sure, but if I come to Springboard first and see how we get on and then maybe talk again about actually targetting some area'.

Relationships with other organisations

Inevitably, it's about personalities relating and individual relationships. My experience of the difficulty working here is knowing which level to tap into. Because we are a voluntary organisation we are, yet again, off the bottom of the pay scale as regards social work. Yet, in a sense, we are expected to contact high management first and work down. When I came here, what I was doing was running groups. Getting Springboard off the ground was a new experience for me. I was never sure which level to tap into and there was a difficulty with contacting the health board, in that we ended up getting enthusiastic grass roots responses from the community psychiatric nurses but it's taken quite a long time to ease the way with the people higher up who felt that they should know about it first and not second. That was a mistake which we made which has taken a bit of rectifying. Although, sometimes, it's quite good to stir people up and sometimes there are effective ways of doing it, some times there are destructive ways of doing it. The key is trying to strike the balance.

Social work — again it's knowing who to tap into. We cover two area offices and we visit both of those a couple of times a year and speak to social workers at team meetings or whatever, but there's got to be more to it than that. You've got to keep things up and keep reminding them what we are doing. We are getting quite a lot of referrals from the Haddington office. I think it just takes a while and it's about personal relationships and it's finding the time to get into the office and meet people and make sure they know what we are doing and what developments there are.

When I moved from Liverpool to Lothian, there was no money in Liverpool so we were definitely stuck with the statutory stuff and facilities weren't good and there were still small children in residential nurseries. When we came to Lothian, it all looked terribly rosy, there was plenty of cash and there were developments. There was time, at that point, for there to be links with work in the community and that all the time wasn't spent on statutory work. Since we have been here, the cutbacks have just kept increasing. The social workers are very much stuck — they have to do the statutory work and there's not a lot of freedom for them to get into developing things and I think that's a pity, but that's the way it is.

Although we have contact with both the offices, when we were discussing something like Springboard and enquiring if anyone could come along to the planning meeting, locally we got no response whatsoever. It's the social workers at the hospital who are getting involved. In Musselburgh, the area officer came to the meeting and said he thought it was a great idea and it's the way they should be looking and that he's just hoping that, their mental health officer and one of the seniors might be able to be involved, but it seems that most of the time is at management level.

The whole reason behind the planning of it is that it is shared jointly by four, five, six professionals. Each person will put in less time although they maintain the contact with each other. That was very much the question that the health board were asking: 'What is it you want in terms of time'. It's difficult when you have the idea. You are then accused of, well 'What do you want from us?'. This was what we got, 'You get money from the health board through your funds, can't you just get on with the job. Why are you asking me to attend a meeting about it?' We are saying 'Because then, we will develop a project between us which is relevant and which will be a resource for your workers to use. If we develop it alone, it may not be relevant'.

When we first thought of the whole concept of Springboard, we felt it was important that we emphasised that, although we have instigated it, it doesn't have to be ours. Ideally, we would like to be able to put in for independent funds for it which was the idea of giving it a separate name, it could evolve its own management committee and get its own funds.

Future prospects

We have to put together our progress report for next year's funds and I don't think there will be a problem getting funding for next year. I think the problem will come the year after that because, if the project takes off in East Lothian, it will depend very much on whether we are seen to have a separate role from it in the year after that. The health board have no money, they are not putting any money into the project though they are hoping to be able to work co-operatively. I think they are hoping, for instance, that hospital staff will do sessions at the project so that it won't cost them money, but they will be using their funds in different ways and more effectively as regards community work. We had already been warned the endowment funding was for 3 years. This is the third year and we don't know whether that will be forthcoming. We can only see our prospects in terms of funding and, I suppose, our funding in terms of how relevant our role is seen to be. If it can be said that there is somebody else doing the job which isn't costing them anything, then we will probably be on sticky ground.

Training

Yes, one of the things that I have missed, in fact, is regular on-going training. What we are doing is — we have a group workers' group which meets. That's the volunteers and the workers who work with any of the groups. We are trying to get a day's workshop for that group to explore, I suppose, its own function and the group processes going on within that. We also want to do some work on groupwork skills in the sense of taking those outside of the group workers' group to groups that we work with. So, we are planning a training day in the spring with maybe a follow-up and then in the autumn. What we want to do is develop that into a training which we can open up to other workers within the area — to social work or health or whatever. So that would have the spin-off of bringing money in to pay for the training and having joint experiences with other local workers. That's a new thing we're hoping to get off the ground because, otherwise, the only training we were getting were things that came into us that we thought we would like to go off and do.

Our total training budget for last year was £300 — I am on a course at the moment, the Scottish Institute of Counselling human relations course. They can't fund me to do that, I am having to take on extra freelance work to fund most of that — they are giving me £100 towards it. That's been great. I think I definitely needed something — some sort of input from outside. I think that is a problem with an agency this size.

Points to ponder

▽ The possible limits to self-help developments.

▽ Funding constraints on the projects level of operation.

▽ Sources of client recruitment.

▽ The user groups.

▽ The role of the workers.

▽ The relationships with other professional bodies.

13 The Buc-Up club project — Newton Aycliffe

Organiser: Rosemary Raine Howe — Newtown Aycliffe Volunteer Bureau Volunteer worker: Carol Watson — Vice-chairperson of the Volunteer Bureau

Keypoints

This account is included because it illustrates how:
▲ *the club grew out of the worker's recognition of the personal psychological and emotional needs of some of the volunteers of the parent project;*
▲ *the parent project's attempt to address the needs of volunteers within the existing staffing and other resources;*
▲ *the additional psychological and emotional demands which the growth of the club placed on the worker and the manner in which these were resolved.*

Worker's background

Before I came to work at the volunteer bureau, I was a secretary and then worked my way up to personnel officer within a manufacturing company. I was there for 10 years. So I would say that my background is that of a 'people person'. (Rosemary)

My background was nursery education, but recently I have worked for victim support scheme which is a charity supporting victims of crime. I am also a trained homeopath. My working life then, is around counselling and helping people to move on from being a victim to becoming more independent. (Carol)

Background to the project

The Newtown Aycliffe Volunteer Bureau, is an umbrella organisation which has several different strands to its activities. We run a sitting service, matching volunteers with elderly and disabled people. This service could include giving relief to carers, taking people out for walks in their wheelchairs, taking people shopping, befriending, or, walking the dog — anything really. We basically fill the gaps that the statutory services are not able to carry out. We also carry out a recruitment service for volunteers generally.

We operate an adult basic education project which is run in conjunction with the education department and helps people with reading and writing difficulties. The volunteer bureau is used both for recruiting volunteer tutors to help the students and recruiting the students from various sources which can, and do, include our own volunteers of course.

We run a dial-a-ride scheme which is a scheme using volunteer drivers who transport people who are unable to use public transport. This works on a mileage basis, and the client pays the driver at the end of the journey.

We operate a resource facility which is for all voluntary groups. This facility includes a photocopying service — at a reduced rate, a typing service and a poster design service.

We also do basic word processor training which is for our own volunteers. This again is principally to help those of our volunteers who are particularly keen to learn this skill but who have not got the confidence to enrol at a college or take employment training. We give our volunteers a taster and if they enjoy it and get the confidence on the machine, they very often go on to enrol at a college or, take employment training.

Then of course there is the Buc-Up club which is another service provided through the volunteer bureau.

The Buc-Up club

The Buc-Up club is short for building up confidence. The idea for the club came about after the volunteer bureau had been running for about 6 months and it became apparent that the kind of people who were coming through the doors to register as volunteers were people who had had some kind of trauma in their lives, or some problem that they could not cope with. They were obviously turning to voluntary work as a means of getting back on the 'road of life' again. However, it was very difficult for me to use these types of people as volunteers out in the community when in fact they needed help themselves. So from that awareness, we organised an afternoon once a week where the volunteers who wanted to attend could come along and talk about their own problems to each other. At first, we called it the group therapy session — which was horrible. I later came up with the name The Buc-Up club which sounded a lot nicer, unusual and meant that the volunteers felt as if they belonged to a club rather than a therapy group. The Buc-Up club has now been running for almost 3½ years.

Club users

We accept volunteers from age 16 and there is no maximum age limit. The majority of volunteers that we have are women, but in the Buc-Up club there are also two men who attend regularly. The club members tend to range in age from between 30–50 years although we have one young volunteer in the Buc-Up club who is 17.

The average attendance of the club is around eight people, but, we have had as many as 16 attending at any one session. We have our regular people who have been coming along from day one. We also have had volunteers who come along for a couple of weeks and then attend occasionally.

All the members of the Buc-Up club are volunteers of the bureau. However, they do not have to do any volunteer work if they do not wish to. We do ask them to register as volunteers when they come along and we do take up two references for each member as we would do with any volunteer of the bureau. Buc-Up club members then come along on a Tuesday afternoon. Very often we find that the people who are attending the Buc-Up club, and who are also doing some kind of voluntary work in the community, talk to other people in the Buc-Up club, and that gives others the confidence to think perhaps that they too could have a go at volunteering. For my part, the volunteer's involvement with the Buc-Up club gives me an opportunity to get to know the person as an individual. When they first approach the volunteer bureau, they might want to be friends with an elderly person, as part of our sitting service, or they might want to do voluntary work 5 days a week. As we have to be very careful when placing volunteers, both to protect the volunteer as well as the person requesting the service, normally I would suggest that they come along to the Buc-Up club which would give me the chance to get to know them and later, when the time was right, I would suggest that we have another chat about volunteering. Sometimes, however, the members will themselves know when the time is right and decide to offer themselves as a volunteer in the project.

Activities

The Buc-Up club meet every Tuesday afternoon in the volunteer bureau from 2.00 to 4.00. Each week Carol and I try to plan something for them to do on that afternoon. Sometimes it is very difficult to plan as we do not always have the time. Very often we play things by ear and see how the session goes.

Some afternoons it is very lively and there is a lot of laughing and we play games such as charades, or we write some things up on the flip chart for discussion. Sometimes Carol and I will go to the library in search of ideas, or on other occasions we might go through the 'agony column' of a magazine to get ideas and have the group discuss the problems that people are writing in about. Each of us decides what answer we would give the writer and then compare our answers with the advice given by the magazine. Very often the advice given by our members is better than the advice that has been given by the experts.

Sometimes the discussion sessions can become very serious, for example when a volunteer is actually prepared to talk about her/his individual problems which might be about bereavement, losing a job, a drink problem, anything that concerns the individual. What does seem to be of general interest for discussion within the group is when individuals start to talk about their psychologists, psychiatrists or community psychiatric nurses. They very often swap experiences that they have had and will talk about the tablets that they are taking. Carol and I both believe it is good that the members feel they can talk openly to one another about these things.

Sometimes we have guest speakers coming along. One very success- ful occasion recently was when we invited a psychologist who is based at the local Mental Health Centre. I think he was actually more nervous than the group on that occasion because it was a totally different situation for him, in so much as he is usually in control in the doctor–patient relationship. However, we had done a lot of preparation with the group the week before he came along, and the group had a list of questions to ask him on the flipchart, so that the normal doctor–patient roles were reversed. Some of the members were talking about personal things which had happened to them when they had been to see a psychiatrist or psychologist. They were wanting to demonstrate that they were not adopting the patient role on this occasion but that they were engaging in the discussion on a basis of equality with the speaker. The members of the group were talking about their individual experiences of the medical services. They asked him the difference between a psychologist and a psychiatrist; and if he, as a psychologist, felt it was fair for a psychiatrist to assess a person's problems within the space of 20 minutes or, half an hour. Most of them had experienced that situation and believed that seeing someone once a month for such a short period was not long enough to actually get to know the person and their problem. Overall, I think that meeting with the psychologist was one of the most successful that we have had.

After the session was over, he rang me up later to say that, although he had been nervous, he had enjoyed the session very much and was delighted with the visit. Since that visit, he speaks very highly of the Buc-Up club.

Professional relationships

The Buc-Up club was actually in operation for some time before the mental health centre opened in Newton Aycliffe. At the time we thought it was wonderful to have this facility in the area, but some of the residents were not quite sure about that. However, it meant that we actually got to know the people who were setting up the project in the early days so that a working relationship developed from that time, and of course, inviting the psychologist up to the Buc-Up club has helped tremendously. We also have a representative from the mental health centre as a co-opted member on the management group of the volunteer bureau, so that, even if they are unable to attend our meetings, they get the minutes every month and are kept updated as to what is happening within the volunteer bureau.

We also get quite a few volunteers referred by psychiatric social workers, community psychiatric nurses, or from the local mental health centre with whom I work quite closely. It is a two-way process. The mental health centre will contact me if they have an individual that they feel would benefit from the Buc-Up club and I would ask that person to come in to see me prior to attending to Buc-Up club in order to discuss their situation and needs. I would register them as a volunteer, but explain at that point that there is no pressure on them to do any actual volunteer work. However, I feel that, by getting them to register, they feel part of something and even joining the Buc-Up club can again make them feel part of 'a family', and that in itself helps. However, referrals can also work the other way. If I get a person who wants to register as a volunteer, but, who I feel is not quite right or ready for the volunteer bureau or for the Buc-Up club, I would try to encourage the person to go to the mental health centre for help and even go so far as suggesting I make them an appointment. This has worked in the past. Sometimes we might find that we will get them back again, but at a time when they are more able to cope with the volunteer work that we do.

Benefits

I think that people have obtained a number of benefits from being associated with the Buc-Up club. Some people have actually stayed with the group from the beginning although they have taken on different roles during that time — first as members of the Buc-Up club and then later as volunteers of the Bureau. Also one of the benefits is that, after a while, members develop enough confidence to become the core of the group as well. We had a new member recently whom the group have taken to their heart. That core of people who have remained with the group are quite useful in that they help to support new members ease into the club situation.

It is also satisfying from our point of view to see somebody blossom and get over their problems, and see the improvements that have taken place since joining the club. When you think back to how the person appeared on the first day they walked through the door and then look at the improvements that have occurred in that person you see the benefits that have taken place. We have had one lady who started in the Buc-Up club but has now gone on to employment training and it is really wonderful to see people develop in this way.

Training the Volunteers

Training which the volunteers receive depends really on what they are expected to do. If they are going to become involved in our sitting service — we match up volunteers with the elderly and disabled people, we meet with the volunteers monthly and provide training on such things as emergency first aid, handling techniques, etc. We also have speakers coming in to give talks on a variety of topics and issues such as benefits available to the elderly or the disabled, talks on crime prevention and topics which would help them in their voluntary work in the community. However, not all of the training is actually done by ourselves in the volunteer bureau. If some of our volunteers are going out of the bureau to work with a project such as victim support, that project would provide their own training.

Role of the worker

There is always one of us there in the group to act as the coper, either to sit back and let things happen, or, to step in and help but not necessarily control, to sort things out if they start to be difficult for anyone in the group. With all of the problems within the group, and they are vast, you will inevitably touch on a subject that hits a nerve. You have to be aware of that and try to control it or perhaps steer away from the subject if you find that one volunteer is getting particularly agitated or upset. Usually the group itself will help the person, but we have had occasions where volunteers have got up and walked out because they have not been happy with the discussion. At that point I usually go after them and try to talk to them. Sometimes we will pick that up later because there is always one of us around, albeit not always in the bureau. If we don't see the person that day then we may see the person the following day. However, we do not like to use the term counselling in these situations. We prefer the term listening. We don't advertise counselling as part of the Buc-Up club service, but we do not leave anyone high and dry if things are brought out within the group and people are distressed. When that happens, we make some time available after the Buc-Up Club in order to help them sort out their feelings and to enable them to go away feeling okay about things. (Rosemary)

Funding

The Buc-Up club is financed through the general funding for the volunteer bureau. The funding for the volunteer bureau, however, is always very difficult — that is a sore point. It gets more difficult as time goes on. We have been running and operating for over 4 years. The first 2 years we had government funding through the Manpower Services Commission but that was withdrawn and then we became independent. We managed to get a donation from joint funding which is health and social services and that covers about one-third of our running costs. These running costs include the salary of myself, (Rosemary) as full-time worker and one part-time member of staff as well as the normal administrative running costs. However, we have to fund-raise in order to raise the other two-thirds we require and that involves writing to local businesses, to industry, writing to charitable trusts and applying to various agency's for grants. This is a constant process that we have to do in order to survive.

Although we act as a recruiting service for tutors to the adult basic education courses, we receive no financial support from Community Education although we have tried to receive some money from that source. We do, however get some travelling expenses for tutors, and we are reimbursed for stationary if tutors use the copier, but there is no actual funding into the project itself.

Every year we have to satisfy the different criteria and different interests of the joint funding bodies. You are assessed as to where the money has gone and this is possibly where the numbers game comes in. For instance, in the case of the clients who are referred to us for the sitting services and the dial-a-ride service, I have to keep a record of where that client came from, whether it be a social worker, or a health visitor and at the end of the year submit the numbers and try to ensure that both the health and the social services are getting their fair share.

Some people have been attending the Buc-Up club for a period of three years. The Buc-Up club was created specifically for the volunteers and although we might, as an organisation, have to put forward numbers, these figures generally relate to the overall running of the volunteer bureau. The Buc-Up project is just something within the Bureau that we do ourselves, so there is no real pressure there. The fact that people keep coming back obviously indicates that it satisfies an unmet need.

Issues

I think the burnout which I was experiencing was probably a combination of the demands of the Buc-Up club and the overall demands of the volunteer bureau as a whole. I was getting to the stage where I was waking up on a Tuesday morning and thinking, 'Oh heavens, it is the Buc-Up club this afternoon.' When a person gets to that point, then you really have got to do something about it. Having run it for 3 years, although it is a self-help group, you are still needed to be there. They need someone to keep it going and it is very, very stressful. As a worker you feel totally drained after the 2-hour session. Because I know each of the members individually and have spoken to them on a one-to-one basis before they came along to the Buc-Up club, I am aware of their particular problems and needs. It means that I am constantly wary of what someone else might say that is going to upset another individual in the group and it seems as if, as a worker, you are on edge all of the time. If you see the discussion going that way, you tend to want to change the subject, or, not to pursue it. We may move on to talking about bereavement, or, child abuse, or, alcoholism, which might trigger off intense feelings in some other members. I feel that a period of time out is actually beneficial to the worker, in order to recharge our batteries. (Rosemary)

Definitely. Yes. We had recognised this earlier on and I take full responsibility for that — for saying 'Well I will help you with the Buc-Up club' but then not doing it. When we began the Buc-Up club, 3½ years ago, Rosemary and I started off thinking that there would be the two of us in the group rather than just one person. Sometimes I (Carol) would be able to attend and at other times I would not be able to get to the meeting, because of work and time commitments. However, we both recognised at the time that this could be a problem that we might have to look at again. (Carol). So we both discussed the situation again and we then thought it was actually more beneficial to have one of us work with the group week and week about rather than having the two of us present in the group every week. (Carol)

It was quite easy for me to rejoin the group. From the very beginning the Buc-Up club was something which I had been interested in and I suppose I have also acted as a support for Rosemary. I knew the people involved in the Buc-Up Club. It was easier for them to accept me coming into the group and doing some sessions with them than it would have been for a total stranger — they would have fought that quite strongly, although, at one time we did consider bringing in another professional. I think it is working quite well — I feel better for having that break. (Rosemary)

I think there might be one other point worth mentioning for anyone who is thinking about setting up a group like the Buc-Up club. The Buc-Up club operates on a Tuesday afternoon, but we obviously have the people who attend the club who are also involved in other voluntary work attached to the bureau and so we see them at other times of the week as well. Ideally, you should have a drop-in facility so that volunteers can come along at any time and have a cup of coffee and a chat. However, we do not have the facilities here to provide that — although it does happen. People do come in and they will want to talk to you. However, we have other work to do — you really have not got the time to spend chatting with them. I think if somebody is going to consider setting up a project like this, they should be aware that this situation is inevitably going to arise, and consider ways of meeting that situation.

Successes

If you are talking about the success of the Buc-Up project then you would really have to talk about the individuals within it. We have seen people come in who are very emotional, very distressed and do not want to carry on living. A number of times we have heard somebody say 'I'm just going to top myself.' and then as a result of the support that they receive from the group, they are able to cope better with their situation.

I think one of the other successes is to see a volunteer who might come along thinking only of his/her own problems. When they start talking to another member of the Buc-Up club about the problem — then we know we are getting somewhere. They are starting to think about other people and not just themselves. I think that is a big turning point. It is almost like a process. Quite often you have people come to the Buc-Up club feeling depressed, down and not able to cope. Then a few months go past and they actually approach Rosemary and say, 'I would like to do some volunteering now, perhaps go and visit an old person'. The experience of volunteering really helps them to feel a sense of their own worth. Just to see them blossom — to see the person opening out and coming out of their shell is success enough. (Carol)

While the majority of our members do progress, there are a couple who have fallen by the wayside, but then the Buc-Up club has just not been for them. One lady came along for a couple of weeks and she actually came into the bureau and told me that the Buc-Up club was just not for her — she could not handle it. But that is fine. We know the club does not suit everybody, but for the majority it is successful. Perhaps there are a few people who will only ever come to the Buc-Up club and never actually get around to doing any volunteer work but this does not matter. We see the members' confidence and self-worth improve, and after all, this is the aim of the 'Buc-Up club'. (Rosemary)

Points to ponder

▽ The development of the club as a result of the worker's awareness of the personal needs of the volunteers of the parent project.

▽ The way in which resources to mount the club were met by the parent project.

▽ The skills required for effective groupwork in such settings.

▽ Increase in demands on the worker over time as new needs were identified with club members — counselling, one-to-one support and drop-in facilities.

▽ The emotional demands of the worker's role within the Buc-Up club group and her need for personal support.

▽ The benefits to the volunteers of the club.

14 The University Settlement — The Day Care Dementia project

Trish Combe

Keypoints

This account, told entirely in the words of the project co-ordinator is interesting because:
▲ *it illustrates the development of one project out of an earlier project;*
▲ *there is a significant support role played by health personnel in the training of respite day-care staff for the project;*
▲ *it reflects something of the vicissitudes which can confront any initiative;*
▲ *it highlights the importance of on-going management support for the workers.*

Background: the companion service

The beginning was in 1985 when the consultant psychiatrist at Royal Victoria Hospital, contacted the settlement to ask if we could provide students to sit at home with sufferers of dementia to give the carer a break. My predecessor did quite a lot of research of various projects that have worked with volunteers which flourished and then flopped because there wasn't the commitment or the staying power. We could not rely on students to provide the service because they usually all disappear for their summer vacations. So the idea was shelved and no one thought any more about it until the Scottish office came up with their Section 10: Care in the Community initiative and circulated this amongst the voluntary sector. We applied for funding to employ people and now we have a paid staff to go and sit with sufferers.

Training

That companion service was set up in December 1985 and the first companions were trained at the Victoria Hospital. The companions for the companion service have two full days of fairly intensive training. The psychiatrist does something on the nature of dementia and the different types of dementia. The clinical psychologist does a session about behaviour problems as well as normal ageing so that people can draw comparisons between the illness and the normal drop in the level of functioning that one can expect in old age.

The physiotherapist demonstrates lifting techniques should a client have a fall. Occupational therapists have a big input with activities and the types of things that you might engage a sufferer in doing. Also, what not to do: not to push people to do something that they might fail at because that can cause frustrations. They also do a section on safety in the home, things to look for, worn mats lying around, really just common sense.

The sister from the day hospital gives information and instruction regarding coping with difficult or inappropriate behaviour. One of the nursing staff offers a first aid input. We also have on-going training for the duration of their time with the project. That happens one evening a month and is usually attended on a rota basis by a member of the original Victoria Hospital training team. It can be fairly formal in that someone will come and give a talk on current research into dementia, for example, or it can be very informal. The last one we had, the consultant came down and he sat and chatted with the companions about problems they might be having with their clients. He also gets feedback about his patients in the home situation, how they are coping at home so it is a two-way thing which benefits everyone.

The service

Some people have an evening visit if the relative wants to go out. Some people have two visits a week because their need is particularly great and they can't get, or they can't avail themselves of the other services, because their relative is objecting to it. The sitters will do a maximum of 4 hours at one 'sit' as it were. I don't like to call it 'sit' because it is more than that. It is not simply a respite service for the carer, like a babysitting or minding service. The companions are working with these people maybe doing crafts or games or even taking them out, going shopping, a whole range of activities. I think to call it a companion service is a bit of a misnomer really.

How much time is allocated to a particular family really depends on the need and on the availability of staff and, at the minute, we have a long waiting list.

So that, is the 'nitty-gritty' of the companion service.

The co-ordinator

I am a psychologist and previously have worked with victim support before I joined the dementia project. I came to the post in September 1986 and it was part of my remit to find funding beyond the Section 10 money. At that time, the project was situated in part of the Victoria Hospital catchment area and had six companions visiting 15 clients. I had to go and see local councillors and sound them out about further monies and I was invited up to the city chambers to meet some of the councillors on the social work committee to put forward our proposals.

The message I was getting was that they were not going to be prepared to fund a very small geographically limited project.

They were all saying 'Expand to cover the city and we will consider it'. So, we had to do that and after that the project mushroomed. We got money from the social work department backed-up by money from the mental health foundation and various other small trusts who were approached and also some money from the health board.

The second year of covering Edinburgh, we had money from the social work department and health board and some other trusts and we are now, thankfully, on to the joint funding programme for the companion service.

The companion service, to date, had something over 800 referrals and we have 25 staff who are covering that. It is not enough, we still have over 100 on the waiting list. More money is needed, that is the bottom line. We never get our full budget of course from the health board and social work joint funding, and we are always trying to raise funds elsewhere.

The day care service

Establishing the need

However, about 3 years ago, I did a small research study saying to the carers 'What else would you like? We are not saying it's available, but what would be your priorities in asking for extra help in caring for a relative?' Overwhelmingly, they said day care, they wanted extra day care. The hospital waiting lists were long. However, hospitals were sometimes inappropriate for their relative in that there are some very severely demented people in the day hospitals and their relative might have been mildly demented, although still a handful to cope with. So we looked into it and approached various trust funds and eventually got some money through a charitable trust which enabled us to fund a project for 1 year.

Finding the premises

At the time, through a colleague, I was informed that the Church of Scotland had a property at Milton Road which had been offered to their charity but, they did not have a purpose for the property. I telephoned the officer in charge of Queens Bay Lodge, who had been the one to offer the property, and said that we may be able to use it and he was very keen on this.

The Milton Road day centre is a small property annexed to Queens Bay Lodge which was no longer used everyday. It is a three-roomed cottage with bathroom, shower and kitchen and ideal for our purposes. We wanted it to be a small group service because people had said 'Oh, these big institutional settings, my relative does not like to go'. We thought we would provide an alternative to that, and this was ideal for our purposes.

After a lot of discussion, they said 'Yes we could go ahead'. Lynda, the organiser at that time, started recruiting volunteers and things got underway. We were then contacted by the board of social responsibility in the Church of Scotland who did not feel that they had enough information so things had to be put on hold for a while and a report had to be submitted that satisfied their board of social responsibility that what we were doing was in line with their objectives. That was done, and then the chairman fell sick so the committee could not meet and so-forth. After a lot of hiccups they finally gave us permission to use it on two days a week, and that operates on Tuesdays and Fridays.

We went to Craigentinny social work team and said 'Look, we have the money, we have this property, we will take referrals' and we already had contacts with all the social work area offices because of the companion service so that it was quite easy to make the contact. There was not a great deal of 'Look, we are here'. We were already known to them. It was really just a case of saying, 'Look, we are providing this as well now.'

Guthrie Street and the gas explosion

Meanwhile, there were also plans going ahead for a day centre at Guthrie Street in a property owned by the University but leased to the settlement rent free. We had architect's plans drawn up and had applied to UVAF (unemployed voluntary action fund) for funding for the Guthrie Street project. The UVAF gave a substantial grant for 2 years' running costs, the core costs, not capital costs. We had to find the capital ourselves. So we made various applications and got some money from a variety of sources. We targeted lots of trust funds, picking out the ones which were relevant. Meantime, Lynda had started her recruitment campaign for volunteers. All of that had to go on before we could say, 'Here is the end product'. And then of course we had the gas explosion which completely demolished the building at Guthrie Street which really set us back. The UVAF had granted the money for a city centre project because that was where we had identified a need and was also where the Guthrie Street premises were located. So we then started thinking about what on earth we were going to do. We had to start looking for other premises for which we did not have the money to rent.

The Marionville Day Centre

We went to the social work department to discuss with them where would they identify another area of need that might be acceptable to UVAF and they were targetting areas like Morningside where they were very short of day centre facilities. Morningside, of course, is notoriously expensive and any property which was coming up was just way beyond our reach. Eventually, I telephoned the district council and asked if they had anything at all that might be suitable for use as a day centre that we might lease from them and within a week, I was offered a couple of properties which might be suitable. One sounded wonderful, it was at Dumbiedykes which was still central. However, it turned out to be on the third floor so that was no good and the other was at Marionville. They also offered us another property down at Restalrig which we avoided because, at that time, the joint project of social work and health board was going ahead with the Restalrig Dementia Centre, which has since been shelved because of the funding difficulties. We avoided the Restalrig one and the Marionville one was wonderful and I must say, the district council were superb. They said that there was a little bit of money if any redecoration was needed so I went down to see the house and there was some gloss paintwork which needed touching up. I telephoned and said we could do with a bit of gloss paint and when I went back again, they had actually redecorated completely with woodchip paper and paint. It was really nice and fresh.

I think they were sympathetic probably because we were going to be providing a much-needed service. The need had been identified, not just by ourselves, but by everyone working in the dementia circles who will tell you that there is not enough provision. The district council have a 'special lets' department which certain properties can be let out, I believe they rent out to voluntary groups, Barnardo's and suchlike. We did all the signing of the contracts and they said 'Yes, we could have it'. They also suggested that we might apply to their general purposes committee for the rental for the first year, which we did and that was granted. We now had 1 year's free rent on the place which was terrific. We have also been invited to re-apply for the rent — whether or not it is granted again is questionable, but we have been invited to re-apply.

By then, we also had the recruitment sorted out. The Royal Edinburgh Hospital took the responsibility for the training of volunteers for the centre because it is in their catchment area. We went back to UVAF and said 'Look, this is not in the central area as it is defined by social work, but we can still take people from central area because we have the accommodation 5 days each week and we have our minibus and would be able to transport the people from the central area. I also had a meeting with divisional officers of the social work department and sorted out the three areas in Edinburgh that we would cover from Marionville. Lynda was still here at that time and we started off 2 days a week building up to the third which is just about to happen, providing respite care. Eventually, we will have the Marionville Day Centre running 5 days and we can take up to ten people on each day.

Volunteer and employment trainees

Lynda did a lot of leg-work. She had leaflets made up and targetted shops, libraries, doctors' surgeries, everywhere round-about saying 'Please can we put a poster and some leaflets here?' and, I think initially five people volunteered and dropped out one-by-one which I think illustrates the concern that people have about using volunteers on a project that is so important and needs such a lot of commitment. I am not saying anything about volunteers because they do wonderful work, but I think it is a situation where you really do need to have reliable people who are going to turn up because, if they are not there, the thing can't happen.

We had a bit of difficulty finding enough volunteers to staff the projects, and were actually approached by the training agencies of the employment training scheme. Various projects in the settlement were involved with the training agency and they approached us, and said that they had certain people who were expressing an interest in the caring professions and could we possibly accommodate them. They initially approached us for the companion service and, at that time, I said no because we did not have any funding to take on extra people.

We were really very grateful to the training agencies. They send along, from time to time, perhaps ten people and one of the project organisers and myself do the interview fairly thoroughly and select out the people that we think might be suitable. They then go and have their training at the Royal Edinburgh Hospital which is a bit different from the Victoria Hospital training for companions in that it is staggered training and they have more placements in the day hospitals and in various community projects before they are actually working in our day centres. They have quite a bit of experience before we let them loose, as it were! They have proved to be very good. We have had two or three people who have dropped out for one reason or another, but overall, a very good, reliable staff.

The funding we received was given on the premise that we would use volunteer staff. No one was prepared to actually pay staff, they will pay the organiser's salary and an administrator's part-time salary but no one wants to pay for day care staff. So I have mixed feelings, I am not terribly in favour of the employment training programmes because I think they are exploited a lot in industry and elsewhere. However, I feel that we can offer a bit of training to these people if that is where their interest lies. There is no good someone coming to us saying, 'I have nothing else to do so I will do this and see if I like it'. That's why we have a fairly in-depth selection procedure to identify the people who really do have an interest in this and I think we can provide, or at least show them the alternative. Many of the people that we have have been working in nursing homes or as auxiliaries in hospitals. We can show them the community side of it and the differences. I think we can be more flexible than the statutory organisations or even the private sector can. They are restricted, of necessity, whereas we are not.

They are placed with us for a maximum of a year and we have, in fact, been able to offer a couple of them work with the companion service; those who have been willing to take part-time work. So it is working nicely, networking quite well. The trainees work alongside the volunteers.

Day care clientele

The provision

There are two elements to it. There is the respite or relief service being offered to carers but there is also something for the sufferer.

We aim to provide something for the client when they are at the day centre as we do with the companion service and I think that is where the occupational therapy input of the training sessions comes into its own in that we do hope the people will have increased socialisation. They may never see anyone apart from a relative who is caring for them, and at least coming together with another group of people will increase that. Also, to provide a bit of stimulation, it is not easy for a carer who is there 24 hours a day to be stimulating and provide things for them to do. There are so many other things in the day just to get through the day. So I hope that we can provide a wee bit of that too. They do gentle exercises that people might otherwise not be doing. We don't have them hurdling over horses, but sitting down and doing various things. Lynda did quite a lot of that with them, she went to classes to find out the proper methods to use. They also used the Museum of Childhood quite a lot, they have reminiscence packs which they give out and that can generate a lot of conversation and a good reminiscence session with the clients. It's great.

The illness

It is the short-term memory deficit which is usually the first thing to be obvious. dementia is really a slow deterioration to death. It is a terminal illness. It is a loss of, as the name suggests, the mind. The brain cells start to die off, and there are patterns of behaviour, although everyone is an individual and everyone will display different behaviours. There are patterns such as loss of short-term memory and disorientation in time, place, and eventually person — you stop recognising relatives. They may wander out because they don't know what time it is, 2 o'clock in the morning they will get a shopping basket and get dressed and take off to the supermarket because they are disorientated in time. Incontinence problems, a lot of people eventually suffer from incontinence, which is dreadful for relatives to cope with.

Everyone at our day centre is primed to expect the occasional accident. I don't think we have anyone at the minute who is terribly incontinent. We have, as I say, the odd accident and Kirsty was just on the phone the day before yesterday to say that we had this horrendous mess and could she go and buy some rubber gloves! That sort of thing is coped with. If someone is very incontinent, the chances are the relatives will provide pads and so forth which can be changed there.

The day centre in Marionville I see developing to its limits of taking ten people each, 5 days a week. In terms of other day centres, it is really only money that stops us from having various day centres dotted around the city because I think the small community concept offers a really good alternative to the institutional type.

We provide a relatively inexpensive service compared to hospitalisation. I think this is why we have the backing of most of the medics if not all of them involved in the care of dementia because we do provide a service that is cheaper than the hospital service. It is also felt, although very difficult to research and prove empirically, that we do tend to keep people out of hospital, particularly with the companion service. Relatives cope for longer if they are getting this community support. So, in that respect, I think it is saving quite a bit of money.

There is also more personal attention in these smaller units than might be possible in an institution. What we try to do at the day centres, and it is not always possible, is offer a one-to-one ratio, but two-to-one is quite acceptable. If one member of staff is dividing their attention between two clients, it is still more attention than they would get elsewhere.

Skills of the worker

I suppose with the setting up of the day centres I had made a lot of contacts through the companion service and that was just going out and talking to people and telling them what we were about and what we were intending to do, selling the project if you like. We can do this cheaper than the social work department.

I don't think I have any special skills, not what I would call skills. Networking . . .fund-raising. You may identify things that I may not call skills, just part of what I do.

Management skills, selecting and recruiting people, the monitoring of staff needs are very important dimensions of my role, not only now but since I took up post.

Staff support

I think it is very important that all of the staff feel that they have the support and backing of whoever is in charge of their particular bit. I am very fortunate in that our director is always available. I also have a monitoring group who I meet with once every 6 weeks at the Victoria Hospital who are the original steering group. They take part in the training, they are professionals from the health service and social work department. I have that support in my role and I think it is important for the organisers of the day centres to feel that they have, in turn, my support and for the workers there to feel that they too have the support. I meet regularly with the girls and they meet regularly with the day centre workers. If there are any problems to be sorted out, and the girls feel they need a bit of support, I will go down and talk to the work staff. Any changes that might happen, I will go down and inform everybody of what is to go on, if for no other reason than it takes a bit of pressure off the girls who are organising. I think, with Helena coming in and Lynda going, that was a change and obviously Helena had ways of doing things that were different to Lynda's and they had to be fitted in with, and there were difficulties in adjusting to someone else coming in with changes. I think everybody needs the backing and I don't think anyone would say that they did not get it. I certainly have a lot of support from my director here, and from the monitoring group at the Victoria.

The monitoring group

The steering committee originally set up to look at the companion service have very little to do with the day care service. The day centre doesn't really have a steering committee. The setting up and everything was done by the settlement — myself, the director and the management group that meet. There is a monitoring group of professionals from other areas. We have Dr Phanjoo, consultant psychiatrist, a community psychiatric nurse, a health visitor from the Royal Edinburgh Hospital, the officer in charge of Queens Bay Lodge who is the new officer, we also have the ex-officer because he was the one who was there when we started up and who also volunteered some of his time now that he has retired to driving the bus for us for Milton Road and the day care organiser from Craigentinny.

Support of statutory bodies

We have no financial support from the health board or social work department for either of the day care centres. That's not to say we will not be asking them for it, but at the minute, they have no input into that at all. They jointly fund the companion service but they have no input into day care.

We actually approached the social work department in our funding application of 2 years ago and said that this is a need that had been identified and that we were prepared and able to go ahead and provide it and would they like to give us additional funding to do this. They said no, it was not something that they were prepared to look at at the minute because a review was going on in the region of all day care facilities and, at that particular time, they were not prepared to fund us. However, we had this money from the anonymous trust fund for Milton Road which gave us a year's running costs and we have had donations from relatives and so forth since which have enabled us to carry that on. We are always seeking funds to keep the Milton Road one going. The Marionville one, as I say, is funded by UVAF for two years and social work have been involved in the planning of that so we would hope that they might see fit at the end of the two years to contribute.

Inter-agency communications

Through the companion service, I attend two or three social work area offices, they have liaison meetings with the consultants from the hospital. These liaison meetings involve almost anyone who is involved with the dementia sufferer from the home carer, health visitor, district nurse, psychiatric nurse, day centre organisers from the statutory services, social worker, myself if we are involved through the companion service and they meet once a month to discuss what is best for each. . .we have case loads to go through. So we have a constant contact with professionals. It may be the social worker from the hospital who is involved. If they are based at the hospital, and these liaison meetings are between the hospital and the social work department. The social worker from the hospital will be the social worker who is involved if their patients go in for respite care at a day hospital and so forth. So that there is constant contact .

I am in regular contact with almost all of the area offices about clients and we liaise on what we might provide.

Communications are excellent both ways, yes, and not just with the social work department but with health board personnel, you know, the hospitals, day care centres, whatever.

Future funding

The difficulty is that, at the minute, the projects are three separate entities. There is the companion service, the Marionville Day Centre with funding from UVAF and there is the Milton Road one with funding from somewhere else. The ideal would be if they could be seen as part of a whole and the funding was given for all of them.

The joint funding that we have for the companion service is supposedly fairly secure and I think it probably is as secure as any funding is in light of the present financial climate because we do have a lot of support from a lot of people.

The organisers

I would think probably the organisers will stay 2–3 years. Both of them are very keen to see the thing up and running and working well. I know that Kirsty has intentions of doing social work eventually and whether that is this coming session will depend on whether she is accepted. Helena, I think, is still debating what she wants to do. I don't think she has made up her mind yet. Certainly, in terms of the time with the project, probably a couple of years.

I think it was deliberate that we chose people who were young and enthusiastic. We wanted organisers who would be a bit innovative and creative and could offer suggestions as to how things could be done.

It's working well. I'm pleased with what's going on.

Other day care developments

There are lots of Churches who are offering one day's day-care specifically for dementia sufferers which is terrific and they have the volunteers from their congregation coming in and that's great. I think to set up something like the Marionville Project would take more funding than would be available to just any little group as it were and I think that is where the involvement of perhaps an established charity is essential because the funders are not going to hand out substantial amounts of money to little community groups.

Lessons learned

I don't think there are any short-cuts. I think planning is of the essence and should involve all the professional people that are willing to help. I don't think you can do it without them, I think if you did you would be providing an inferior service.

Certainly something that we are going to be offering in the New Year is that the settlement as an organisation is taking over the management and setting up of training and we are actually going to be employing the health board and social work professionals to provide training sessions which will then become a package for sale to other groups who want to have personnel trained. That is in the planning stages at the minute, and it is something else which we will be able to offer quite soon.

Points to ponder

▽ The importance of interagency contacts.

▽ The initiative of the key worker in researching, identifying and responding to the 'need'.

▽ Putting funding packages together.

▽ The level of financial support from the statutory bodies — social work and the health board.

15 Day centre for dementia sufferers
Kirsty Gillies and Helena Guldberg

Keypoints

This account is included because:
▲ *it provides an insight on the day-to-day operations of the Day Centre;*
▲ *it spells out the aims and objectives of the project with respect to its user groups;*
▲ *it illustrates how referrals are made and places taken up.*

Background: the workers

Both Kirsty and Helena are graduates with degrees in psychology and with some experience of working with psychogeriatrics in hospitals, experience which they both gained during their vacation periods from the university. Helena has also had experience of working part-time with the companion scheme which provides respite care for carers of dementia sufferers for periods of 2/4 hours in any one week. Kirsty had undergone the training associated with the work for the companion scheme, and had additional experience of working with non-demented elderly in residential homes. Both workers are similar in age and both have only recently taken up their respective posts as organisers for the two day centres.

> I came into the post in March 1990, taking over from the worker who had set up the Milton Road Day Centre from the beginning and who had moved on to Marionville to set up that project, and once it was up and running Helena was appointed to the post. Helena has been here since August 1990. Both day centres are for dementia sufferers. Our job is to manage and develop the service. (Kirsty)

Since coming into the post, Kirsty and Helena have sought to deepen their understanding of community day care provision for dementia sufferers by visiting other day centres for dementia sufferers in Edinburgh. Their experience from such visits indicates that the routines established by the various day centres follow very similar patterns.

Objectives of the day centre provision

One objective of the day centre is to provide respite care for the carers. To give them a day to themselves. The second aim is to provide stimulation and socialisation for the sufferer, and we do accept clients who live by themselves in the community in order to help them to retain the skills they still have and to combat the isolation and loneliness of living alone. (Kirsty)

Monitoring the day centre projects

As far as monitoring the day centres is concerned, there is a monitoring group which meets once every 6 weeks and reviews the progress of each day centre. That group is made up of Trish Combe, the project co-ordinator: Helena and myself as day centre organisers: Dr Phanjoo, psycho geriatrician of the Royal Edinburgh Hospital: Kirsty Ball the health visitor: a representative from the social work department, Katrina Morris, Lewis Grant, officer in charge, Queens Bay Lodge and David Turner who helped us get the Milton Road premises for our first day centre. (Kirsty)

The project's finances

The finances are managed by the university settlement. The funding covers salaries, heating, lighting, telephone costs and lunches. There is also an allowance of money for the petty cash to cover the cost of buying incidental items for each of the day centres. That way we do not have substantial amounts of money lying around the place. (Kirsty)

The employment trainees of the day centre

As with other voluntary agencies which make use of employment training as a source of workers for their respective projects, recruitment, selection and training of such trainees were matters which had been seriously considered and built into the day centre provision by this particular agency.

Recruitment and selection

The trainees for the day centre are selected initially by the Edinburgh and Lothian training agency (ELTA). They send along to us people who express an interest in care work or working with the elderly. They come to see us and then have a further formal interview with Trish Combe the project co-ordinator, Helena and myself.

The skills we would look for, and wish to develop in our volunteers/ trainees, are common sense, patience, listening skills, communication skills, initiative, reliability and trustworthiness.

I (Kirsty) hold the part-time post of day centre organiser and part-time post of day centre administrator. Therefore, I do most of the paperwork for ELTA, keeping the petty cash books, typing letters and so on. There is a fair amount of paper work involved with the running of the day centre.

Training

> If they are suitable, they then go through a fairly rigorous programme; visiting different day centres within the community and working under supervision at both our day centres. They also go to the Royal Edinburgh Hospital for two training sessions and have a talk there with Dr Phanjoo the psycho-geriatrician; the health visitor; the psychiatric nurse and the social worker.
>
> Dr Phanjoo talks about the nature of dementia and what to expect when working with dementia sufferers. (Kirsty)
>
> The others talk about the work they do regarding dementia sufferers and the role they play within the psycho-geriatric team. The trainees then have a talk with the occupational therapist and have a look around the occupational therapy department to see what facilities are on offer for stimulating dementia sufferers. (Helena)
>
> Finally, they have to do a placement of 2 days a week for 3 or 4 weeks at a day hospital so they can compare community care with hospital care. (Kirsty)

Over and above the formal training programme, there is the ongoing in-house training which takes place within the individual day centres.

> Not every client has the same level of dementia, and that can be a bit of a problem for new trainees, which gets easier with training and experience. The trainee needs to learn how to adjust to the different needs of the different clients. For example, when you do a quiz with a client, you do not just simply stick to the quiz book, you make up questions that are sufficiently difficult for some of the clients and also questions which they are all capable of answering. If you continually ask people questions which they cannot answer, it is a very disturbing experience for them. You need to go by what you know about the client's general background and their capabilities. (Helena).
>
> It is the same with some of the other activities. You can persuade people to go for a walk, and you may feel they will enjoy it once they get out, but, you do not do that with people whom you know do not enjoy walking or who find walking physically strenuous.
>
> You have to spend time in getting to know your clients and their likes and dislikes. (Kirsty)

Benefits to trainees and volunteers

> Both volunteers and trainees benefit from working at the day centre. they receive a basic training from the psycho-geriatric team at the REH and gain much experience in the area of working with the elderly suffering from dementia. They gain experience of working in a day centre and in the area of caring. Many trainees and volunteers also grow in self-confidence and they all have fun. (Kirsty)

The number of employment trainees

There are nine members of staff, all employment trainees. We would, however, like to attract more volunteers to the day centre. The intention is to offer respite day care on a one-to-one basis, with one member of staff to one client, or, at a push, two clients to one member of staff.

The staff at the two day centres are separate only in terms of who organises them on the particular day. The staff attend both day centres. They go to Milton Road on a Tuesday and a Friday and are based at Marionville for the remainder of the week. (Kirsty)

Client Numbers

When I came into the post, Milton Road was open two days a week, with five different clients attending each day. Now we have ten clients attending on each of the 2 days. We would rather provide a respite service for 20 carers over the 2 day period than a service for half that number over the same period. However, in cases where there is some kind of crisis and the carers could not cope any more, we would take the same client on the two separate days. However, we would prefer to spread the number of places we have at each day centre to accommodate more clients. Both day centres cater for dementia sufferers from the local community, and I cover the Portobello area. Clients who attend the day centres can do so for as long as they are able to remain in the community. However, we have reached our maximum intake at Milton Road and have a waiting list. It is very sad when you cannot offer a person a place until another person goes into long-term care. Although we can refer people to other day centres, most of these are also fairly full. (Kirsty)

The situation at the Marionville day centre is similar in terms of the numbers of places available on any of the 2 days on which it is presently open and in terms of the policy of spreading the number of recipients of the day centre provision. However, unlike Milton Road, it does have the possibility of extending the day care provision to other unused days of the week, and commencing in November 1990 that Centre will open for a third day accepting ten clients from more central parts of the city. The Marionville Centre would then open on a Monday, Wednesday and a Thursday, the Milton Road Day Centre on a Tuesday and a Friday.

At the present time both day centres will continue to be able to share trainee staff and the use of the minibus without overlap or straining the resources of either centre. However, if the Marionville Day Centre is able to recruit clients for the full five days of the week, Monday through Friday, then transport difficulties might arise. However, we can fully utilise the trainees which we have at the moment. The contract that they have with ELTA is to work 9.00 am to 5.00 pm Monday to Friday. Eventually, we may need more trainees but, there is a constant supply of trainees available from ELTA. We would also hope to attract more volunteers, particularly unemployed volunteers, to work at the day centres. (Kirsty)

The referral system, criteria for selection

Referrals

Our referrals come mainly from the occupational therapist, but, a referral might also come from a GP, consultant, the social work department, a home help and sometimes from relatives. (Helena)

Selection criteria

The clients all have to have a diagnosis of dementia. That is the first criterion. Otherwise we cannot accept them until that diagnosis has been made. (Kirsty)

Secondly, they have to be living in the local community, although that can be flexible. (Helena)

However, there are certain problems with the accommodation in Marionville which means that the clients would also have to be fairly mobile. Look around. We do not have the facilities here for people who are in wheelchairs or who have severe physical disabilities, or for people who cannot get into the minibus. (Helena)

It is unfortunate that we cannot accept people with severe physical disabilities. However, our staff are not trained in lifting techniques and, as you can see, the dining/activities room is quite small and we could not fit a wheelchair in there. That is also the problem with the toilet. (Kirsty).

Assessment

When we first make the visit to the client's home, there is an assessment form which we complete. The visit is usually to make an assessment of the client's physical ability to walk about the home and to gauge the level of confusion and disability. We also speak with the client and with the relatives or with anyone else who is with the client at the time about any hobbies, interests and dislikes, such as food, which the client may have. (Helena)

Our referral forms which are completed by other professionals usually have sufficient information in them, but, you can only learn what people like through personal experience of them.

On that first visit, we usually offer an invitation to visit the day centre. If someone refuses to accept, we cannot force them. However, we may go back at some later date and try to encourage them to visit the day centre, but that is not always possible.

However, if someone was keen to come along and was physically mobile, we would be happy to accept them. (Kirsty)

Cost to the carer is 75p for each day a client is here, but that is the total cost for the whole day and is to pay for the client's meals. This may have to be increased to £1.00 in the near future to help cover rising costs. (Kirsty)

The day centre routine

Meals

When clients first arrive in the morning, they are given tea and toast by
either of ourselves or the trainees. We organise a rota for each day centre
of who is to make the tea and toast each day and the same applies for the
lunches. Clients get a hot two-course meal with either soup or pudding.
We, Kirsty and myself, do the shopping for food, etc for both centres
about once a month. (Helena)

Activities

Given that one of the day centres is a former three-apartment ground floor
tenement flat which accommodates nine clients and possibly up to six staff,
the best utilisation of the available space had been a consideration which
had been resolved to the general satisfaction of the workers.

We have two main rooms: the living room area which is all seated and
the room set aside as the dining room with tables and chairs and which
doubles up for the use of those clients who wish to do board games,
dominoes, whatever. The third small bedroom serves as an office and
a place for conducting individual interviews.

We split up according to what the clients want to do. If they want
to have a sing-song, there is sufficient room for everyone to stay in the
living room. A couple of staff will also spend a bit of time in the kitchen
preparing the teas and toast and the lunch, but the kitchen is too small
to let the clients help. (Kirsty)

Whilst there is no cure for dementia sufferers,the staff firmly believe in the
positive contribution which involvement in the activities and the regimen of
the day centre held for the client users.

Although there is no cure, you can , perhaps, slow down the progression
of the illness. If people are isolated and don't take part in any social
activity, they not only get depressed and lonely, but, their memories
will go even faster. Coming here not only keeps them happy in terms
of socialisation, the activities also jog their memories. We also like to
vary the activities, not only for the clients but for ourselves. If you do
the same thing continually, people will just get bored. (Helena)

I think as well as maintaining the physical and mental abilities
which the clients still possess, the day centres are also providing a safe
environment where dementia sufferers can come in and feel secure and
happy. Every day in life they are out in the real world so to speak,
and every day they are coming up against things which they cannot do
any more. They cannot remember how to use money, or, how to cook
meals, or, how to put their clothes on properly, or, the shops do not
look familiar, or, they do not recognise where they are.

But when they come here everything is gauged to dementia sufferers. They are never put in a position where they are unable to cope
with something or do not know the answer for something. They may
recognise your face from before, but they will not necessarily remember

your name. So we all wear name badges. That way, clients will not be put in the position of saying, 'Sorry I cannot remember your name'. (Kirsty)

Collection arrangements

We have two drivers for the minibus who are well experienced and trained in working with dementia suffers. Two trainees go on the minibus to do escort at the beginning and end of the day. As part of the rota, I also participate in the escort duties, but only at the end of the day as I need to be present at the day centre to take phone calls, receive visitors and to supervise the volunteers/trainees. Participating in escort duty provides an opportunity to have direct contact with carers, and to build up relationships with them. (Kirsty)

The workers who are allocated each day to go on escort to pick up clients from their homes and bring them to the day centre in the minibus have a sheet with a list of who they are going to collect that morning. The sheet will also give the names of the client's doctor and the name of the person to contact in the event of any problem emerging.

Last week when we went to pick up one client he was very disorientated. He is usually ready with his suit on, knows who we are and knows where he is going. But that morning he was visibly quite ill and upset. Obviously, we are prepared for such situations. All we had to do was get on to the doctor and ask if he knew anything about Mr X and was told that the doctor was already on his way to the house as he had visited the client the previous day. I think by now, most of the trainees are trained and ready for difficult situations emerging and are very responsible. (Helena)

Clients in stress

I think in a situation where a client is becoming stressed whilst at the day centre, often the best thing to do is to remove them from the stressful situation and then try to analyse why it is they have become upset. For example, it may be that a general quiz is going on and the person is unable to answer any of the questions and they may get upset and very stressed that their memory is not what it used to be. In that instance, you can give them questions which you know they can answer, or simply remove them from the situation and find them another activity whilst the others are getting on with the quiz. (Kirsty)

Incontinence

We do have a couple of clients who are incontinent at one of the day centres, but, that is not really a problem. Incontinence is something that can be managed simply by taking the person to the toilet every 1 or 2 hours. That way the clients do not have the embarrassment of having wet themselves and all of the problems of having to change all of their clothing. In cases where a client is incontinent, I would certainly have a meeting with all the members of the staff and let them know that this was the case, and either appoint someone to make sure that the client went to the toilet on a regular basis, or I would usually take responsibility for it myself. (Kirsty)

Attendance at other day centres

In relation to possible stress factors for the client, the subject of the client's attendance at other day centres during the week and the possible negative effects of this were aired.

> Most of our clients actually go to various community day centres for dementia sufferers. They may have a place at a different Centre on any given day of the week. However, we are working with dementia sufferers who have severe problems with their short-term memories. If you did the same thing with them every single day of the week, probably, most of them would not remember what they had been doing.
>
> I think that those clients who are more aware know where they are. Those who are more severely confused just know they are at a day centre, and sometimes they get the names all mixed up, and are not terribly sure where they are, but, they all seem to enjoy themselves.
>
> On the odd occasion some clients do become very confused about where they are. However, I do not think it has anything to do with going to different day centres. I think it is just the nature of the illness. Some of our clients, when we take them home at the end of the day, do not even realise they are home. But those are the clients who are more severely demented. (Kirsty)

Management and support

In common with most other work groups a few problems have arisen with the trainees over aspects of the work, or, the management of the project itself. One of the most common problems has been that of the rota system and the sense of dissatisfaction which some trainees have expressed of the number of times which they have had to spend on kitchen duty, or the fact that some felt they have not as yet experienced all the aspects of the centre's work. Occasionally the difficulty may be that of working with a particular individual attending the centre. In an attempt to deal with such matters before they become an issue, the project organisers have joint group support meetings with staff and trainees to try and identify and ventilate emerging difficulties for individual workers.

> There is a good system of support for all the members of the staff. We have support meetings with Trish Combe the co-ordinator of the project and we ourselves have regular support meetings with the trainees in which they have an opportunity to speak about any problem or dissatisfactions they may have. We also use these meetings to update trainees on what is happening with our clients.

In those instances where individuals are unable to express their views publicly within the group context, meetings with the organiser on a one-to-one basis are also a feature of the ways in which these day centres are managed. However, one of the day centres experienced an initial difficulty with the transition brought about by the departure of the original organiser and a replacement with a new member of staff.

> I had a few problems at the start with some trainees reacting to the change. It was not just that we were seen as young females, but that we had come in after the project had been going and we had not trained them from the start. I think it has been quite difficult for some trainees adjusting to someone new. They had been used to one person and her way of doing things and someone else comes in and changes how things had been done. (Helena)
>
> Every trainee was asked how they felt about working with a young woman in charge and everyone said that that was fine. (Kirsty)

Skills required

> I think that what is needed to be an effective organiser would include the following skills of:
> organisational skills, open communication, patience, sense of humour, good listening skills, good observation skills of mood of individuals and events, etc. (Kirsty)

Carers' view of the service

This project had set out two main objectives for its work. The first relating to the needs of the carer, the second the needs of those being cared for — the dementia sufferers. From this account, there is ample illustration of the benefits to the sufferers which were built into the service provided: support, stimulation, socialisation and personalised attention. Moreover, the experience is one which most dementia sufferers found non-threatening and enjoyable.

For the carers, the benefits of the service provided were equally evident to the workers of this project.

> The carers are delighted with the service offered. They enjoyed having a day's break from caring and they can relax to do things of their own interest knowing that their relative is in safe hands. Often carers have no contact with home helps, support groups, day hospital, etc, and we may be the only service that they receive. Carers feel that they can talk to us about problems or ask us where to go for help if they are not coping with their home circumstances. Again, many of them feel that this support is invaluable.

Points to ponder

▽ The background of the two organisers.

▽ The significance of client numbers.

▽ Ratio of carers to clients.

▽ Attention given to needs of individual clients.

▽ Development of the service provided.

▽ The management of care staff.

▽ Benefits provided to both carers and clients.

16 Parkinson's Disease Society — self-help group: Durham

Secretary: Mrs Joan Wilkinson

Keypoints

This account is interesting because of the simple and undramatic way in which it illustrates:

▲ *the gaps in the support service provision to people with Parkinson's disease in the community;*

▲ *the self-help efforts of an elderly group of volunteers who were either themselves sufferers of Parkinson's disease or carers of a relative with that disease;*

▲ *the relative absence of support from the statutory services in meeting the community needs of these individuals.*

Project Background

My name is Joan Wilkinson, my husband has suffered from Parkinson's disease for 16 years. I am the secretary of the Durham branch of the Parkinson's disease society. I was not exactly a founder member, but I was the second meeting member for this particular support group. The group was started by a friend of ours who has Parkinson's disease and her husband. We felt we needed a society in Durham for other people in similar positions to ourselves. There were four of us at the very first meeting, we now have a membership of about 46 regular attenders. Sadly of course, we lose some of our members through bereavement, but generally we are a happy group.

We founded our branch in 1986 and were inaugurated as a Parkinson's disease society in 1988. We wrote to all the doctors, the health centres, the nurses of course, and the health visitors and asked that they would contact or inform Parkinson patients of our intentions of starting a branch — although actually we had started our branch, but in a very small way. When we first began our Durham branch, we very much appreciated the services of our society development officer. He guided us through our inauguration to the Parkinson's disease society. He gave us advice on advertising, fund-raising, supplying us with information leaflets and posters, and generally issuing society guidelines. Since setting ourselves up as a branch, we have had assistance from our society — the Parkinson's disease society — for any small expenses we incurred, but this really only amounted to the cost of the rental of the hall, because other expenses such as postage we were able to raise ourselves. We have very few expenses really, it is just mainly postage and letter writing.

The voluntary worker's role

My role is to co-ordinate between the society and the members by writing and helping them with advice from headquarters, helping arrange holidays between headquarters and the patient and their carer because we care as much about the carer as we do about the patient. I write monthly letters to each of our members inviting them to our branch meetings. I do not organise the programme for the meeting, but, I make sure that the speaker attends. We organise fund-raising events which are mainly street collections, usually three times a year. This, of course, entails letters and telephone calls. I generally keep in touch with people on the telephone monthly. For our general members, I type the letter, have it photocopied at the library and then distribute it to our members. I also try to organise transport which is one big headache.

Branch meeting place

We meet every month at Bowburn — the community centre in County Durham. The centre is only 3 miles from Durham city and is the central location for our Durham branch. We really could not find anywhere in Durham itself that was accessible for disabled people apart from Dryburn Hospital, but we felt that a hospital was not quite the right place to meet. Perhaps, by the time you have gone to visit your consultant, or you have other appointments at the hospital, it gets a bit depressing, so we avoided that and we chose instead to meet at Bowburn which seems to be accessible to everyone. Bowburn Centre has good parking facilities and a ramp for wheelchairs and everything else is on the level inside the centre building. Bowburn Community Centre is the centre for carpet bowls within the area, so we are able to bowl on their carpets and they were very kind, they lent it to us free of charge. We had a pleasant afternoon carpet bowling. It was entertaining, because we were surprised how many disabled people really wanted to join in that activity. We did not damage anything and it was a very good afternoon.

We now have a permanent booking at Bowburn and the charge is quite reasonable — it is only £2.50 per hour or £3.50 for two hours.

Activities

I think there are about 44 users plus the carers, although we do not always have full attendance because of course some people are poorly that day. They come when they can.

We really meet to support each other, give advice and to help each other when we can.

We have a chairman, a treasurer and a committee of about seven members. We work mainly to raise funds for the society for research. We would like every penny we get to go to research, but it is not always possible. Since we became a branch, we have raised and sent £3500 to headquarters — for research only. Fortunately, we were able to select a piece of equipment to be used to benefit research into Parkinson's disease and this we donated to the neurology department of Huntersmoor Hospital at Newcastle. They bought a computer system, which of course, will benefit more than us really, but it will also benefit research into Parkinson's disease.

We have a speaker at every branch meeting. Usually before our committee meeting in November, we ask for suggestions from our own members about next year's programme. They usually come forward with ideas such as opticians, chiropody, market garden, the Red Cross and so on. The Red Cross have come and given us advice on how to handle patients, physiotherapy, occupational therapy, etc. Those who have travelled abroad come and show us their slides and tell us about their holidays. In October we will have a gentleman who lives in the north east and who has walked from Lands End to John O'Groats raising money for multiple sclerosis who will come and talk to our group. We also have an input on handicrafts. We have only had to cancel one meeting because of the weather and that was in February and we were all snowed-in in County Durham.

We have educational talks from nurses, doctors and from other disabled people such as the multiple sclerosis group. We have also had the Red Cross Society come and talk to us.

Next month the Head of the Neurology Department is coming to speak to us so that is quite an interesting meeting. Generally, when we have a neurologist come to speak, everyone will attend. We are all hoping for news on the latest developments and good results from the research, but, at the moment, there is very little forthcoming.

We just support each other. We have outings. Once a year we are allowed to use a disabled bus with a lift for disabled people which we get from the Sherburn Hill Hospital, and that is when we have our outings. We can take 17 disabled members on that outing plus others in cars who are able to walk. Last year, we went on a visit to the post office sorting office which was educational and also the National Garden Festival. This year we visited a historic church near Bishop Auckland, and we had tea while we were out. We had hoped to take a stroll down to the riverside, but the weather prevented that. It was rather cold.

We also organise a Christmas party, but usually have a caterer to do the catering. However, that is the only time we make use of an outside caterer.

As far as the branch activities are concerned, we do not make any difference really between the carer and the patient, both are regarded as the same. We are quite keen to organise holidays, but the holidays are usually only partially funded. Of the funding 50% comes from the Winged Fellowship Society who offer holidays for handicapped people. They only offer half price for a holiday at their centre. However, if the member's means are very small we would cover the entire cost of the holiday, but, of course, the person would have to answer a few questions. But the offer from the Winged Fellowship is there and they have been very kind and generous. They can also organise transport through the British Red Cross to enable the carer and the patient to holiday at the centre, but that costs a certain small amount for mileage cover.

Benefits

I believe that membership of the group offers a number of benefits to the carer and to the patient. For a start, I would say that at least they know that they are not alone. We are all in the same boat, whether you have a husband to care for, or a parent, or a wife, you just share the same problems. We just seem to cheer each other up — we all get along very very well. We have had holidays together which was the first holiday I have ever been on with friends, and I was really quite surprised at how well that went. We had a happy time. We try now to encourage as many people as possible to go on these holidays and some do try to take advantage of them. Others perhaps, if they feel too ill, feel better at home, so we try to encourage day outings as well. We sometimes visit each other's homes in the evenings. We have just become good friends.

Apart from just really cheering up members, we can also advise them on where they can get help on how to care for the patient.

We also have a voluntary welfare officer who is interested in our members. She keeps us in touch with any welfare benefits we can gain to help the disabled person. She visits, perhaps once or twice a year, any members who are unable to attend our branch meetings. Sometimes, but not in ours, there are branches of carers' assistants who will come and sit with the patient while the carer goes out, but we have not got anything like that organised here.

In November 1990 we urged all our branch members to write to their Member of Parliament requesting them to support Mr Jack Ashley MP, who presented a 'written parliamentary question' in March 1991, requesting exemption from prescription charges for sufferers of Parkinson's disease who do not qualify for free prescriptions.

For other local people who are not already members of our branch of the Society, one of the biggest problems for anyone who may learn that a member of their family has got Parkinson's disease is getting that immediate support. We try to pass on this information through the health visitors or through our own advertising. We have leaflets in libraries and health centres. There is also our volunteer exhibition in Chester Le Street once a year of volunteer organisations, and we have leaflets there with my contact name on explaining what our branch does and the help available to the Parkinson patients. People can also contact the Parkinson's society headquarters address for information. When anyone contacts me, I send them a society quarterly newsletter, a book of hints for day-to-day living for the patient and carer which includes such things as washing, turning and dressing the patient. I

would also send out a leaflet stating the aims of our society and about
our local branch.

We just try to support each other as best we can.

For £1.00 a year you can also become a member of the national
organisation and for that you receive a quarterly newsletter which
gives you the latest news on research into Parkinson's disease, the
developments in the research, what is going on at headquarters, what
happens in other branches, and also keeps you in touch with publications
on the disease. Individuals take out the subscription and automatically
become a member of the society which entitles them to any information
that there is.

Funding

Our general funding is raised from street collections. We generally have
two or three street collections a year and from each of those we can raise
anywhere between £200 and £400. Last year we raised quite a lot, but
this year we have only had one street collection although we do have
two more organised. The next one is on 3 August 1991. We have to
have an official permit for street collections and also have to notify the
police. You are not allowed to approach people in the street. You
have to stand passively to collect, although you do give it a gentle rattle
now and again — you are not supposed to, but we do. It is surprising
because some people will come up and give you a bank note — put a
pound in or five pound note in and say

'I had a school teacher who was a marvellous person and he
developed Parkinson's disease so in memory of them I am giving you
this donation', which is very nice of them, and very kind.

We also have raffles, but it is really within our own groups. We
could use the national society's lottery's licence, but we just organise
this raffle among our own members and raise the money there. We
have 'coffee mornings', market stalls where we sell home-made cakes,
sponsored runs, memorial collections and donations.

We also raise funds through our branch meetings. We only expect
a small donation from our coffee or tea that we supply at our branch
meetings — but people are very generous, they usually put a £1 in or
possibly £2.

We have not yet applied to the health board for any grants. At the
moment, the branch is just really sowing the seeds. It is really just a
case of getting our project off the ground. The question of applying for
funding may come up in next year's budget.

We do not get any support financially from the social services,
although we do get advice, any advice we need, they will come and
help us with that.

Professional relationships

The medical profession has had very little involvement in the development of our self-help group. It was negative really, we did not get any
support. I suppose really that they are too busy themselves to start a

branch such as ours. We did have support, however, from health visitors. They came and saw what we were doing and were quite interested. Because, I suppose, it also offers a channel of support for their patients. They did show some interest but again it was very little really. We did it all ourselves. I do not think that the doctors and the hospitals are particularly interested in the work of our branch. I do not think they would be interested in spreading the word about our branch. I think that any medical contact to our branch is mainly through the health visitors which I suppose is their prerogative as part of their therapy role.

Transport

Transport is a major headache for us. Mainly because many Parkinsonians who have been drivers in the past are now unable to drive. I suppose it is also a sign of our times that the carer, who is generally the wife, is herself unable to drive. This problem will eliminate itself because the younger carers are generally able to drive.

People ring me up and say that they would love to come to our meetings, but that they have not got any transport. So how do you arrange it? As part of our welfare service we contribute a small sum towards the taxi fare to get people to our branch meetings. We feel that is part of our welfare role — sharing some of the money we raise, but that is really a very small amount. However, we have not anyone who comes to our branch outside a 10-mile radius of our meeting place. A journey of 10 miles is pretty costly. You see, you have got to think of it as a double journey — there and back again.

We do not have any help for transport from our society either. We do have a group of volunteer drivers who will come and assist any patients to get to meetings, but these are a bit costly. I will not say too costly because sometimes it depends on the mileage you see. And I think some people are rather reluctant to go into that expense.

We have asked the social services for assistance but they have done nothing to help. We have a volunteer driver service, which we have used once or twice, but again some of our members found it rather expensive.

Transport then is our biggest problem. We did arrange a meeting with the Durham County Council last year and held one or two meetings with the Handicapped Society or the Handicapped Committee to try to see if they could arrange to give us the use of a bus with a tail-lift for disabled people. There is not any such project at the moment, but as a result of that meeting we did go on to have a larger meeting with the representatives of Cleveland County 'ring a ride' scheme. This scheme is funded and controlled by the Cleveland County Council, and based in Middlesbrough. That group have organised a transport facility by buying a fleet of disabled buses with tail-lifts for disabled people and these are used as taxis really — although you must arrange your journey the day before. It is a marvellous transit service for disabled people and I think there are seven buses. But Middlesbrough is a compact geographical area and you can arrange such a service as that. Here in County Durham we are a much more scattered area and it would be more costly to organise. I think it may take a few years for such a scheme to come into the County Durham budget when there is more money available. However, at the moment we have just sown the seed in the mind of the council and we will have to wait and see if the idea ever gets off the ground.

Volunteers

Our biggest problem is transport — and it would be wonderful if we could have more volunteer transport drivers. We do have an occasional son or daughter who will come and pick someone up and perhaps their friend as well.

All our branch members are either sufferers or carers, their ages range from 50 to 76 years.

Our vice-chairman whose father, now deceased, suffered with parkinson's disease for 25 years.

Our treasurer, does a tremendous amount of unseen work accounting, banking and totalising coinage from our collecting tins. He also cares for his wife who is seriously ill at home.

Our chairman is occasionally invited to speak to other charitable organisations of the work of the society. This service is provided free of charge, sometimes a small donation is given to show their appreciation.

It must also be noted that some of our committee and our members not only care for their Parkinsonian partner, they have aged parents to care for too.

Our voluntary welfare officer visits hospitals and nursing homes to distribute informaton and advice on caring for Parkinson patients.

When we have a delegate who is able to attend conferences or annual general meetings held in London, usually twice each year, we cover their expenses.

Unfortunately, illness can affect the degree to which volunteers can remain active on behalf of the branch. Our chairman, who is a marvellous person, her husband is very ill, so she cannot be involved as much as she would like. She does keep in touch, of course, on the telephone and makes decisions and we have committee meetings every 2 months to keep things on a steady, even keel.

Sometimes, when the patient dies, the relative will continue to support the branch. Our welfare officer lost her husband last year and she now devotes a tremendous amount of time to visiting. She is the right person to do it. She is an ex-nurse and knows how to handle people. I do a lot of work locally on the western side of Durham and she does the eastern side because she lives in that area. Although she is just a voluntary worker, she has been trained by our society to advise and inform. She goes on training days or training weekend seminars twice a year. She is really there representing the Parkinson's society branches.

However, it is difficult to increase the number of volunteers to share the workload. Obtaining volunteers is a very slow process really. Its mainly through new members joining, and it depends on whether their families have any other commitments. Generally, you see, the young people, both male and female, are working these days — so that makes it difficult for them to volunteer.

A lot of our fund-raising is generally on a Saturday so relatives sometimes spare us an hour for our fund-raising efforts. There, again, we are also rather short of street collectors because of the nature of our illness. Most patients, themselves, cannot help us. Their carers are unable to come because they are already caring for someone who has Parkinson's, so we have to rely upon their family members to come and support us. Generally, we have about seven or eight collectors. Between us we work for about 4 or 5 hours with very little break, trying to catch the shoppers before they spend their money.

Another possible reason affecting the number of volunteers for the branch is that people can only come forward to help us if they are available. Our branch meets in the afternoons, on a Monday afternoon, and that perhaps is a difficult time for volunteers to come and help. On our very first evening meeting, there was a howling gale, lashing down with rain, it was deplorable – only four people turned up. It was decided that there would be greater likelihood of more people being able to attend in the afternoon, so we now meet on Monday afternoon, although we keep raising the timing of our meetings in discussions at our committee sessions. However, we keep coming back to the afternoons. I think most Parkinson's patients do not like coming out at night. Mainly I think because — it is rather strange, but in my husband's case and, in general, in other Parkinsonian cases — patients have more strength in the mornings and that strength peters out by teatime. So, when it comes to the evening time, they just want to collapse. So in the afternoons, we can get through the meeting which lasts for 2 hours and it is a pleasant occasion for everyone. I enjoy it, and I think other people do too.

Members' involvement

Everyone on the management committee has a relative who has Parkinson's or has the illness themselves. In fact I do not know anyone who comes to our branch meetings that does not have some association with Parkinson's disease. We have patients who are on the committee. We have one lady, aged 76, who is our catering officer. She has Parkinson's disease and she organises all the tea/coffee and biscuits and the raffles which we have every week — all of which helps us to cover our monthly expenses.

We also have a very good vice-chairman who organises our programme for the year. Our ideas come from our branch members, but, he is pretty good. He has loads of contacts and is a nice fellow. He attends our meetings and occasionally, when he is able, he brings a patient with him.

Future

As far as the future is concerned, it is really volunteer drivers that we are desperate for. We would have more branch members if we could get some more volunteer drivers. You see, you also have to remember that Parkinson's disease patients cannot get a bus — or very few can. Even for those members who are able to travel by public transport, we are such a scattered geographical area that it would possibly involve two or three buses in order to get at our centre, which would be too arduous a journey for patients to make. Parkinsonians only have a certain amount of strength each day. If they have used that strength up in the morning, it has just gone for the rest of the day. Until we get that transport, we just do what we can. We just support each other.

Points to ponder

▽ The ages of the volunteers' committee.

▽ The problems which living in a geographically scattered community presents Parkinsons' sufferers or their carers gaining access to the support and resources of the self-help group.

▽ The limitations of funding to the project.

▽ The problem of attracting volunteers.

▽ The problems related to transport.

▽ Spirit of caring and resilience expressed in the account.

17 The Integration Trust Ltd — Esh Valley, Co. Durham
Parents: Mr Angus Millar and Mrs Joan Millar

Keypoints

This account, told entirely in the words of Mr and Mrs Millar is interesting because it illustrates the:
▲ *efforts of a small group of parents and their attempts to develop a residential care facility for their severely handicapped children;*
▲ *tenacity of the parents;*
▲ *imaginative use of funding to finance the project;*
▲ *limitations of the existing provision for profoundly handicapped individuals within the community.*

Background

We have four children ranging from 35–22 years old, some married and others living away. Our youngest son, David, is very profoundly handicapped and we, like all parents in this situation, were very anxious about what was going to happen to David when we can no longer take care of him.

In the late 1970's when the development of long-stay facilities were being curtailed, I remember Dr Jean Robson, who was David's paediatrician answer to my concern about David's future when we were older, if good provision was not made for youngsters like him, saying that nursing/care provision could be made in our home.

No significant widespread provision of such community support seems to have developed in the 15 years which have elapsed.

Here, in Britain, when the informal care network breaks down which is inevitable as parents become physically unable to provide the care, owing to increasing age and/or illness, the system's response is to place the handicapped or disabled person in an institution. Initially, this may be viewed as a temporary measure, but, in many cases, particularly where there are serious and profound disabilities, the move becomes permanent. However, the developing view for caring for the handicapped and disabled is that traditional institutionalisation is neither an efficient or an appropriate way of meeting the needs of this group. That certainly is the view that has long been held by the handicapped and disabled themselves, their professional support networks and by ourselves as parents.

We got the idea for this scheme as a result of the noises that the Government was making perhaps 3 years ago. We had read the Government White Paper *Caring for People* which acknowledged the major contribution of the informal carers and the Government's own recognition that the demographic trends in the population will have implications for the future availability of carers to undertake such work. It seemed that the idea was to raise the profile of the handicapped a bit more and to encourage people to think of alternatives. There was a feeling, which was put about at the time, whether that feeling had any real basis behind it. There was another thing, that the Government would like to empty the institutions.

Occasionally, David has been taken into hospital because we could not care for him at home. The most recent occasion was when I was in hospital with appendicitis. However, when David has had to go into hospital, when he comes out, he is totally different. He has stopped responding and becomes withdrawn. His real interest in life is people, and he gets great happiness and joy from going out and meeting normal people. Institutionalisation just finishes him and to envisage institutionalisation as an inevitable future for David is not only unappealing but is totally unacceptable.

Client choice

In 1989 after considering many possible solutions to the long-term needs of our son, David, my wife and I decided that a framework should be developed within which David's future and the future of similarly handicapped and disabled young people might be secured. It was important that both David and ourselves should have some say in what that future would be. We consulted with the parents of similarly handicapped young adults and their social and professional networks and decided to investigate the possibility of setting up a project which would establish our children in their own house, where they would be independent of us, but supported by well trained carers and the available community services. We saw the project as being the first of several which would tailor the services to the needs of the individual rather than the more familiar tailoring of the individual to the services which is criticised in the Government White Paper *Caring for People*. However, the idea behind this project is not unique and has been applied in practice and with success in British Columbia, New Zealand and in Scandanavia.

Developing the idea

We first read about a scheme called the linkability scheme in one of the Sunday papers and got further information on that scheme from

Geraldine Granath who lives in the village and works for the Spastics Society. What interested Joan and myself was that the linkability scheme actually worked in a way that we hoped to operate. The parents set themselves up as a company limited by guarantee and as a charitable trust and managed to get accommodation and staffed a home which provided accommodation for young people in Chorley. However, they had an advantage over us, because they had the assistance of a Spastics Society fieldworker's professional full-time support who had been given a year's sabbatical actually to develop the work and, also, because Chorley did not have any established provision for handicapped of their own. The linkability group took about 2 years to get their scheme up and running.

Three years ago Keith Wilkinson, who was the social worker attached to the community mental handicapped team, and ourselves discussed the possibilities of Joan and myself doing something similar and I was amazed that he did not think the idea was impossible. We took it from there and we have been working on the project since that time. First by finding other youngsters who were similarly situated and whose parents were prepared to let them go into a house of their own.That is not an easy decision to make because there is a very close relationship between disabled young people and their parents. All sorts of emotional feelings and fears are raised at the prospect.

We initially thought that perhaps we could build a house, but that was going to be too expensive. That was really going to take away all of the funding we could possibly raise. We also gave some thought to the numbers of people who would use the project and decided three would be okay. One of the things I am most anxious about is that the group has to be small enough to look in the community as if it is a normal household. If you have four or five or six people living in the house, you have created a small institution.

The development of Project One to facilitate three young people living in the community was deliberate and made on these grounds.

1. Each of the young people requires high level of personal care and meeting these needs in a dignified way made a small group size essential.
2. Spending much of their time in wheelchairs it was considered that three people in wheelchairs would stretch the space in a normal house to the limit.
3. The trust hopes that the young people will live in a situation which responds sensitively and quickly to their individual needs. It was felt that a household size of three, given the severity of their handicaps, made such a response to their needs possible.
4. Another important consideration which should not be overlooked when deciding the size of a project is an estimate of the number of handicapped people a particular community might absorb, thus achieving integration rather than segregation within the community. It is felt that this number is inevitably small and that three is near the top of it.

The user group

We found that we were able to identify three young people, including our son David, who would benefit from such a project. The three young people are:

David age 22

David lives at home in Esh Village with my wife and myself. David was born with spina bifida and hydrocephalic. These conditions have left him with multiple disabilities and handicaps. Because of a scoliosis which has developed with time, David sits in a moulded seat in a wheelchair and needs to have his position moved frequently to release stress and prevent the development of sores. Despite his disabilities, David is a very sociable person responding to, and participating as best he can in, social activities. Each weekday David attends the special care unit at the Durham ATC. The rest of David's care and his socialising depends on my wife and myself, with our few hours of support and respite funded by the independent living fund (ILF). Before the arrival of the independent living fund, we got spasmodic help from Crossroads. Someone would come in and look after David. The community mental handicapped team were also very helpful, particularly at times when Angus, my husband was in hospital. Other than that, we have tended to rely on ourselves rather than on other resources.

Jean aged 40

David already knew Jean, one of the other young people in the group, through their attendance at the same adult training centre. They are very fond of each other. Jean has a lively and sociable personality and lives at home with her widowed mother, Helen, in Croxdale. Jean has been very severely handicapped and disabled since early infancy owing to vaccination damage. Each day Jean attends the special care unit at the Akley Heads ATC. Jean is quadraplegic, spending most of her waking time in a wheelchair. Until very recently, Ellen, Jean's mother provided all of Jean's care. However, in the last few months some support care funded by the ILF has become available. However, Jean's mother Ellen is about 76 or 77 years old and so time is running out for Ellen and Jean in terms of how long that care can be sustained.

Dorothy aged 27

Like Jean, Dorothy has been quadraplegic since early infancy, owing to vaccination damage and, while she can walk a little with assistance, she spends most of her waking time in a wheelchair. She needs help to eat, dress and wash. She is cared for at home in Esh Winning by her father, Bill who is a widower getting up in years. Each weekday she goes to the special care unit at the ATC at Harelaw between 9.30am and 3.30pm. Bill, supported by some help, funded by the ILF, however, provides the care.

Dorothy's, Jean's and David's medical, social and family networks are aware that the three young people become withdrawn and significantly less socially interactive when they have been in hospital for any reason. The other parents, the medical and social networks and ourselves felt that an alternative to institutionalisation should be developed before the inevitable collapse of their care network occurs and hospitalisation is imposed on them as part of the crisis management process. The solution which was considered appropriate was that Dorothy, Jean and David should be enabled to live in a house on their own where, supported by appropriate care and community service, they would live independent dignified lives.

The Integration Trust

We had put together the name the 'Integration Trust' because, concurrently with doing the spade work of hunting down the resources, we were also going through the process establishing the project as a charity, which was not an easy thing to do.

We decided to set up the trust because the project was eventually going to be in a position where it was going to have to employ quite a troop of carers and, since David and the other young people are going to be here after we have gone, there had to be some basis for continuing the management process. We were advised by people like Keith that we should set up a body which would not be identified solely with ourselves and it has taken us 18 months to process this through. We also took the advice of our lawyer because we were considering seeking charitable status and one of the things that the book Phillips (1988) advises is that, if you are going to own property or to employ people, this is what you should do.

Obviously, you could not have your charity for just your own three people. This was the big problem we faced with setting up the charity, a charity has to have a general community benefit and cannot have specifically named beneficiaries. On the application form which the solicitor received, we had to put down the people who would benefit from the project and the people who would administer the trust. Initially, it all looked like a family concern, so this was why it took such a long time. Eventually we had advice from Barbara Lithgow at Charities Commission who was very good. On the other hand, the inland revenue were very lacklustre about the whole thing. At first they were not going to allow the project to be tax-free. Actually, it has all worked out all right and we got it through not so long ago. We won through in the end.

We succeeded in persuading the Charity Commissioner and the inland revenue by making adjustments to the persons named as trustees. It was not on to have ourselves as trustees. The trustees must not be related to beneficiaries current or potential, which is what we have now achieved. People we knew who were not related to the youngsters, like the headmistress of the special school, who, as well as knowing David, knows 60–70% of the group who would be potential clients of the trust. She is one of those people who would instil confidence, not just in the youngsters, but in the parents. There is also another lady who teaches young people with special needs who is one of our trustees. Because we felt that we were having legal hassle, one of the things that we also decided to do was to get our lawyer in on the act as a trustee.

Locating the community

We thought hard about where we would like to locate the project. We would like the house to be in Esh Winning or in Langley Park which is the village down at the bottom of the hill. The reasons for this are that both are small communities and have a sense of community. They have a kind of ambience. There are other places where you might not like to try and set up this type of project because the environment would be hostile. You get the feeling in Langley Park that the community might, in fact, be supportive. Also it is so near Bill and Ellen, the two other parents and ourselves. The training centre is also just 5 miles along the road.

Developing the project

A bid was made to the local health authorities (we had to deal with two, since Dorothy and Jean lived in the Durham district's area and David in North West Durham) to get support for the project from the health authorities' joint funding budget. The DHA allocated funds to convert a property but were unwilling to contribute to care budget. NWDHA rejected the first application but after a fairly heavy canvass of the authority members and, in particular, those members of the authority who participated in the joint care planning team's allocation of the joint funding budget, they agreed to match the DHA's contribution on a pro rata basis.

With this money available we canvassed local authorities seeking allocation of a property for the project. After a very hard canvass and, using our local MP to intercede, Derwentside District Council councillors agreed, first in principle and then in practice, to allocate a property. We had to provide clarification of the significance of limited company among other things before agreement was reached. Initially, it seemed possible that the care budget might be met by independent living fund but the capping of ILF's activity in April 1990 has resulted in ILF indicating that they would contribute the maximum permitted amount towards the budget. This amounts to 45% of the required budget. We have continued to negotiate with the health authorities and with county social services to secure the remainder. The health authorities have agreed a further £15,000 contribution from joint funding in each of the next 3 years.

At each step, heavy canvassing has been necessary. After another round, we have been assured that the residual money will be found by social services.

The big problem in securing the care budget is that neither health nor social services know if money will be provided to meet the community care costs and they are unsure into whose court specific care needs and provision will fall. As far as I am aware the criteria setting out what is health care and what is social care, despite being promised by the DHSS 12 months ago, have not yet been promulgated, and in this grey light before the dawn no sector is prepared to take responsibility.

Initially, our steering group consisted of the parents, two members from county social services and Geraldine Granath of the Spastics Society. We would invite additional people to the meetings whose expertise and influence was thought could be beneficial to the project.

At a meeting to which we had invited Simon Priestly, Durham Area Health Authority's Community Services Manager, when we were seeking support for the project from joint funding, it became apparent that, however appealing the project, a hard battle was to be fought to secure its implementation. Simon, who agrees that institutionalisation is an inappropriate outcome to the long-term care of Dorothy, Jean and David, by acting as devil's advocate at that meeting strengthened our determination to seek a solution which was considered more appropriate than institutionalisation for these three handicapped and disabled young people.

A great deal of interest has also been shown in the trust by parents in the region who are currently caring for young adults with handicaps and disabilities at home and who, like ourselves, view the future prospect of their loved ones with concern. Both social services and local health authorities who see the work of the trust as pioneering and as an answer to the increasing problems of how best to incorporate the needs of the disabled into their community care plan, have shown great interest and are prepared to support this pioneer project financially. They also support the spirit of our work which is to provide a new initiative sensitive to the special needs of the long-term caring for physically and mentally handicapped people. All of this is in keeping with the objectives set out in the legislation on community care.

Now health and county hall know who we are, and it seems as if our hopes for the project will come true.

Funding

In terms of costs, we are looking at a gross care budget of about £88,000 of which figure the youngsters, with their severe disability premium plus their independent living fund money are providing somewhere around 50% of the running costs. We have employed an accountant to do this calculation and have had a set of accounts made up. We talked at length with Keith of the mental handicapped team and his predecessor about the kinds of staffing which a project of this size would require. We have also gone to courses run by care training agencies which Keith has told us about. In fact, every time a course or something comes up which may relate to the project, we hear about it.

One of the things which we will possibly have to negotiate is the structural alterations to any property we may be given to house the project. They might say 'it is your property', and at that point we would have to initiate consultation with their architects. Or, it might be that one of the other possibilities is that one of the housing associations would enter into the picture as they have expertise on this kind of development. The questions we will be asking ourselves, our trustees and others involved in developing the project would then be, 'Who's our friendly architect? Let's see if we can persuade him to do the job on a charitable basis'.

At the moment, the majority of the money is in fact coming from the kids, from their grants. The independent living fund money would come to the youngsters rather than to the trust. The health board have contributed something and I think that some of the unmet money could be overcome by using community services like the Befrienders and Crossroads. Befrienders are organised by county social services and provide assistance for social activity. Since socialising is part of the care budget, if this service was available to Dorothy, Jean and David, the amount required for this aspect of the care budget would be reduced. It is a matter of using the community services. We are trying to investigate these and other possibilities. It is all very political.

The money has actually come from the Health Board. However, the question of, 'Who, is going to pick up the tab to keep the project running?' that is the problem. If the community care thing had gone through as it was supposed to do in 1991, when it was imagined that all sorts of money would have gone to the social services, the situation would have been clearer, but it did not happen that way. I now doubt if this is going to happen in 1993 — who knows?

What appears to be happening is that, with the changeover in the health structure, it seems that health is taking more of this type of initiative over, and we are hoping they will pick up the tab, but we do not know and we feel we must take our chance. We do not particularly want to do this bearing in mind the extent of the young people's handicaps. Obviously, everything involves negotiations with the planning department, social services, the health board, etc. The criteria distinguishing between health and social care have not yet been published by the DHSS and this creates a great area from which both health authorities and the social security department hang back. So these are the main areas of concern.

Keeping up the momentum

Of course, there are still times when you get disheartened and sometimes you need a kick to get you going. Right at the very beginning I was sceptical about the future of the project. However, because of the activity of Berle, the lady from next door, who canvassed every County Councillor in North Durham at 7.00 on a Sunday morning to get the initial money to adapt the house, that changed my thinking on the project.(Angus)

Angus, woke up to the fact that no one was going to give him anything on a plate and that we had to work very hard. (Joan)

From then on, I just set in. I was due for retirement, so I took on a new job and this is what I am spending my time promoting — The Trust.(Angus)

Sometimes there are other 'kicks' that you get from people who perhaps questioned the project or your commitment to the project and that has actually strengthened resolve. Most of the time, however, you simply have to motivate yourself. One of the things that happens is that you get into troughs and you say to yourself, 'Come on, go!' and you pick up the file on the project to see who is the most likely candidate to target for information, help or resources. You get into a juggling situation, getting commitments from various agencies and you think 'you are there' then everything goes 'on hold' and all the time you are working to get the next piece put together and when that is done you have got to go back and chase all round the circle again so that you can feed the next ball into the juggling. That is why it gets very frustrating. You say 'To hell with this!' and 'I'm going away for a week on holiday'.(Angus)

We also talk to each other and to our other children, to neighbours and to friends. The other two parents, who are marvellous people, perhaps do not have the same professional ability as ourselves, perhaps because of the jobs that we have done in the past. It is basically thee and me. However, Bill and Ellen, the other parents can obviously see the advantages of the project and are very supportive in what we are doing.

Consultation with clients

We would like to be in operation by Christmas 1991. David knows what we are talking about, but does the ostrich on it. He will pretend he does not know, or want to know. Shirley, David's ILF funded carer, who looks after David, is very good. He occasionally stays with her. She has a son of the same age; David loves her. David's life, so far as it can be, is perfect at the moment. He cannot possibly fully appreciate what it is that we are attempting to do. What we are trying to do is almost to ease David and the others into the situation of independence long before they require to be there. It is trying to pre-empt the trauma; by being around to support the transitions.

The legislation on community care which was enacted in 1990 stated the aim of community care as enabling the handicapped and disabled to live in their own house or in small family-sized groups, where, supported by the appropriate care and community resources, they could live independent lives. To live an independent life in one's own home is a natural ambition of everyone, but only by developing responses sensitive to their needs will it be possible for the handicapped and the disabled to aspire to this basic human goal.

One of the things that has driven us on is that we would like — in consultation with David, the other young people in the project, and their parents — to have some say in what the outcome of the collapse of the current caring network is going to be. Bill's and Ellen's carers will both go on to the new house, and David's carer would certainly be there voluntarily.

None of the young people is going to be shut in; they will be looking outwards. It is rather like young people going into their first flat. Yes, that is the idea. All youngsters want to go away from home to a place of their own, the problem with the handicapped is that they need services to live and this is what we are trying to provide.

Benefits

One of the things that the charitable status requires of the trust is that we demonstrate that we have a wider benefit to the community. We feel that we have achieved this by showing that the Integration Trust was set up in order to facilitate present and future developments which will enable many more adults with physical and mental handicaps to live independently within their community. We see this project as only the first of several.

One of the things that you realise when you meet and talk with other parents of handicapped young people, as we have done, is that there are no general categories in this business. Everybody's needs, desires and aspirations tends to be different. However, there is one thing which is constant in all these people that you meet. That is the concern people have, if they are parents caring for handicapped people which is, 'What happens when the current care network finishes?'. You die, so you cannot do it forever, and it is going to leave your handicapped person at risk. Given David's handicap, and others like him, the immediate response of the system would be to put him in an institution because he needs feeding, etc. They would do it with the best intentions in the world, saying it was not going to be permanent. However, one of the difficulties is that there are very few intensive care set-ups. There is one in North Yorkshire where people with profound disabilities could, in fact, be sent. However, that would remove David from the community that he knows and would place him somewhere where he is a stranger. I feel very strongly that people like David, Jean and Dorothy belong in the community. When I take David out, he knows more people that I do. In fact, his social network is huge compared to mine. We should be working to retain that for David, Dorothy, Jean and others like them.

We also think it is important to share our experience and ideas with other groups of parents and also to become more knowledgeable ourselves about what is happening elsewhere in order to help the project. We have attended seminars and courses on personal future planning with representatives from Canada, and from Newcastle and have also met with another group from Darlington as well as meeting with, and talking to, professional workers at these and other meetings and courses on work with the severely handicapped.

Progress

Looking over the past few years, it is possible to detect areas in which our work has been successful as well as the setbacks which a project of this nature almost inevitably experiences. The successes which we are able to identify are listed below.

- Derwentside District Council have agreed to provide a house which can be adapted to meet the needs of young people and their carers.
- The local health authorities have agreed to provide money from their 1990 joint funding budget to cover the capital costs of converting the property.
- The trust has developed work schedules and job specifications for

the carers and is developing monitoring procedures to ensure that appropriateness of the care provision.

- The independent living fund has agreed to make their maximum contribution towards the care budget for the project.
- The Durham Area Health Authority and the North West Durham Health Authority have agreed to make contributions from their joint funding budgets towards the care cost of the project over the next 3 years.
- The Director of Social Services for the county is prepared to seek authority to meet the residual care budget costs of the project.
- The trust has been registered as a charity in order to provide a basis which will enable other integrated living projects to be developed and provide a structure to ensure the future maintenance of the projects.

Points to ponder

▽   The gaps in service provision to those with multiple disability.

▽   The concern expressed by parents for the long-term care of their handicapped children.

▽   How the idea for the project first arose.

▽   The networking abilities of the parents in attracting support and resources to the project.

▽   The setting up of a trust to secure the future of the project.

▽   The skills of the parents in working through the complex process of establishing the trust.

18   Livingston and District Epilepsy Group
Jane Aitken

Keypoints

This account of the development of the Livingston and District Epilepsy Group project is interesting because it again highlights:
▲ *The importance of the commitment and energy of the key worker(s) in sustaining and developing a project;*
▲ *The genuine regard for clients as a whole;*
▲ *The problems of locating permanent funding for staff;*
▲ *The importance of the contributions made by volunteers and employment trainees to the delivery of the service.*

Worker's background

My background was in accountancy. I worked with a large electronics company as office manager for 18 years before I decided to train for the social services. During my training, I was sent to various organisations and hospitals, including Craigmore Hospital in Inverness, where I worked for 6 weeks. It was there that I undertook two case studies on two female patients — both with epilepsy — one a girl aged 9. That is how I became interested in epilepsy and, although I did not really decide that I was going to work with people with epilepsy at that stage, I did learn quite a lot about the illness. After I qualified, I saw this job advertised and it appealed to me because I thought there was a challenge to it. However, when I came to the interview, I was alarmed that there was no provision for children, and I was mainly interested in children. One of the things I asked during my interview was whether, if I was successful in getting the job, there would be an opportunity for me to set up a facility for children. They said that would really be up to me and that is how I came to be in this work.

Background to the project

The project for which Jane is director had originally been set up as a self-help support group for epilepsy sufferers in 1982 and had subsequently developed over the space of 3 years to offering advice, information and a drop-in facility for carers or sufferers of epilepsy.

These premises were first opened in 1985 and had been going for about 2 years when I first came here in 1987. It was largely an information and advice centre, although there were also a few people who suffered from epilepsy who used to stay for at least a part of every day. However, I could see the potential and, after I arrived, the care side of it built up. It gradually came that more and more people were being referred to this place and it became a day care centre almost by accident. Before we knew where we were, the place, which is a five-apartment council house, was overcrowded which meant we had to look at our numbers and the basis on which we would accept further referrals.

Referrals

People are referred here by local general practitioners; from St John's; the Northern General and Gogarburn Hospitals; local health clinics; social workers attached to the hospital; as well as a lot of self-referrals and family referrals. We have people referred from throughout West Lothian and not just from the Livingston area. We also have a lot of people referred to us who have epilepsy as a result of mental handicap. However, their epilepsy is the least of their problems but, try telling that to some of the other agencies who refer them our way. When they get someone who has a lot of handicaps they will say 'Oh, but they have epilepsy. So it is your problem'. They see epilepsy as the *problem* but, in most cases, epilepsy is not the key problem.

We allocate places at the centre according to needs. I, together with a health visitor and a care assistant from the adult day centre do an assessment on applicants when they first come to us, and establish what we can do for them by finding out what their needs are. We also try to assess the length of time they should be with us and look at whether they require 1, 2, 3 or 4 days per week at the day centre.

We then sit down and discuss each case with our selection panel which includes the local community nurse and the development officer before allocating anyone a place at the adult day centre.

We have reached the stage where we allocate 22 places at the adult centre on a daily basis, Monday to Friday, 9.30 am to 5.30 pm.

Home visits

We also undertake a number of home visits in order to assess the need of the individual. A number of people do not wish to attend the day centre for epilepsy, but, nevertheless, still need help. We would go out to the home and, if necessary, help them to link with more suitable agencies. For example, a number of people develop epilepsy as the result of a stroke and doctors often refer these people to us. There is no way in which we could undertake to do daily visits to these individuals because there are not enough staff here. In these cases, we would try to help get other agencies to go and visit these clients in their homes on a regular basis. Again, because of the work of the adult day centre, a lot of these home visits have had to take place in the evening and sometimes, especially in my first year, we were working 16 hours a day.

Staffing

For the first year, there was me and my part-time clerical assistant, or, one and a half members of staff. I also had the support of three community development workers in Livingston. The social work department funded the post for myself and for my assistant as well as giving money for overheads for the adult day centre. The premises themselves, a corporation house, were provided rent free from Livingston Development Corporation.

However, by the end of the first year, 1988, we had around one dozen users coming to the adult day centre as well as about eight families attending the children's centre, as we do not deal with children on their own, we work with the whole family in the early stages. We found that we could not possibly continue running both centres on the basis of one and a half members of staff. There was no way we could continue. Fortunately, we were able to get a voluntary contribution and the assistance of our national body who helped for the salary of one full-time worker — a state registered nurse — to work with the children's centre. We required a qualified nurse because of the nature of the work which involved these young children.

However, in 1990, the social work department stepped in and funded a full-time post for both the children's centre together with funding, hopefully permanent, for a day care assistant in the adult day centre. That means we now have myself, two full-time care assistants at the adult centre, a full-time worker at the children's centre and my part-time clerical assistant. We are also trying to get support funding, but that is practically impossible.

Employment trainees

At the present time we have five employment trainees between both centres. To be absolutely honest, without the trainee workers I would find it very, very difficult to run the project. The project would still continue but it would be very limited. There is no way without employment trainees that I could bring in 22 adults to the day centre.

If we need someone, we contact the training agency, but, if the training agency get someone they think is particularly suitable for this project, they contact us. If I felt that we were needing an extra pair of hands, as I have done in the past, and they could give us the hands, and we could train them, I do not, and I would not, hesitate to get in touch with the training agency. We work very closely with the training agency here.

However, we get employment trainees, train them and then they go away on to something else, so there is a big turnover with trainees. In order to try to deal with that situation, we started an on-going training programme for all of the staff on a Thursday. I use the Thursday training day as a means of keeping staff and myself up to date. I train the employment trainees along with the rest of our staff on how to care for people with epilepsy. We also train them in different craft skills — they l earn to work sewing machines and knitting machines. We train them in the general running of the two centres and in working with people who have special needs, e.g. how to handle a person when they have a seizure. Many of our clients have had behaviour problems, and we try to train the trainees in how to deal with them when they take them shopping, etc. Also, a number of our children, as well as some of our adults, are incontinent, so the trainees have to learn how to deal with that situation if they are going to learn to care for them.

The trainees basically have got to do the same type of tasks as the staff who work here on a permanent basis. We make meals as well as snacks for our day care users, and our trainees learn to do that. Nearly everything the care assistants do, the trainee does, for that is what they ultimately hope to become — to be care assistants.

I feel that, with a project like this, it takes a long time for people with special needs to get used to the trainees, and they are just getting used to them when the trainees change. A year with a project like this is not long enough. I would recommend at least two years' training for trainees to get the best out of their placement.

Volunteers

We have a pool of 12 volunteers, five of whom are really reliable. You know, you could call on them practically any time, and they would come. The others will come when it is suitable, as they have other commitments. Some days there will not be a single volunteer and on other days there will be as many as three or four volunteers. It all depends on whether we have something special going on such as an outing. Then we call on all our volunteers to help us out.

You get commitment from volunteers when they are here, but you cannot look at a volunteer as being the same as an employee. You cannot expect the volunteer to be here every day.

Transport

The centre is open from 9.00 am to around 3.00 pm daily. The clients do not start arriving until around 9.30 in the morning and the minibuses are usually away by 4.00 in the afternoon. The actual arranging of transport has nothing to do with ourselves. The people from Gogarburn Hospital come by minibus, other come to the centre via social work transport, and other users come by public transport. We do have our own minibus which is used for outings or for children when they cannot be brought to the day centre for some reason and that has been a great help. However, we have only had the minibus for a year. Lothian Regional Council gave us a grant of £18,000 to purchase the minibus. We tried for 2 years before we got the grant and the local Councillors worked very hard on our behalf to obtain it.

Day centre users

We have 22 people here every day except for a Tuesday, on that day we do not have so many as we bring in people who are quite profoundly handicapped. Tuesday is a games day. This is to encourage them to use their limbs and increase their mobility. It is about helping them to communicate and we do that by going for a one-to-one ratio.

We have three people who attend the adult day centre 1 day a week and 14 people who come 4 days per week. The people from Gogarburn Hospital attend 3 days per week, but, they could do with attending 4 days per week.

Compared with the hospital, I think we are offering a lot. I have visited the hospital where these people are sitting looking at each other, and that is not something which happens here. These people are given a lot of attention on a one-to-one basis, taken out for walks and taken out into the community. I would say we are enhancing their quality of life 100% by their attending the adult day centre.

We have taken people here whom the adult training centres could not cope with because of their epilepsy, or, because of behavioural problems attached to their epilepsy. Obviously, if there was someone who has epilepsy whose behavioural problems were so bad they were a danger to themselves, or, to others within the centre, then we could not have them. It has not arisen yet.

We have got quite a high profile. A number of parents and adults who come here say they could not cope if this centre was not open. Obviously, medication helps. In 80% of all cases, medication can control epilepsy, but, the Centre is geared to those people who are not controlled. These are the people who have the problem.

The children

When I first came here, there was nothing for the children. The adult day centre was the centre parents were referred to for information on epilepsy. There are a number of people here who have severe physical handicaps as well as epilepsy, others have epilepsy as an illness on top of a mental handicap which makes it even worse. I became aware that parents coming here to the adult day centre with their children, looking for information, were seeing the adult users and saying to themselves, 'Is this the future for my child?' In most instances, that was not the case.

We decided that we would have to get somewhere for the children and that had to be a different centre. I went to the Livingston Development Corporation (LDC) and after a lot of begging, they eventually gave me another house at 62 Mowbray Rise. We opened the children's centre in 1987. We got the house, but we did not have any money to run it, and we had no staff. There was myself and one part-time clerical information officer and we ran both the adult day centre and the family centre at that time with the help of community development workers. To begin with the children's centre was just a drop-in centre. We were open four mornings per week which was the only way we could do it. My assistant, the information officer, and myself, worked the family centre and the adult centre and that situation continued for a year. At the present time, we have between 10 and 12 people attending the children's day centre and, during the school holidays, there could be as many as 30 people including brothers and sisters coming in to the family centre.

Education and the parents

One of the things we have tried to do is to educate parents, but it is very natural for a parent to be over-protective. This over-protection I would say accounts for eight cases out of ten, for the adults who use the day care centre. These people have found it difficult, almost impossible, to cope on their own. What we have got to bear in mind, is that the people who are attending the children's centre and the people who are coming to the adult centre are people who, for one reason or another, are people who are not coping with their illness. Epilepsy to them, in a number of cases, has become an illness it should not have become. Hopefully, as you educate parents they realise that the child with epilepsy is simply a child who should not be discouraged from going swimming or taking part in other sports activities.

There is also the difficulty of getting parents to acknowledge epilepsy as an illness and sometimes for schools to recognise this in children. I can think of the case of one young girl who started off with 'absences' which lasted only a brief time when nothing registered. But, say the child was in school and the teacher had said to her '4 and 4', the child had taken a momentary absence at that point and by the time she had come out of it, if the teacher had gone on to '5 and 5 makes 10', the child who had had the absence thought 4 and 4 made 10. It also happened with spelling and with reading, so you can imagine the damage it has done to the child if it happened 20 or 30 times in a day. Of course, in most cases, absences can be contained by medication. There are a few children who go to school, have a seizure in school and the parents will not admit it. They are perhaps ashamed or blame themselves in some way. I have gone out to families and the mother has said that the child has been taking 'these little turns' and I will say, 'How long has she had epilepsy?' and the parent will completely ignore that I have said epilepsy and will just say, 'She has had these little turns, these little dizzy turns'. They will just not accept it. It's dreadful. That is why it is so important that a place like the children's centre deals with the whole family.

Worker's motivation

I think that you have got to have a lot of resilience for this job. You've got to be able to pick yourself up, have a lot of dedication and to care about people who have a handicap. I would say that this is the main thing. If you're sitting on the end of the phone and there is a mother who phones you up in desperation and tells you that she is at the end of her tether with a child who is hyperactive, there can be problems initially when children first go on medication, you cannot turn your back on the family or whoever it is that has epilepsy. Not only are

there difficulties associated with the condition, some people experience
a lot of social pressure. They just cannot come to terms with the stigma
attached to epilepsy and find that very traumatic. Indeed, there is quite
a high percentage of suicides because people cannot come to terms with
the illness.

Professional support

Both the adult day centre and the children's centre have benefited from
support of a number of professional groups.

The Livingston Development Corporation has been 100% behind
the project, without them and without the support of the community
development workers, we would never have managed. I had never
worked in the voluntary sector before and they offered me advice.
These people were my contacts. They told me the best people to lobby.
I was only here a year when I tried to get the children's centre off the
ground. The Livingston Development Corporation came forward and
gave me all the help they could. I would say that the corporation has
been great.

National Epilepsy Week, which is a big event for the national
organisation was launched by the children's centre last year. TV cameras
were present and a celebrity launched the event. Without the assistance
of the Livingston Development Corporation there would be no way we
could have done that. The corporation laid on the workmen to remove
fences. They did absolutely everything for us. They were fantastic. The
community workers also gave tremendous support. In the beginning,
the community development officer was my main source of help and,
without her, I would have been floundering all over the place. I would
have eventually found my feet, but she helped me a great deal. I often
think I would have given up at the start if it had not been for her.

The community development officer is also very supportive in giving
advice and obtaining funding for our centres.

In the children's centre, we also get a lot of support from education-
alists; psychologists and the consultant paediatricians at St John's and
the Sick Children's Hospital have given us a lot of support. The local
doctors too are very good. If we have a problem; if someone has taken
a bad seizure in the centre, we can have the doctor from the local health
centre down here within a very short time.

We also have sessions for the parents and the carers at the children's
centre. We wait until we have about eight new referrals and then we
hold a session one night per week. We ask parents or the carers exactly
whom we could bring in to help. We then draw up a programme and
invite the different professionals to talk to them. Never once, since
we opened in 1987, have we asked a professional to come who has
refused us.

Funding

Our only source of funding comes from social work other than a few
small donations from fund-raising activities. We have a Christmas fair

for fund-raising and we 'shake the can' in the summer as well as selling the crafts we make at the centre at the local galas. We did manage to get something from the health board — £1000. I kicked up such a fuss about having no staff in the children's centre and at one stage we thought we were going to have to withdraw the centre completely simply because the staff we had could not cope any more and the health board gave us £1000 towards the salary for an additional worker.

Management committee

We have a very mixed management committee. There is a social worker; a health visitor; two people from industry; a representative from the development corporation; a doctor and a community nurse. We also have a local minister as well as parents of children who have epilepsy, parents of adults who have epilepsy as well as local people who have epilepsy themselves. It is a very democratic committee. Everyone is allowed to have their say and we listen very closely to the person who has epilepsy since they know what it is all about. These are the people who have had the experience.

Future developments

When the centre started off, there was really nothing much to it. However, it was the first of its kind. We were pioneering if you like. We are the only drop-in centre for epilepsy in the whole of Scotland and, whilst it started off very small, we now provide a very good service. You prove yourself and I think it becomes known. Now we think, where do we go from here?

Our future plans at the moment are in line with the White Paper on community care. We hope to offer an outreach project for children and families who have epilepsy that will cover the whole of West Lothian. There are a lot of people who are slipping through the net and a lot of people who cannot afford to come to the centre. This is a very deprived area and I am not talking just about this particular local community. I am talking about West Lothian itself. There are a lot of deprived areas within it and a lot of people who have epilepsy. We are here to help them and, if they cannot afford to come to the centre, it is up to us to go out to them. At the moment they are just not getting the help that they need and we cannot afford, at this present time, to do all the research that is needed for the children with epilepsy and to go out into the community to find out what exactly is required. Whilst I would say that the educational needs are being met, I think it is the emotional and social needs which we have really got to provide for the future.

Points to ponder

▽   The almost fortuitous development of the project.

▽   The pace at which the project developed and grew.

▽ The number of hours per week worked in the first year of the new
   worker coming into the project.

▽ The attention given by the worker to ongoing training for staff and
   volunteers.

▽ The importance of interagency contacts.

▽ The support role played by the community development workers.

19 Leominster mobile day centre — Age Concern

Magda Praill and Geraldine Duncan

Keypoints

This account is interesting because:

▲ *it illustrates how the priorities of one national agency, the Rural Development Commission can be tapped to promote a service development;*

▲ *it emphasises that development in rural communities can be at the forefront of innovation;*

▲ *it illustrates how diverse, small communities can be drawn into a network of collaboration;*

▲ *in some circumstances, and with appropriate negotiation and planning, initiatives taken by one project group can foster developments by other service providers.*

Background

Leominster District is a predominantly rural part of the county of Hereford and Worcester. Something like 18.5% of the population in Leominster are elderly. This is the context within which the notion of the mobile day centre for the elderly was originally explored in 1988. The organising secretary for Age Concern at the time instituted enquiries with 16 parish councils in the district. Five parish councils replied to the letter of enquiry about the provision of a mobile day centre and indicated their commitment to the project as it was envisaged.

After some delay in proceeding with the plans, a strategy committee was set up under the auspices of the Rural Development Commission. It appeared that the commission had some money available for developments in relation to rural transport facilities. Since there were already some discussions taking place with the local health authority about the development of the service, it was decided to prepare and submit an application to the Rural Development Commission for the funds to purchase the vehicles required by the scheme.

> It was quite good timing — October 1989. We were looking to get an application into the Rural Development Commission in January 1990, which didn't give us much time. We had approached some parish councils in 1988 to see what their reaction would be; whether they felt

it would be appropriate to have such a project based in their villages. We had a fairly clear idea of what we wanted to do with such a project. The sorts of things we had in mind were foot care, hairdressing and health checks. That side of things seemed to be more interesting to them than the day care side initially.

So we had something to start up from in October 1989, which was fairly solid and we drew a very hurried application together. That was the hardest thing; we knew what we wanted to do but the writing of the report, the budgeting, was a nightmare. We had no idea where to start from.

We had a vague idea of where to start in relation to the minibus, but the caravan we wanted was going to be something totally different from anything we had produced up until then. There was a project down in Hampshire which was in the process of purchasing a similar sort of unit, but they had a bath on board. That was discouraged very quickly, mainly because the size of the caravan would have been such that, in the areas we were trying to take it to, i.e. deep rural locations, it would have limited us in where we could go. Instead of a 22' caravan we brought it down to 16'. In addition, we did not see bathing as a priority, the social side and the health side were the bigger priorities. In any event, district nurses provide a very good bathing service.

The revenue side was easier in that we had a fair idea of what we would have liked, which was two full-time employees, an organiser and a driver. However, that was not possible with the future revenue funding in mind, so we had to go for part-time.

We knew more or less what the mileage was likely to be and had a guestimate at the fuel costs. Then it was just a question of costing the administration on top of all of that. And, in one of my many discussions with the area manager of social services here, we went through in some detail the budget that I had produced. My budget was obviously fairly high, so some reduction was possible. However, as those costings were produced some little time ago, it is obvious that things are going to be quite tight, since the same budget carries on for the next couple of years. There is no inflation proofing allowed for.

The capital funding and the revenue funding were two different aspects. Help the Aged were prepared to help us fund-raise, on condition that we identified revenue funding to continue. We could get, through the Rural Development Commission, three years' revenue funding or a proportion of it, 25%. After that, it would cease. So we had to have a commitment from the social services department and the health authority. On the capital side, we had to raise something like £40,000. We were lucky in that 25% came through the Rural Development Commission and the rest Help the Aged raised for us through two or three major trusts. In fact, we had all the capital funding identified by January/February 1990, but still no commitment from local or health authority. This went on and on and on. In fact, by about July 1990 we really thought that the project would have to be shelved. It became a question of the fund-raiser seconded by Help The Aged, Marne Durnin and myself pestering. We were also acquiring more detailed information from the research that was being carried out. It came down to us saying that, unless some kind of commitment was given very soon, £40,000 which might otherwise be spent on services for the elderly in Herefordshire would be lost, and could they afford to say no! The letters that we eventually received, although not a firm commitment, were sufficient for us to proceed with our application.

Research

The presentation of the project was strengthened by information acquired through a research programme. That helped to identify demographic data as well as establish a framework for an evaluation of the project over its initial period of operation.

> The research side was through a contact in the heath authority who was setting up as a consultant. He offered to do this research work, collate it and produce statistics at the end; one of our volunteers offered to do the leg work for which she gets paid — which entailed quite a commitment. She has personally spoken to every parish council involved and issued a short questionnaire to every person over 65 in that parish catchment area. This is usually done through the post office in the villages concerned. We are having difficulty with one at the moment in that there is no post office in that area. We have now been able to do it through convoluted means. We now have identified a lady volunteer who is willing to distribute questionnaires in that area.
>
> We had a good response. In some villages we nearly had 100% return of the questionnaires. I think, on average, it has been something like 50 or 60% return altogether.
>
> The actual research project is going to be written up by Help the Aged who are jointly funding it with the Rural Development Commission. They have put time and money into these sorts of projects before but no evaluation has been done up until now, so this is a good opportunity for them.

Parish councils and the project

Since the success of the project depended, to a considerable extent, on the goodwill of the parish councils and local people, clear efforts have been made to generate a sense of partnership and goodwill with them.

> They wanted to see a project such as this based in their village. Very often there is a village hall they want to be used obviously to support the people who live in the village.
>
> The parish councils we have been working with have been very supportive and, in some cases, have given grants. Others have been supportive in negotiating with village hall committees to get the village halls free. In the budget, it was part of our planning that the village halls would be rent-free as a grant in kind from the parish councils. In the application to the Rural Development Commission we had to demonstrate that the parish councils were giving the project their support.
>
> We now have six parishes identified in Leominster District and two more identified south of the Wye in South Herefordshire. We then

have one other day available and there are two other areas who have
approached us since the project was initiated.

We try not to be swayed by the enthusiasm or otherwise of the
parish council, since it can be a negative factor as well. Some of them
don't want it to come because they think it will cost them money. Some
of them don't seem to quite understand the principles of the project,
despite lots of explanations.

We knew where the elderly population was because the person who
was doing the research work had all that information through the health
authority. He collated that for us. So the approaches we have made have
been to those areas where there was a high proportion of elderly people.
Which is why the other two places which were approached subsequently
were not identified originally.

We recognised that the research can be misleading. Take Weobley
for example. It is a high population for a village, because it is a large
village, so the numbers of elderly people will be quite high, but, in
relation to the rest of the village, the proportion looks lower than other
areas. So it can be a bit deceptive.

The survey questionnaire

The questionnaire distributed to people over 65 in the villages offered
respondents an opportunity to respond to a series of simple questions about
the provision of services, as well as giving them some opportunity to make
more general comments about issues covered by the survey. In part, it sought
to ascertain the extent to which potential users would have taken advantage
of the service when it was made available. The questionnaire indicated that
the plan was to provide a range of facilities which might include some, or
all, of the following:

- Day care and lunch in adjacent village hall
- Foot care
- Hairdressing and nail care
- Health checks, eyesight, hearing, blood pressure, etc
- Health education
- Advice, information, counselling.

In addition, the questionnaire indicated that transport to and from the
centre would be provided, and invited the respondents to indicate the extent
to which there existed or they would like to see development of social
activity.

It was part of the project's original idea to provide a facility which other
groups could make use of in the village when it is there. For example,
the Department of Social Security could have sessions in the caravan.
The CAB could offer a link service. In addition, health authority services
could be linked with it, including, for example, specialist advisers on
incontinence.

We also haven't cut out the rest of the population. For example,
the facilities could be used for the provision of vaccination services for
children, and an approach has also been made by the health authority for
use of the facilities in health education in relation to immunisation and

sexually transmitted diseases. They might use it by either, borrowing the unit itself for something specific like that or using it as a base in the village for health visitors and district nurses. This is something that they haven't decided yet.

Discussions are also taking place with the social services department about the ways in which their home care services might be linked with the project's facilities.

Management of the project

Management of the project is overseen by a committee which has, in essence, the same composition as the steering committee established to develop and initiate the project's work. Involvement of the local authority social services and the like in the development of the project is now extended into representation on the management committee itself.

It is quite a busy time at the moment because it is now really getting under way. Decisions have to be made when you come across things that you haven't thought about or have to change from the original plan.

The management committee has approximately 12 members, representing all of the main funding bodies apart from the Rural Development Commission. They are kept in touch.

The management committee is a sub-committee of Age Concern Leominster, so is accountable to the executive committee. The project organiser is accountable to the development officer as general manager of the organisation.

Initiating the service

We received the caravan in April. It has been quite frustrating in that it has taken longer than we expected to get the logistics sorted out. We had been to village halls to look at the facilities, but not until we had actually got the equipment could we look to see where basis such as plugs and taps were — some village halls do not have disabled access, so that had to be sorted out by village hall committees. In Leintwardine, they had to redecorate the kitchen.

Geraldine's time has also been spent contacting key volunteers in each of the villages, and getting them together to discuss what roles they would be playing. It has been an important part of the project that the day centres themselves would be run by local volunteers. We want the villagers to feel that it is their day centre.

Staffing

We have Geraldine on 25 hours, and Barry on 30 hours.

(Geraldine) I do the initial starting off, identifying village halls, approaching Parish Councils and village hall committees, identifying volunteers, and then pursuing referrals and making it all happen — meals and professionals, staff who might use the caravan unit and so on.

Barry, in particular, is my deputy and is the driver as well. I don't do very much of that, although I do a bit. Barry's role is to deliver the unit, hitch it all up and with the minibus, go and collect people and then assist in the running of the day centre.

In some places, the bus is used to collect meals.

Facilities and services

We can offer hairdressing, foot care, hand care, and health visitors, district nurses and social services home care staff might use the unit as a base as well.

We identify a hairdresser in the area who, perhaps, already visits people in their homes, but would be willing to come and do it in the unit for a morning or a day, once a month, or so. The benefits agency want to use it as well, and address some of the problems that they feel there are, but which don't get to them because of the isolation of the people involved. The Citizens' Advice Bureau, as well, are interested in offering a service.

Those were the services intended before I came into the post. When we started in Leintwardine, we had a library assistant who brought books, so we had a library service available. I think the service is going to be like Topsy, and grow. The librarian is actually a volunteer, although she is also a librarian with the local authority. This service is operated with the informal agreement of the chief librarian. It provides us with access to large print books, for example, which are particularly useful. It was just something that we hadn't identified as being a role for us to play, but it has developed, inasmuch, although they are there at Leintwardine on a Friday whether we go or not, because we have a specialised audience, she has a specialised selection of books.

Timetabling the service

With a peripatetic service of this kind, some decisions have to be made about the length of stay in each particular village location. The project staff have reached some conclusions about the best way in which to manage this.

We arrive at 9am and aim to have the clients there for about 10am, leaving at about 3pm.

Initially, when we planned the project, we intended to cook the meals ourselves. In fact, the caravan included fridge and cooking facilities, but then the Food Act came in which says that people who are selling meals have to prepare the food from a registered kitchen; a caravan would not be an appropriate location. That was when we contacted the WRVS. We had already spoken vaguely to them about the possibility of them using the day centre as a way of finding out how they could extend their meals-on-wheels services to the villagers. Because we were looking at the caravan as being available only once a fortnight to each village, there was also a possibility of offering some kind of lunch cover in the intervening week, so that there was still the regularity of the service.

The WRVS already provide a meals service from their own kitchens, which will have to be registered. So we approached them with the idea of them providing the meals for us to the day centre, and they have been extremely helpful.

There is a charge made for each day — £1.25. That is the standard social services day care charge. The meals cost just 0.75p and they themselves are heavily subsidised by the local authority. So, in effect, the users are getting a very reasonably priced meal. They have to come in heated containers and they can only travel a short distance for that reason. We must never reheat them. They are brought out during the course of the day, either by a volunteer or by Barry, the driver.

Volunteers

Initially, the contacts I have had have been through Age Concern in any case, so I have been fortunate in that respect. I have also contacted people through the researcher, because in her efforts to distribute the questionnaires she has had help from the parish clerks, some of them have been very helpful. They have been able to identify a figure in the village who has taken the project on board and wanted to become involved. It isn't always easy. We have just launched one at Monkland where the volunteer base is very small. No one is prepared to take on a keyrole, there but I am sure it will happen when the project is going. In some places people are very *au fait* with the whole thing and they followed it through and understand what it is all about. They can see the potential. But in some places they really don't know quite what is involved. Initially, if that is the case, Barry and I have to go every time, and we will start it off with those volunteers we can recruit, and in a little while, I am sure, we will find somebody to take over a key role. Then we will support them with volunteer training sessions which Magda already holds, but will probably do it in the villages that we go to. Because part of the attraction for volunteers is that they don't have to come to the town. They haven't got to drive, and some of them can't. We are opening up opportunities for them, as well, to be volunteers in areas where they might not otherwise be able to.

Staffing ratios

After some consideration about specific requirements in relation to staffing ratios, project staff have arrived at some notion as to what is an appropriate level of staffing for a given population of users.

It does depend very much on the frailty or otherwise of the clients. We started with about 19 clients at Leintwardine and we have eight volunteers, not including Barry and me. That would just happen because they were all very keen to come and we were not going to say that we didn't need their help, in fact, nobody was superfluous. There is a great deal that we can do.

Of course, we have the experience from other day centres which we operate that helps us to know what kind of staffing is required.

Very often it depends on the competence of the volunteers and their self-confidence. So it depends entirely on the sort of people you are catering for and the types of volunteers that you have available.

Background of project staff

Magda, who is the organising secretary for Age Concern, was trained originally as a bilingual secretary. She then married and brought up four children and looked after an elderly relative. She was then absorbed into Age Concern. Geraldine was trained originally as an electrolysist and worked for nearly 20 years. She has had work experience in both private and NHS clinics and was also a tutor for the Institute of Electrolysists and had quite a lot to do with elderly people.

Relationships with other professionals

I found that quite difficult to start with. I hadn't had that sort of background at all and hadn't had any reason to be in contact with them. After a while I made a point of speaking to people to tell them something about what we had in mind. Then, really, the way you build up the relationship is to prove that you can do what is required. I don't think anybody asked me once what experience I had.

Of course, the more you do the more you come in contact with the statutory authorities. A lot of my work, as well, is representing the agency in the voluntary sector in various committees which include representatives of statutory agencies. Because it is a scattered population, we are covering over 400 square miles, we are still bumping into the same people all the time and we are all working towards the same ends. Because the funding is in fairly short supply, as long as your organisation can produce what it says it can produce, at a competent level, you are taken seriously.

Of course, given that the project staff themselves undertake assessments of people referred to them by health and social service professionals, there is a potential for conflict between the assessments and demands of professionals and the views taken by project staff.

It hasn't happened yet, although we have rechannelled one or two potential referrals and turned them into volunteers. Some of our volunteers are over 80. To start with, people weren't sure (social workers, particularly) what kinds of clients we are catering for. They would have a referral that they weren't quite sure what to do with so they would just pass it on to Age Concern. That sort of referral we would not support through a direct service, but rechannel perhaps into working for us as volunteers; social workers now have a clear idea of what we can do and what we provide.

The local social services staff have been very supportive. The area manager would like to fund everything, but obviously can't, and I appreciate his situation. He is working to a very tight budget which can be reduced by another £10,000,000 at the drop of a hat, and has been recently. So he is in an impossible position. At the same time, that doesn't stop me from pushing for something that I feel very strongly about.

GPs are a little bit detached from us. I think they are detached from most similar organisations, but they are supportive; we have had some very encouraging letters from them, for their project, for example, and sometimes referrals directly from them. Occasionally they are inappropriate referrals again. It is like most things, if they happen to have seen something about you the previous week, then they are more likely to refer a patient to you who seems to fit the bill. They haven't really got involved in the mobile day centre. We keep them informed. It is naturally very important that they know what is happening.

Health visitors are the same. Their remit is more for children, anyway, in this area. The elderly population they don't spend as much time with. Both health visitors and district nurses have become fairly heavily involved in the mobile day centre. They haven't defined their own role, but they are certainly involved with the referrals. They have come to the launches of each centre as we have gone along. I think we have finally produced a project that they can identify with, because they are very much working on a village level as well. They can see the potential there.

Early difficulties

It can be frustrating, when I think everything is going well and then can't get a hold of a certain person for weeks, which can hold up the start of the day centre. There have been times when research and questionnaire returns are such as to make me think that they are all ready to go, and then, when I don't visit them and to meet a couple on the parish council, they don't appear to know anything about it, even though they have had the researcher visit them to talk about it before.

There are two areas like that particularly, where I am still waiting to discuss details with the village hall committee.

A big problem at the moment is the potential for the project to expand rapidly. Some of the research work has identified two villages south of the river, which isn't our area, Age Concern Hereford covers it. We had always said that we would leave 2 days free a month for villages south of the Wye. We were aware that they were very poorly served and, to be honest, it had to be appealing to social services that we would be covering the majority of Herefordshire, not just north Herefordshire. The researchers started by contacting these two villages they have had questionnaires sent out now and the potential is very great. But, there were seven other parish councils who were also interested, and the researcher contacted them. Our biggest worry is that we raise people's expectations and then can't produce — having done that once before, then encountering delay. So we are addressing that at the moment with Age Concern Hereford with a view to looking for funding to purchase another unit.

The research project will probably be extended if we can get funding for south Hereford as well. They would then take on the operation of their own day centre. The research is being funded jointly by Help the Aged and the Rural Development Commission.

Users

Our usual age group is, of course, the over 60s. With our involvement in vaccination, health education and other groups, our criteria are obviously not that strict. We wouldn't say, 'It is our caravan, you can't use it if you are under the age of 60'. If, for example, somebody else comes along, who might be disabled in some way, there is no reason why they shouldn't be able to take advantage of the service.

The criteria would include elements of frailty, isolation, disablement, and carer support — where we would be giving relief to somebody who is looking after a relative, giving them the day off.

It is very difficult to put down strict rules and regulations. In one of our other day centres, we had somebody who was very severely handicapped by Altzheimer's Disease, but her husband used to come with her. When she first came, she wouldn't let go of his hand, he had to be there all the time. But after she had been going for about 3 months she was happy for one of the volunteers to sit with her, and her husband could actually then go out for half an hour or so to do some of his shopping. So it depends entirely on the individual, and how the volunteers feel about coping with that situation.

We have to look after our volunteers very carefully. If they feel that they are going to be asked to do what they are not capable of doing, they are not going to be volunteers. But, having said that, if they are given the support and the time to grow into a role like that, they get a lot out of it. We have another volunteer at a day centre who is actually helping a stroke victim to talk again. She couldn't say anything, and this particular volunteer got some cards which they have been working on together, she is now beginning to learn a few words. The volunteer actually interprets for her sometimes.

It is difficult to say, 'No you can't take anybody who is going to disrupt the day centre', because they may not disrupt it if there is somebody there to give them the attention they need.

While the project staff and volunteers might encounter no difficulty in dealing with incontinence, elderly people who are confused and liable to wander off present a more challenging prospect.

But again, as long as the volunteers are aware of the situation, and somebody can be identified to keep an eye on that person, it is no longer a problem; it is a question of giving the volunteers the information they need.

Volunteers' support for paid staff

Some elements of the project's operation do depend on the services of the paid part-time staff; duties in relation to driving the unit to the village centres are normally undertaken by a paid driver. However, the project is fortunate in having a volunteer driver available to provide back-up in the event of illness or other circumstances.

One of the other men that we interviewed for the driver post, he only interviewed because it sparked his curiosity, was really very interested in the project, he wasn't actually looking for a job as such. He wrote and said so after he had been turned down for the post. We contacted him to see if he was interested in assisting us as a volunteer.

Geraldine's post is not, perhaps, quite so desperate because her work is more general, can be covered, so long as there is a volunteer who is prepared to take on the running of that particular day centre.

Relationships with other voluntary organisations

It is a new project, it is a big project, which means that several different organisations have been working together, voluntary and statutory; because it is a new role for us all, we are learning. We are learning by our mistakes, let's put it that way, as well as the successes.

It's breaking boundaries, and, therefore crossing into what other people might see as their territory, that is a problem. Some groups might get territorial about their role, in general, and they might see us as threatening it, because we are catering for so many aspects of life all in one.

Advice for individuals in groups involved in developing equivalent, innovative cross-boundary projects might well want to consider how ideas are communicated and discussed with groups who might otherwise see themselves threatened as a result of the developments being undertaken.

I have always found it difficult to be confined by boundaries. In an area like this there is more than enough that needs to be done, by everybody. And still people are being let down. But you can't say because Mrs So and So lives 2 miles down the road and into Shropshire that she can't come to Leintwardine, which is only just 3 miles down the road. Instead, she would have to go to Cravenarms which is 10 miles down the road. So I spend a lot of my time talking to other organisations to say, I know that this is something that you do, but are you actually doing it in this area? If you are not, is it alright if we pick up Mrs So and So and take her into our day centre. So long as they know what we are doing, and they know that we are going to contact them before we do it, to check with them first, there have never been any problems.

It gets a bit more difficult when you have identified areas of work. As I was saying, we have no desire to cook meals. WRVS have been cooking meals for years, they are the experts, so it is obvious for us to go to them and say would you be able to help us out with this project to provide the meals. The same could be said for the Red Cross. They do hand care, although they don't do foot care. But we do foot care. We know what they do and they know what we do. The Red Cross runs day centres and we run some day centres and the WRVS run some day centres. It is a question of who is able to set up what in which area.

Communication is the essence. If you talk to people beforehand, they
are drawn in straight away and they are part of the project. If you say,
right we have got this project set up, we are going to do this, this
and this, problems arise. One area where we have had difficulties is
about acknowledgement of what is being done by whom. It is an Age
Concern project, and it always has been, but heavily dependent on the
input from other organisations. Age Concern Leominster has to be seen
as the managing agency but we endeavour at all times to acknowledge
the initial roles of other organisations within the project.

Wider associations in the development of community care

In an area like this when there are so few people who are able to provide
a service, you are never having to actually tender for services as you are
usually the only organisation prepared to offer a service. It might change
in the future, with the development by private, residential homes. We
have set up a liaison group in the Kingston area involving voluntary
organisations, independent and private homes and health and social
services, and meet quite regularly. We have identified what services are
provided and what services we would like to see provided. Hopefully,
we should be able to talk about who should provide the services and
how. From my point of view that is how community care ought to be
planned. Otherwise, it would be just a dreadful mishmash, with huge
gaps left and it is always the poor client who is the one who suffers. So
I am hoping that this is quite a good positive step forward.

The problem is time. People have a limited amount of time available
during the working day, because of limited budgets, you have a limited
number of personnel, it is yet another meeting. It entails a whole
afternoon by the time I go down there, have a meeting for an hour
and a half, and come back again. It has time implications for all agencies
involved.

The Age Concern staff have been consulted by the local social services
department in relation to the development of its community care plan.

They have tried their best. Quite frankly, I think they are as much at
sea as we are. They have had several meetings over the last 18 months
for voluntary organisations and for the private sector. Social services
have explained that they are setting out to produce a plan. This time
last year they were setting up this wonderful system to go into 1992
for their implementation of the plan, only to have their entire budget
cut. How can they work in that sort of situation? They are ploughing
on. We have had another meeting recently dealing with the outline of
their plan, but not actually what is in it.

There are other gaps. Social services don't know everything that is
provided at any one time and, up until recently, didn't seem to have
much idea about how to go about finding out what's available.

It is difficult. A meeting is set up at County Hall for the whole
of Hereford and Worcester. You have 50 odd people there and there
are probably another 150 odd people who should have been there
but couldn't. How do you get anything constructive from a meeting

like that? How does anybody put anything particularly forward that they think ought to be incorporated into a plan? They have had smaller meetings in the seven social services areas. But, the one for Herefordshire is for the whole of the county, so there again you still have a large number of people that you are dealing with. It is all very much 'suck it and see'. But it is very important that everybody lets everybody else know what they are doing; to ensure that precious time and energy is used as constructively as possible for the benefit of those needing support.

Points to ponder

▽ Rural politics

▽ Relative deprivation in rural communities

▽ The vulnerability of elderly people, isolated from main centre services.

▽ The impact of volunteers on services for close rural communities.

▽ Privacy and confidentiality.

20 Scottish AIDS Monitor (SAM)

Charles Anderson and Paul Lockley

Keypoints

The following account is based on interview material and material culled from written reports and unpublished papers by SAM staff in the period 1990. In the discussion, the focus is on the buddying aspect of the work of SAM and concentrates primarily on the training for the buddy network in Edinburgh, Glasgow, Dundee and Stirling.

This account is included because:

▲ *the project reflects the community's ability to respond to the changing needs of individuals within society in imaginative and caring ways;*

▲ *it reflects a dramatic growth in the scale and scope of the project's activities;*

▲ *it emphasises the importance of selection and training of volunteers to the befriending relationship;*

▲ *the active role of the client is stressed in the buddy relationship.*

Background

Scottish AIDS Monitor (SAM) is Scotland's largest national AIDS charity. Starting off with a pump-priming grant of £6000 from the Scottish Home and Health Department, SAM has grown in size to the extent that in the financial year 1989–90 the total income received amounted to almost £225,000. This sum does not take account of the income generated by the connected fund-raising charity SAFE Scotland Ltd. Today, Scottish AIDS Monitor employs seven full-time professional staff to supervise the training for the various volunteers; welfare rights officers, prison worker and an educational roadshow manager. SAM also employs five staff including a director to take care of the very important administrative side to the work being undertaken by this agency.

In 1983, Scotland had no diagnosed cases of AIDS. None the less, SAM was set up by a small group of men concerned to protect the Scottish gay community from the eventual arrival of a disease sweeping America's gay centres of New York and San Francisco. However, by 1985, SAM became aware of the dangers of needle sharing among the drug-using community as a route of HIV infection and, having identified the drug user link with HIV before any of the other agencies, quickly adapted its service delivery. Volunteers with drug counselling backgrounds were enlisted by the agency, and staff for training, counselling and advice services were specifically recruited from drug agencies.

SAM continued to work in the gay community as the sole agency providing their information and HIV counselling needs. SAM buddies were working originally with most of Scotland's AIDS patients, and also with individuals who were HIV postitive, the vast majority of whom were, in 1986–87, gay men. However, as the decade drew to a close, Scotland saw the emergence of a heterosexually spread HIV mini-epidemic. Now, the great majority of people choosing SAM for support are heterosexual; being either current drug users, ex-drug users or whole family units where HIV has affected one of the family members.

In 1989, SAM began its prison work — a ground breaking project in the UK context, whereby SAM buddies were able to befriend prisoners who wished outside support following HIV infection. Another innovation was the launch of SAM Roadshow, an educational and safer sex travelling exhibition.

In 1989–90 the Scottish epidemic grew geometrically. Actual figures of AIDS cases were 247 at the end of the year. Homosexual men accounted for just over half of the total cases of AIDS (compared to over 70% in the UK as a whole). Next year, it is anticipated that homosexual men will account for less than half of any new cases. Conversely, heterosexually transmitted spread of HIV is indicated to increase. This is a most worrying trend in the epidemic, with Edinburgh showing some of Europe's most alarming statistics. At the end of March 1989, there have been 131 cases of heterosexually transmitted HIV in Scotland. In Edinburgh approximately 15% of all new cases of HIV have been caused by heterosexual intercourse in the past year.

Scotland with one-tenth of the UK population, has 16% of UK HIV positive population and Edinburgh accounts for almost two-thirds of all Scottish HIV cases. Of the 100 or so HIV positive children in Scotland, 75% live in Edinburgh and 35% of them are of school age. A study by the Muirhouse Medical Group in Edinburgh estimates that heterosexually spread HIV infection will become the main cause of HIV infection within 15 years, overtaking, by then, the homosexual and drug use epidemics.

Volunteers

In 1989–90, SAM had a total of 218 volunteers spread throughout Scotland. The volunteers work in all of the different fields of SAM activity. The breakdown is as follows:

Office work	5
Buddies	91
Phone liners	32
Fund-raising	42
The quilt project	13
Prison volunteers	24
Roadshow volunteers	11
Total	218

The 'buddy' network

The workers

Paul Lockley came to SAM with an impressive history of drug counselling
in Scotland. He is the author of the Scottish Health Education Group
training pack on HIV and AIDS and brought considerable experience and
understanding of HIV in the drug-using community to SAM. Paul's remit is
to train all volunteers with the information necessary to carry out their tasks
in SAM as well as to supervise the volunteer support provided by SAM.
On-going supervision of volunteers is considered important by SAM because
situations inevitably arise which are not anticipated in the initial training
and supervision provides an important point for resolving these problems.
In this role, Paul also gives an invaluable oversight of the dynamics of the
volunteer service delivery — and incorporates the lessons in the continually
evolving training programmes. Paul trains buddies for the buddy network in
Edinburgh, Glasgow, Dundee and Stirling. At the end of the 1989–90, there
were 91 trained buddy volunteers throughout Scotland. Charles Anderson,
who is currently a lecturer in the department of education at the University
of Edinburgh is a consultant trainer with SAM and is also one of the
organisation's trustees.

The thoughts I will be putting forward on buddying are those shared by
quite a number of different people over the years. The principal responsibility
for things at the moment is held by Paul Lockley who, as training officer, is
responsible for training, supervision and support. Paul is based in Edinburgh
but works all around the country.

The idea of buddying started in Scotland in the mid-1980s. When I
joined in 1986, there was already one group of people who had had some
training and were beginning to work with people who had HIV and AIDS.
I was part of the second group to be trained and became involved with both
direct counselling work and training work from that period. (Charles)

The buddy model

What happened in the early stages was very much informed by what was
going on elsewhere. The model at the time was very much influenced
by American organisations such as the Gay Men's Health Crisis in
New York and the work which was done by West Coast organisations
providing care and support for people with HIV and AIDS. However,
I do not think anyone actually went across to America at that stage.
Certainly, in more recent times, people have been across to see what
was happening but that was really more of a comparative exercise. Right
from the start there was an acute awareness that, whatever system of
befriending or buddying was involved, we have very much to meet
local conditions which were obviously different from those of major
American cities.

The objective of the befriending scheme is to ensure that the person
being befriended has support of a non-formal medical type. That is not
meant to be derogatory of the support which comes from statutory
health services or social work. It is just that we attempt to give a
form of support which is more of a befriending relationship than a

professional one. Buddy services are very much in the hands of the person being buddied setting an agenda of how meetings are established or are to continue.

It is important that people know there is someone there offering a helping relationship which is under their control. When they are faced by a potentially serious illness, or are actually having problems, and may not be able to exercise the same degree of control over their lives, it is important that this helping relationship exists. But it is a very special relationship where people know they are calling the shots. That matters. There are also practical considerations which are important. The statutory services run from 9 am to 5 pm and there is a need for a befriending role which is not from 9 am to 5 pm. People can receive buddy support at any time of the day. Clearly, there are also advantages in the relationship which the statutory services can provide, and it is a matter for the person affected with HIV when choosing the appropriate balance for themselves between the statutory and the voluntary agencies.

The selection of volunteers for the buddy training course

The buddy system now operates all over Scotland. The people selected for a training course are varied in terms of age, sex, sexual orientation, social background and work experience. People who express interest in being a buddy, are sent, with their application form, a copy of the *Buddy Guidelines*. These guidelines set out the nature of the buddying relationship and the code of conduct for buddies. The interview for entry to a buddy training course provides an opportunity for the potential trainee to gain more information about buddying, and a clear view of the demands that he or she is required to meet. The interviewing panel who select participants for a training course are guided by a number of criteria. These criteria include some practical considerations such as the ability to attend almost all sessions of the course, and ensuring that volunteers are likely to stay in Scotland for some time after the course. Attention is also given to the demands of the volunteers' job and existing commitments to care for, and support, others. Principal considerations in selecting someone to participate in the training programme are:
whether the person will be able to work in a non-directive, client-centred manner, how able they may be to work with a range of clients with differing lifestyles, how realistic they are about the nature of buddying, how sure they are about their motivation and commitment to buddying, and how well they are likely to cope with stressful, difficult situations.

An important aspect of the interviewing of potential trainees is trying to get a clear sense of the nature of the motivation that a person has for volunteering, in particular that their commitment to supporting someone with HIV infection will not be subordinated by the satisfying of personal needs.

The interviewing process itself takes quite a few hours. The preponderance of volunteers are women. Most volunteers have had some higher education and range in age from late 20s to mid-40s with quite a lot of variation in between. We would not be prejudiced against accepting young volunteers, but, we would want to ensure that the individual would be able to cope with the situations that would arise.

We look for the ordinary human qualities of warmth you would expect from somebody who's going to be a volunteer in a fairly difficult situation, but also someone who is going to be reasonably calm, cool and collected, and is going to behave sensibly in a crisis. A supportive person who comes forward to volunteer will get a lot out of it themselves. However, we must be wary that they are not being too driven by their own emotional needs. Also what is important, given that buddying needs to take place over a long period of time, is the simple practical consideration that the volunteers are going to continue to be resident in Glasgow or wherever long enough to carry out the work for which they have been trained.

Buddy training course

Successful applicants go on to take part in the fairly lengthy training course before they begin to work with a client. The training which Scottish AIDS Monitor currently provides for volunteers who wish to act as buddies takes the form of a 14-session course, ten evening sessions and four full Saturdays. There's also regular training update 'sessions' held for buddies who have gone through this initial training programme. The training programme covers a wide range of topics. There are sessions on information concerning HIV and on information-handling skills, sessions which allow both general self-exploration by participants and exploration of particular aspects of themselves and their reactions to others, such as their experience of loss and bereavement, issues surrounding sexuality and attitudes to drug use. Some sessions concentrate on developing counselling skills and encouraging a reflective, self-critical approach to counselling work. Given that a high proportion of the clients of Scottish AIDS Monitor are, or have been, involved in intravenous drug use, a considerable part of the course is spent looking at issues surrounding drug use, and working with drug users. Sessions are also held which look at: the ways in which HIV infection is affecting women, working with clients in prisons, the needs of partners and families of people who are HIV infected, welfare rights and patient advocacy.

A common concern of people who are on a buddy training course is that they must know 'all the facts about HIV and AIDS'. This is a very understandable concern and there is an attempt in the initial training course, and in subsequent training updates to present current information concerning HIV, AIDS, the treatment of HIV and HIV-related illness, epidemiology, and the social aspects of HIV.

At the same time, there is an attempt to ensure that volunteers do not exploit the power that comes from playing, even an informal, helping role by setting themselves up as an 'expert' about HIV and AIDS. The trainers wish to be sure that all volunteers would avoid a 'top down' style of presenting information, and would see themselves rather as assisting clients to gain more information about HIV. Part of the training on information-handling is concerned with how volunteers can assist their client to gain skills in planning and putting questions about their condition and treatment to doctors and other health-care professionals.

The need for a lengthy training course

Whilst buddying is seen as an informal, befriending relationship rather than one which involves a formally defined counselling role, it is still very demanding. Buddies often find themselves in difficult or stressful situations; and they require to prepare themselves to cope effectively with such situations. They also require to meet the different sets of needs experienced by people who are HIV antibody positive but are asymptomatic and well, people who are beginning to have health problems, and people who are seriously ill.

If people with HIV infection are to be provided with an appropriate service, it is necessary to ensure that volunteers can work in a competent, caring, non-judgemental manner, and follow the standards of good practice for any helping relationship, including maintaining confidentiality. A fairly long period of training and assessment for volunteers' suitability would appear to be a necessary pre-condition for delivering a good quality of service to clients who are affected in some way or another by HIV infection.

A long training course also acts as a useful test of a volunteer's commitment before he or she is placed in a buddy relationship; gives ample opportunity for participants to examine their own commitment and suitability for buddying as well as providing trainers with a large body of evidence on which to assess the performance of trainees. The other advantage of having a fairly long training course is that it allows individual members to build up confidence in their abilities, and the development of feelings of trust and security within the training group as a whole.

> The training timescale is fairly long, partly because there is so much to cover and partly because we try to use a fairly exploratory type of training rather than a didactic one giving people discrete skills. The emphasis is very much on getting people to think about what they are doing rather than pushing narrow skills training, also that takes time. Another advantage of having training that is spread over a long period is that it allows time for some feeling of belonging within the training group to emerge, which is important given that the training group will later go on to be a support group.
>
> We do all the training in batches. The training itself varies depending on local circumstances, how much need there was for buddies at a particular time and how many people were waiting to be trained. Generally, there are lengthy waiting lists for people to be trained.

Counselling, interpretation and the responsible use of power

To enable buddies to perform their befriending role in a competent and responsible manner, much of the course is concerned with an experiential and fairly informal introduction to various aspects of counselling. From the beginning of the course, trainees are introduced to exercises in counselling skills, and role-playing of a wide variety of helping situations. There is an attempt to avoid practising counselling skills in a way which is divorced from the context of their use. As far as possible, the practising of counselling/helping skills is related to some situation which a buddy might meet.

Role-playing of a range of helping situations provides trainers with opportunities to reinforce the importance of following the rules of good practice in helping. In particular, it allows potential buddies to gain a concrete sense of what is involved in respecting confidentiality, and of ensuring that no harm results to a client from a failure to respect his or her own ways of coping with stress.

In an attempt to ensure that the buddy does work in a way which respects the client's own thoughts, feelings and needs, the course sets aside a lot of time for self-exploration on the part of the buddies. Buddies are encouraged to consider their own reactions to loss, and bereavement, their feelings about their own sexuality and their reactions to the sexual orientation of others, and their feeling and beliefs concerning different groups of clients with whom they may work.

The support group

As the course progresses, the participants spend an increasing amount of time on exercises and discussion which has the aim of ensuring that this training group will be able to go on to become an effective support group at the end of the training. All buddies are required to take a regular part in support group meetings. Support is seen not only in affective terms, of giving individual members care and understanding when they are dealing with stressful buddying situations, but also in terms of joint problem-solving. A support group is expected to discuss a difficult situation that is posed by an individual member, to provide a variety of possible interpretations of the situation and to assess carefully what might be the best course of action to take. It is recognised that a delicate balance needs to be struck during the training course between encouraging individual trainees to have sufficient confidence in their ability to act in a self-directed manner with their clients and ensuring that they will also be prepared to accept support and be open to alternative interpretations of their judgements and decisions. Throughout the course, there is an attempt to enable participants to preview and begin to work out ways of coping with challenging situations that are likely to arise in buddying. Looking at individual difficult situations also enables the participants to clarify the way in which they see their role as a buddy, and to consider the boundaries they may wish, or need, to set on their helping role.

Negotiating the nature of the buddy relationship

It could be very much an issue in the support group and in the supervision how the individual buddies have negotiated with their client the arrangements for meetings. A volunteer may be seeing a person a lot of the time but they may need to consider other occasions when the buddy themselves would have difficulties in seeing clients more frequently, and it would be important that the buddy did not appear inconsistent to the person being befriended. It is important that they have got that right. But there would not be any set times each week for meeting because clearly people's situations vary — it's quite negotiable. For example, when dealing with some drug-using clients, setting times for appointments may have to be very flexible just to keep in touch with that person. Another recurring problem for buddies is adjusting to the fact that the person's needs may be intense at one point in time and quite light at another.

So buddies have to cope with that variability in the practical and emotional aspects of the relationship.

There are sometimes occasions when someone is experiencing a lot of anger, and part of that anger is expressed towards the buddy and that can be difficult. People can take on the difficulties which their clients are experiencing, and so there is a need for support and supervision. The support group is very much set up in terms of both looking at the emotional needs of buddies themselves and also dealing with any problems which may have arisen. The support groups now have external facilitators who are professionally experienced in the helping professions. For example, one is a psychiatrist, one is a lecturer in nursing, another is a very experienced counsellor in this area. We would expect clear communications between these facilitators and SAM's staff but, of course, the support group is also an area for the buddies themselves.

Assessment of trainees

Trainees are encouraged to approach the trainers to talk through any difficulties or unhappiness which they have concerning aspects of their training or of their own performance. Self-assessment of performance is required of voluntary trainees. Some time into the training, participants are provided with a form which asks them to assess their own performance under a number of different headings. This self-assessment is then shared and discussed with the trainers. Trainers also provide individual trainees with their own perceptions of how well the trainee is progressing, and may make suggestions concerning how a trainee may strengthen his or her performance. If, towards the end of the training course, both trainers agree that a trainee is not well suited to buddying, the trainee is counselled out of the course and other ways in which he or she may assist the organisation as a volunteer are suggested.

Matching

On completion of the training period, there is an important matching-up process which takes place between the person requesting the befriending service and the buddying partner.

The process of matching up a buddy with a client and the nature of the buddying relationship is very much determined by the needs and the wishes of the client. These needs and requests are varied. An important consideration in our selection of volunteers is ensuring that there is a sufficient variety in the applicants selected for training to meet the possible requests from clients.

Currently, there are still more men who are being buddied, and the client has to indicate what he is after. The client may want a man or a woman as a buddy, someone younger or someone older, someone who is gay or someone who is straight. Some people do ask for a woman, some for a man, others are not as fussed. Certainly the person who is going to offer the buddying has a choice. Clearly, we would not force anyone to work where he or she felt uncomfortable. At the same time, we make clear at the beginning of the training that individuals may require to work with someone from any of the main client groups. It would not be a case of someone saying they want to work with gay men. We try to match up both sides as best we can. However, the volunteers recognise the limits for that are reasonably narrow.

Once the people are matched, buddying goes on for as long as the person wants it to continue, or for as long as the buddy is physically able to provide it. Then another buddy can be found to act as a replacement. The person would still continue to be buddied even if he went into hospital for quite a bit of the time.

Whilst the vast majority of buddy care is provided to people with AIDS a decision to provide buddy support to the family members and partners has increased the workload. We do not, however, believe that it is feasible to restrict buddy services only to those who are sick. Often, the person with AIDS is content with the emotional and practical support offered by friends, partners and family — but the ability of these informal carers to continue their vital and high-quality work depends on the support offered by such people as SAM buddies.

Responding to training as identified by volunteers

Several training sessions may be held in the 6 months following the end of a buddy training course to deal with any areas which the participants identify as lacking, or as having been covered inadequately, in the initial training. There is also a programme of on-going training for all buddies within Scottish AIDS Monitor. This training is shaped, in part, by the SAM counselling and training staff who may identify areas which need to be examined in more depth by all of the buddies. Suggestions from the facilitators of buddy support groups are also taken into account in the planning of on-going training. After the long initial course, however, the content of training for buddies is determined very much by the buddy's own stated wishes. The aim is to have a training programme which responds to needs identified by buddies and which values and asks them to reflect on the experience which they have gained in working with clients.

The future

Many aspects of the present buddy course have been tailored to meet the circumstances that prevail in central Scotland, and the particular challenges that the advent of HIV has brought to this area of Britain. Any buddy training course will have to be designed to meet the needs of a particular locality; and the shape of the course designed to fit the context of Edinburgh might need to be considerably remodelled to meet the requirements of a very different area in Britain. Any course also needs to be continually remodelled to take account of wider changes in the epidemiology and treatment of HIV, and in the response of statutory services to HIV. For example, if training of

HIV improves considerably in the next few years, the emphasis in buddy training courses may need to move more to considering how best to support individuals with a much improved life expectancy but who face problems of chronic ill health over a long period of time.

Points to ponder

▽   The growth in the project's income.

▽   The number of staff employed by the project.

▽   The responsibilities which the above entail for the management committee or trustees.

▽   The importance given to the matching process and the emphasis on client choice.

▽   The highly professional nature of the training offered to befrienders.

▽   The ongoing training programmes and back-up services.

▽   The availability of volunteers.

21 The Afro-Caribbean mental health project: Manchester

Gilroy Ferguson and Preeya Lal

Keypoints

This account is interesting because:
▲ *it highlights problems in the society's medical and social response to the mental health needs of black Caribbean members of the community;*
▲ *it explores ways in which statutory agencies of health, social services and probation can be assisted in shaping services to take fuller account of the special needs of the black Caribbean population;*
▲ *it highlights the importance of community advocacy as a mechanism for affecting change in service delivery to black Afro-Caribbean groups.*

The Afro-Caribbean Mental Health Project believes that existing services need to be more sensitive and appropriate to the needs of the Afro-Caribbean communities. This will result in the individual having a positive experience of services, which will lead to improvement in service utilisation. To achieve these objectives, the project has set itself six main aims.

1. To encourage existing health and local authority mental health services to become more accessible, appropriate and sensitive to the needs of the Afro-Caribbean community in Central Manchester.
2. To facilitate discussion and exploration of mental health issues by the Afro-Caribbean communities.
3. To establish a machinery for dialogue between the community and the service providers.
4. To promote and support the establishment of self-help groups within the Afro-Caribbean community, aimed specifically at consumers of services and their families.
5. To enable existing health and local authority mental health services to become more sensitive to issues involving race and mental health.
6. To stimulate debate and discussion between community groups such as MIND so that there is greater receptiveness to the needs of the Afro-Caribbean community.

Background

The project really began about 6 years ago when a group, later called the Afro-Caribbean Mental Health Group, which was made up of a mixture of professional workers, local community groups and residents, met as a reaction to the concerns which were being expressed in the community about the high level of psychiatric diagnosis and admissions to the local psychiatric hospitals. A good deal of that initial professional involvement and concern at the time came from local youth workers who were tuning into the fact that a lot of young black people were being admitted to psychiatric hospitals. Because there is quite a strong voluntary sector network in the area, community groups, including some of the local churches, met to discuss this issue as it seemed to them that such a diagnosis reflected crucially on the black community, its culture and behaviour. (Preeya)

Among the first people from the statutory agencies to become involved were certainly the black workers from probation and from the social services because, in every large organisation which is dealing with black people, black workers tend to be allocated to those client groups — it is not necessarily the best thing, but that is what tends to happen. One of the consultants at the local hospital, who has since become very involved with the project, joined in these meetings. He too, in his role as consultant, had become more and more aware of the issues and was prepared to step outside of the traditional consultant's role and join in the discussion with the local community. It just grew from there. There were public meetings held where people expressed their concern. Local black people who had been users of the psychiatric services also came forward at these public meetings to describe their experiences of what happened to them. One of the positive things to emerge from these meetings was the sharing of information on the issue. (Gilroy)

An important source of information was obtained from a study done on local psychiatric hospitals. That study showed that, among the immigrant population in central Manchester, the African-Caribbean people number about 6%, yet in terms of psychiatric in-patient population they are significantly over-represented. The admission figures for the Afro-Caribbean population in central Manchester at that time was, and still continues, to remain around 25%, but in some instances, that figure has risen to nearly 30% and sometimes 40% in the more secure hospital units of the city. (Preeya) Moreover, the study also showed that it was mainly second-generation Afro-Caribbean youth who were admitted to psychiatric hospitals and the regional forensic units. Concern focussed on the way in which such admissions took place, what happened when people were admitted (in terms of diagnosis and treatment) and what happened when they left in terms of aftercare and housing. Having obtained this information, the steering group then used these figures as a basis on which to make a proposal for funding to the project.(Gilroy)

We are not saying that the Afro-Caribbean people don't suffer from some sort of mental illness problem, we are not saying that. What we are saying is, within the context of that statement, there is a tendency for higher numbers of black people being admitted to psychiatric hospitals in relation to the numbers of the black Caribbean population of Manchester as a whole. Moreover, Manchester itself is no different from other areas which have higher than average numbers of black Afro-Caribbean people in the community. What tends to happen it seems is that the diagnostic yardstick which comes out when measuring some type of psychotic disorder is used more frequently than it would be for the more traditional indigenous white population, which suggests to us that the kinds of diagnostic tools that are used to measure levels of behaviour in order to determine mental illness might not be appropriate — in the sense of culture and race, for the Afro-Caribbean population. There might have to be other ways of taking on board people's behaviour which then could be assessed as being mentally ill.(Gilroy)

Funding

Once the fieldwork staff of the social services became actively interested in the issue more people at a senior position in the services became involved and they managed between them to provide the first small one-off grant to employ one part-time worker to act as development worker to develop the project — myself. (Gilroy) From that point the group moved forward and draft proposals were put together for funding and joint finance. The Afro-Caribbean mental health project was formed in October 1989. Joint finance agreed to fund two workers within the project for a period of 3 years with an annual review to ensure the project was keeping to its stated aims and objectives. Later, two non-statutory agencies, the Mental Health Foundation — which is a national body, and the Kings Fund Institute — a national body which is particularly interested in research, also provided funding for one worker each. All of these sources of funding had operational costs, applied to them. In addition to these funds for staff and running costs the health authority for Central Manchester (which is now a trust) also contributed in direct ways by giving us the use of a room at the centre to accommodate the project at a minimum cost and also provide some support. Recently, we have obtained funds from the special mental illness group to employ a case worker, which was one of the biggest gaps in the service that we offered. No one had been specifically appointed to undertake the case work role and people have been coming to the centre for more than a year now seeking help, and self-help workers have had to take on most of that case work.

The particular source of funding to the project has its own set of strings or conditions attached to it. For example, the Kings Fund has an interest in research and they funded a research worker post. The Mental Health Foundation had an interest in setting up a self-help group and in supporting hands-on work, so they funded a worker to work in that area. The joint finance, on the other hand, wants both — they want statistics research as well as hands-on work to be done, hence they funded the post of the liaison person, whose job is to take this information back to the statutory agencies and to negotiate and contribute to the planning process with these bodies. And then there is the post of administrator, who obviously holds everything together because each funding body is very keen on the work being evaluated and a database being set up. (Gilroy)

However, our project is going through the process of becoming independent at the moment. We were managed by a separate organisation called the Youth Development Trust YDT, along with two other projects, but YDT has just had its grant cut by 100% by the social service and so we have lost all of our managers. We will now have to find an alternative way of managing that task. (Preeya)

The project team staff

My job is research and education worker for the project, and I have been here since October 1990. My job is to conduct interviews with people both in and out of hospital in order to find out about their experiences of the services, to feed that information back to the different health authorities, the social services and the voluntary sectors and to try to help restructure services so that they are more appropriate to what people want and need. Also, I help put together training packages and educational information on mental health issues relating to black people which again are targetted at the social services, health authorities and the voluntary sector. (Preeya)

I am the community liaison worker for the project and have been here since its inception. I started off as a development worker in 1989 and have been with the project since, just changing my role in that time from development worker to liaison worker. As liaison worker, I liaise between community and service providers to facilitate greater community participation in service planning and delivery. Basically, my task is to take on board the issues that are identified by the research and by the community and take these forward to planning groups within the health authorities and other services that are offering mental health and social care. My task, as I see it, is to try to convince these groups where the services are required to change in order to make them much more appropriate, sensitive and specific to the needs of black people in the community.

The main statutory agencies that I liaise with are health, social services and probation. Some of these agencies would say that they provide a service for the community and, whilst I would agree with that, I would also make the point that the service provided is not always one which the black community finds appropriate, or one which they can use. In my meetings and discussions with individuals, carers and community members, I am learning their views and experiences of the statutory services and how that experience is one which meets with their needs or is something which can be improved. I then attempt to feed in that information to the planning groups in the health and social services and try to make what is on offer more appropriate, sensitive and sufficiently accessible to the black community. However, the feedback is not always negative and, where there are areas of satisfaction with the services, this information is also fed back into the system.

I also try to get into meet senior management as well as the basic grade workers because you have to have information from both sides to be effective. I then take the opportunity to indicate any shortfalls in the service which have been identified, as well as those aspects of the services which have received favourable comment from the community. It is a sort of dialogue of exchange in which I find out something about their plans for the future, the strategies they are trying to develop and how these plans and strategies match with the information which I am bringing in from the community. I also try to get access to health authority meetings or meetings that have statutory sector/voluntary sector involvement in order to try and play a similar role there. In addition, I also work extensively with voluntary groups, telling them about the project and exploring and identifying with them whether there are common philosophies amongst ourselves and attempting to develop these. We have, for example, a strong link with MACHEM which is looking at the more holistic role of health care for ethnic minority people in Manchester. My work involves a lot of meetings, a lot of dialogue, a lot of report writing, a lot of writing and so on. (Gilroy)

We also have a self-help development and outreach worker who acts as an advocate for individual users, their families and community groups and who provides support for the development of self-help initiatives in the community. However, that worker who is Pat Gray, is also doing case work at the moment. People who came here say what they want when they come to the project — that is they ask for some sort of help and hands-on work such as counselling.

One of the things which we do at the outset of a person making a contact with the project is that we assess on a kind of bottom-up situation. People tell us what they want and we then try to match that rather than ourselves telling people what we think they want and then not matching that, which is a trap the statutory agencies fall into all the time. (Gilroy) However we weren't initially set up for that task. Pat's main task is to arrange a drop-in centre and assist self-help initiatives to build on their established local networks. These self-help groups are, in turn, intended to be supported by workers from different agencies ranging from the social services to the youth services. Some of the self-help groups which are starting in August, for example, will be based at the local youth clubs and will be involved with a lot of young people there. However, that aspect of the work is still at the very early stage because we are having difficulties over space. We don't have enough space here to offer such a facility, and support costs really don't take account of having to find alternative premises.

The other worker, Thelma Brathwaite, is a support and communications worker who looks after the day-to-day activities and ensures that these are in line with the project's aims and objectives.

Volunteers

The thing we are now trying to get together is volunteers. Again, it wasn't foreseen that we would need them and there was no budget for that when we applied for the initial funding. So we are now applying for funding in order to try to get a co-ordinator for that aspect of the work. We started using volunteers in an *ad hoc* way with clients doing bits of work here and there at the project. Befriending is one of the activities which volunteers would be encouraged to take up. Befriending is one of the most needed things really because people can get very isolated when they are discharged from hospital, and there is nothing for them in the community, or nothing which is sufficient or appropriate for their needs. (Preeya)

Training

Finally, as part of our role to encourage health and local authority mental health services to become more accessible, appropriate and sensitive to the needs of the Afro-Caribbean community, we provide a lot of in-service training for staff of the health and social services.

When we first began offering the training a year ago, we started off responding to every request for training that came our way because we saw that as part of getting the project established, well known and accepted. Over that period we had done training with nurses, multi-disciplinary teams, social workers, community groups and other black workers on a whole range of topics. Now, we are in the process of evaluating our work and looking at what we have done. We feel that we have gotten to the stage where we are reviewing the work which we were doing before, which was mainly short sessions — morning or afternoon. However, we have decided that we are now going to try to do a full day session or perhaps a two-day session and attempt to become more established in the training curriculum for the statutory bodies and other agencies. We feel that this change in direction is crucial, because one of the things which we are looking for, as a result of the training session, is some change in attitudes. However, we feel that a morning or afternoon session is not sufficient time for the task or the issues involved. To begin with, as black people talking about other black people's experiences of the social services, we are in a sense, challenging, if not attacking, the establishment. Regardless of how soft your approach, the fact is you are challenging what people are doing. There are some people who come on the training days who will take that information on board because they are themselves sensitive and come out of the experience feeling 'the situation is bad — look what it is that we are doing', unconsciously or otherwise, and try to alter the situation. We feel that a 2-day model would allow us time and space to up-grade where we are in the experiential training. The difference which this additional space of time would make to people undertaking the training sessions would be that they wouldn't have to think either 'I've been bad' and go out feeling guilty about that, or, be so defensive about the situation that they think there is nothing they can do. Instead, we want them to consider how they, as individuals, can make a difference to what is being offered. To help them begin by looking at how they themselves think and act in terms of their relationships with black people. To help them to become aware of the experiences of black people in terms of how black people might perceive a white worker's attitude towards them and

what it is that they bring into the interview situation as black clients or
patients. To help those in training sessions consider how they would
prepare to visit clients in their homes and some of the things which they
will require to consider when undertaking such visits. I am not saying
that black people don't have their own level of prejudices. But, if you
look at racism or prejudice, you will find that very often black people
are evaluated negatively. More often than not their cultures are evaluated
negatively and, subsequently, if there is racism among black people, it
is a kind of defensive racism rather than the attacking, or disparaging or
negative type of racism which they themselves experience. It basically
comes across as distrust when they don't confide in professionals and
fail to make use of the services which are on offer to the mentally ill
person and their carers.

Points to ponder

▽ The importance of statistical and anecdotal information in shaping the
planning and policy decisions related to service delivery.

▽ The dovetailing of the different roles of the project workers.

▽ The advantages and the limitations of particular sources of funding to
the project.

▽ The advocacy role and support services provided through the project.

▽ The awareness training services offered by the project to workers of
other statutory and voluntary organisations which work with black
Caribbean members of the community.

22 Manchester Action Committee on Health for Ethnic Minorities (MACHEM)

Chair: Rohina T Ghafoor

Keypoints

This account is interesting because:

▲ *it raises, for general consideration, the question of how well existing health and social care practices fully address the needs of ethnic and minority groups;*

▲ *it emphasises the importance for health policy-makers and care planners generally, to consult widely with black and ethnic minority groups on factors relating to their health and social care needs;*

▲ *it highlights some of the effective lobbying strategies adopted by local ethnic and minority groups to bring about improvements in health service delivery and provision;*

▲ *it highlights something of what can be accomplished as the result of positive efforts of collaboration by local health authorities and local ethnic and minority groups.*

Background

Back in February 1986, North West Regional Health Authority organised a conference at which they wanted to launch a document which I think was called 'Better Health Care for Ethnic Minorities'. The document had been written by a prominent community member who was also a very senior medical officer for the city. However, there appeared to have been no consultation with the ethnic communities prior to the date the conference was held and some people felt that the way in which the conference itself had been organised was such that the speakers would make their presentation, and all the people who attended the conference as participants would be asked to endorse the contents of the document. Anyhow, a number of individuals and myself, I was in the Race Unit, Manchester City Council and had previously worked for Manchester Council for Community Relations (MCCR), we managed to contact representatives from a number of black and ethnic projects and helped to arrange for them to be present at that conference and so ensure that there was more black participation. Once people discussed the document, we realised that there were a lot of gaps; we realised that one crucial factor was that there had been no prior consultation with the black and ethnic communities and that we were all passive participants. I think there may have been around 150–200 people in total present at the conference — I may be wrong. Anyhow, the majority of those present, including some members of the health authorities, rejected the document. A number of those present felt that the document had failed to look at the specific and most crucial issue of institutional racism. That issue was totally ignored in the document. So that was the starting point for MACHEM.

Some of us, as individuals, decided to come together as a group to discuss the conference document and explore the way forward. Nick Harris, who was then the worker for the Central Manchester Community Health Council organised for other community health councils and Kais Uddin of GMCVS (Greater Manchester Council for Voluntary Services) also contacted other CVSs and CRCs in the North West to come together for a joint meeting which was held in Manchester City Town Hall to explore the way forward from the document. Also present at that meeting were some of the founder members from a group called the Community Health Group on Ethnic Minorities who were the people behind the lobbying and the pressure to form the Sickle Cell Unit in Manchester — they were also involved with MACHEM right from the start.

We started meeting as a group but realised after only the first few weeks that, again, here were a group of professional people meeting around a table discussing the health needs of the black and ethnic communities. We were still failing to involve people at grass roots level and yet the discussions taking place were about their needs and their services. We decided that the role we could play was to support these groups and to resource them. We also realised at that time that it was very difficult for us as a group with representatives from different local authorities in the north west to try to come up with some sort of framework or standard blueprint for everyone since Manchester had three district health authorities whilst other local authorities had only one district health authority. So we then decided to form a separate Manchester group and that was how MACHEM came to be formed in late 1987. We came up with the name Manchester Action Committee on Health Care for Ethnic Minorities. We couldn't call it Manchester Action Committee on Black Issues because of the representation of Jewish and Chinese views within the group as well as Irish issues — those were the political reasons.

For the next few months we just went around trying to involve people in the community, to discover what was needed and why we needed to exist as a project and what they wanted out of the MACHEM group, because we wanted to be quite objective about it. At that time we also had, as members of our group, one or two individuals from the health authority — but very few black members. Mr Rattu, a member of the North Manchester Health Authority exerted a lot of pressure on behalf of the group to build a working relationship with MACHEM, and to raise the profile of MACHEM.

We then decided to form a Central Manchester MACHEM which also had a city-wide remit. We were given administrative support from the Community Health Council (Central) and from GMCVS (Kais Uddin) who is now the honorary member for MACHEM. For the next few months we just had discussions on how we as a project would form a relationship with the health authorities. The group — the few people who were there at that time, felt that one of the most important elements was that, whilst we worked at the grass roots level, we also needed to link that information with the health authority, and so a lot of our work from 1988 to almost 1989 took for the form of pressurising the health authorities and approaching 'chairs' and so on in an attempt to form formal working relationships with the city health authority. That is how we formed our relationship with Central Manchester Health Authority and with North Manchester Health Authority. These groups are now called working parties on services for ethnic minorities. However, we had a lot of initial difficulties in setting up these working parties because initially to approach the unit general manager, as they were called then — they have got new titles now — and the chairs of health authorities, was not an easy thing to do. They would only see community health councils as the watchdog at that time. They didn't believe in working with grass root communities; communities who live within the locality. We had a lot of initial difficulties. We had to involve people like Mr Rattu, people like Henry Gutterman who was there at the time and who knew Professor Moore in the north. It was actually a lot of individual lobbying which needed to be done. People like myself from the city council, using the city council network, Nick Harris, who was a worker at that time at CHC and who was also a city councillor; there was a lot of lobbying, using political networks, chatting in corridors and outside of other meetings and pressurising and because central CHC and GMCVS (Greater Manchester Council Volunteer Service) and myself having support from council to further this, probably enabled that development. But I am not saying it was easy; it was very, very hard and just how hard was made clear when we put a bid together to apply for funding.

Funding

We felt at that point that there was enough work generated and we had built up a sufficient framework to employ workers to support the work of MACHEM. We decided to put in a bid to joint finance to fund two workers. We could have done with more money and more workers, but objectively because of our political network and working with councillors and people on the committee from the voluntary sector, we realised how much money there was in the pot. We knew we would not get any more money out of them. When we put the bid together, we had to be very realistic. At the time we submitted our bid, it coincided with, for the first time, where there had been a lot of black projects putting in bids to joint finance in that particular year, 1989. Prior to that, no black projects had had any joint finance funding. The groups who were submitting at the time included the African Caribbean Mental Health Project, the North Manchester Black Health Forum and the elderly daycentre at Ghandi Hall and those were among the main black projects that were on the table. MACHEM, Black Health Forum and day centre at Ghandi Hall I think that these were the projects that were on the table at the time. However, the usual white committee structure felt, at that point, that they should only give funding to one black project and the question that I put to them was — do they only give funding to one white project?, because there were ten white projects on the table. We said to the committee that they should assess all the projects on the criteria and on their merits and, if the projects fitted with these criteria, they should be granted — we believed that was the way forward, because, at that time, we felt there was some manipulation from certain members to say that one project was more worthy than another. We felt that all projects were important in their own right and that they needed to be there for the benefit of the community. Anyhow, all the projects I named did succeed in the bidding. We had to do a lot of lobbying right until the night before the committee. Things like faxing, sending letters indicating the project was important, briefing the voluntary sector representatives, and so on. It took a lot of lobbying and a lot of work, and we were surprised when we succeeded, because we didn't think we would.

Funding is still the most important factor. In some ways, we have been quite fortunate to have been given the space for the project in this building, so that has helped us. Also having a reasonable rent, security and everything that goes with the premises has also been helpful. However whether or not I am still the chair after the annual general meeting, I want to make sure the project gets more funding.

I am not looking to the project finishing in 1993 in fact, we are hoping to increase our money from that time. I know we are hitting a recession and that it is a very bad time to get grants. But we are determined, as are the workers, to search for more funding. We have had offers from the health authority to do specific tasks with them and they are willing to offer us contracts. However, we feel that they need to write out clearly the contract specifications on what they require from us. I think the issues we may be involved in with the health authority could be things like undertaking feasibility studies on other topics for them. So I feel that contracts will be one of the areas that we will go into in the future. But, we need the health authority to declare that we as a project can also be pro-active. We would also consider the knock-on effects of any contracting work that we might undertake on behalf of the health authorities with respect to our level of joint finance funding. If we were to attract funding through contracting, this could have an effect on the money given to the project to cover the workers' salaries. One way to overcome that might be for us to form a business trust in order to make sure that one source of income did not interfere with another. That would avoid workers' salaries being clawed back. This is a problem at the moment with every grant funding body. The minute they realise that the project is generating income, because they are all short of money, they claw back. That is something that we as a group have got to review in this transition period. The honorary officers of MACHEM committee are meeting to review all of the situations prior to our second annual general meeting which was held on 1st October 1991 and will consider the problem of future funding at that meeting. We need to be very clear that the project's joint finance money will not be clawed back if we do enter into contracts, or, be ready to deal with that situation.

Both the development workers of MACHEM have a primary role and the committee also has a primary role. Neither can do their role without the other and there is lots of work to be done. At the moment, we are mainly working on developmental health policies and so on. But we know that there is a crying need for preventative work, for training work, and there is also a crying need for this new thing which is coming in — contracting within social services, housing, the health authority or whatever. However, we feel that the two development workers and our administrative worker can't deal with everything and anything — we and they have to be realistic. One of the options I will be putting forward is a link-up with the social policy unit at Manchester Poly who may be able to provide a student on placement to undertake specific research probability studies which I think would be supportive to the work of this project. However, that is only an option. Certainly, one of the ways forward would be to undertake research and feasibility studies on behalf of other bodies — but there are lots of options open.

The joint funding which we received was from the three health authorities and the social services. However, once the initial offer of funding was agreed, there was a cash problem with joint finance which meant that all bids which had previously been granted would continue receiving money from April 1990. New projects would receive limited cash from September 1990 but the shortfall of 4 months would be received in 1993. MACHEM, the lay members and all of us had to do a lot of work and lobbying from September 1989 right up to January 1990; when a final decision was made as to which projects had succeeded in being given the grant, by JCC. However, the actual money didn't come until September 1990. We split the money for one full-time post into two part-time posts. We felt that one person couldn't deal with the diversity of groups which were part of the MACHEM city-wide remit.

Grass roots involvement

The way we made contact with, and involved, the grass root members was through people who were directly involved in the CHGEM and through people and groups that I knew through my own work as community development worker for Asian women and children for Manchester City Council. What we did in the beginning was to send out circulars, visit and talk to people and explain what we were attempting to do and why we thought the work of the project was important. We also found out, as a result of these meetings, the different skills which the people of the community held as well as those skills which needed to be developed in those wishing to become more actively involved, because not everyone feels confident about being able to get immediately involved in a meeting with a health authority. We realised from these meetings that we needed to build up trust and confidence. We tried to build up that trust and confidence by holding a number of local meetings. We had one in North Manchester and one in Manchester South. We also had meetings in Moss Side for Central District. At these local meetings we used to just talk at first, discuss things like what people felt was not good about health care and when I talk about health care I mean issues like homelessness, housing — everything and not just health care in a clinical sense and that is how we went about it. In those meetings we spoke about housing problems, diet problems, diet seemed to be the big issue when people went into hospitals. We also learned about the individuals' experiences of the services. We felt it was important that the black community workers find a way to bring that information together and to resource the groups.

From there, the confidence and trust of the members of the different groups was built up and, as we lobbied with the health authorities to meet us on a formal basis, we then formed the committee. So that when we had a meeting with the health authority, prior to that meeting we would have a pre-meeting among ourselves and at that pre-meeting, over a period of 2 hours, we would discuss the documents we had received from the health authority, make sure that everyone was briefed on their contents and that they were clear about the issues involved. Obviously at these meetings, with representatives from local community groups, varied points of view were expressed, but we felt that the strength of the group would be its ability to compromise, to come to an agreed decision and then present that to the health authority and not to start having a discussion amongst ourselves at those meetings, because we felt that to do that would not be healthy for the group. Prior to each pre-meeting, we also used to have local meetings in order to update the group as we felt that we were accountable to them since it was their group (MACHEM) and not ours. We told them what we had been doing in the space between one quarterly health authority meeting and another; what documents we had received from the health authorities for consultation; discussed their views on the documents and issues being raised and from there come to a decision and present their decision back to the health authority meeting.

Over a period of time, we have become quite structured and formalised at these meetings because we feel the group also needed that discipline. At the same time, however, we are also quite aware that we don't put people off especially those at the level of the community who are not used to that sort of bureaucracy. We feel that it is very important to continue with the local meetings because these provide the strength and the information to work from with the health authority.

Selection of staff

The recruitment and selection process took much longer than the lay members of MACHEM realised, but then we felt that we wanted to involve them fully in the selection process and not have the same group of professional people doing everything once again. That meant training and helping the group and I feel quite pleased that was what happened. Although I am the chair for the group, I divorced myself from that role. I acted as a reserve member in the recruitment and selection panel. We made sure that we had three different panels — one for each post advertised. The first post was part-time 17.5 hours for an African and Caribbean community development worker; the second post again for 17.5 hours was for a worker with the Asian community and the third post, which was crucial, was for an administrator and information worker which was full-time. We had three posts and we had three panels to make sure that everyone in the group was involved.

The recruitment and selection panel was the first real experience of that nature for a lot of group members and made them realise that they had now become an employer.

MACHEM membership

We started with a membership of from 5–10 and have built up from that to a membership from at least 70 including organisations and individuals, so we have come a long way from 1987 to now. Within the constitution MACHEM requires one-third of the executive committee officers to retire after a certain length of time including honorary members on the Executive committee. In this way, we hope to involve more and more people and retain expertise of past MACHEM committee officials.

Workers

Besides lobbying, MACHEM lay members are also employers, something they had to come to terms with.

The honorary officers provided support meetings for their staff since their appointment on 4th March 1991 to 25th September 1991, every fortnight, leading to the annual general meeting. As the chair, I had to provide more day-to-day support. That was crucial, although demanding, but very important in the first 6–8 months of transition of the project and having employees.

External expectations

I think that everyone has a very high expectation of black groups. This is certainly true for MACHEM. However, people have to realise that we only have two part-time workers and one full-time administrator, that the lay members from the community are either unemployed, or, have other full-time jobs, and that we have to go slowly and surely, although there is always the pressure of saying 'Rush, Rush, Rush'.

Successes

When you are working here and caught up constantly in the project, you don't feel that you have achieved very much, but when you are assessing what we have done with the health authority I feel very positive. We have put pressure on them to expand the Sickle Cell Unit and I am working very closely with the worker there because there is only one worker. We have also put pressure on the health authority to establish a post for a Thalassaemia counsellor who would be linked with the Sickle Cell Unit worker and would be part of a team rather than be separated and that has happened. The worker was appointed in April 1991. I won't say that it was MACHEM alone who were responsible for getting the additional work to the project, it was through MACHEM and through the Sickle Cell Steering Group. However, MACHEM has a relationship with the health authority and I am sure that helped the application, but I will not say it was just MACHEM.

One of the other things which MACHEM has done, specifically through pressure and lobbying work with the health authority for central Manchester, is the setting up of a pilot scheme where an interpreter is based at the antenatal clinic for two days a week. The worker also made contact with GPs to make sure that they referred the women on those days when the interpreter was present at the clinic. A lot of work went into that. The pilot scheme has proved successful, and there is a demand that the workers' hours should be extended. From that, the health authority appointed a link worker/co-ordinator who spent last year up until this year looking at the future need for interpreters. Kais Uddin and myself worked very closely with her together with the health authority which indicated the kind of collaboration which was being done. The report was completed this year and they are now in the process of interviewing. MACHEM has been involved together with the health authority in helping draw up a job description and will be present at the panel. It has been a joint piece of work and I don't think that would have happened 5 years ago. Now the health authority is appointing part-time Punjabi, Sylehti, Chinese and Somali speakers. We also stressed that there should be one part-time person who would work with the African Caribbean community. Almost everyone has the view that the language problem is only related to the Asian community — it is not. There is a problem within the African Caribbean community and with the Polish community — nobody has gone into that - for example, we are now beginning to realise that, within the elderly Polish community, there are a lot of problems for those who are making use of the psychotherapy services, because there is a language barrier for the oldest generation because, as you get older, you remember your first language and this creates a problem when they seek medical services. They are also the first generation here. Those are some of the languages used that we still have to work and lobby on. So it's not just looking at languages as an Asian problem, it is a problem of the whole community. The interpreters are funded through the health authority and will be accountable to them. What MACHEM will try to negotiate is, while the day-to-day management would rest with the health authority, there should be a support management group for these interpreters because the health authority itself is not aware of the issues experienced by the interpreters.

But, I would like to stress that we do not look on interpreters in isolation from the rest of the health service provision. Our main aim is that the health authority goes for positive mainstream employment policies and takes positive action with their staff training and development programmes. We are just in the process of trying to negotiate with them an equal opportunities post or the training post under positive action. Whether or not we will succeed I don't know but we are negotiating that because we don't see interpreters alone as the solution to the difficulties. For example, St Mary's Hospital has been signposted in mother tongue languages — Bengali, Chinese and Urdu. They are also translating all of the information on antenatal care but again we feel that the emphasis is on language.

It is positive — yes. People can read and find their way around the hospital and the services, but the main thing we have to tackle, which is the hardest thing, is the institutional practices of racism and so on. People within the health authorities still don't like to use the words 'institutional racism', they get very defensive. We are not talking here about buildings, we are talking about the practices which have to be reviewed. They have to review their inner attitudes. At the moment, both central and north district health authorities have come to a point where they have worked on the theory, developed an employment strategy, have worked out guidelines on a variety of issues, the next hardest task for later this year and for the next few years is together with the NHS restructuring which has come about now and which has slowed down the whole process, is the implementation and the monitoring of these strategies.

Contracting

At the moment, we are now entering a world of purchaser and provider roles to the health authority and, very quickly, both lay members and grass root members will have to face that concept and that change. At the moment, I feel it is important for us as ordinary members or as professional people on the MACHEM group to provide continuous ongoing training to grass roots people so that we come along together to participate effectively and make MACHEM more positive and effective. That would involve looking together at what provider means and what purchaser means, what assessment means and what quality means. I, myself, am not very keen on the term purchasing. I was never keen on it politically. I feel that, now it has become a reality, we have to come to terms with it and if possible work around it. We have had meetings with the purchasing consortia, with Professor Moore and Keith Osborne who is the chief executive and have negotiated a MACHEM representative on that body which I feel is quite important. I didn't think that it would happen, and at this point I think it is a crucial factor. Having a representative on the consortium body would mean that we can be at the meetings, and will have the documents, and will be able to work at them and make an input.

At the moment there is a lot of uncertainty about the role of the purchaser and that of the provider. If the consortium for example, say they want an assessment of the needs of the population in central Manchester — the majority of whom are black ethnic, we seriously

need to work with that. There is a great deal of poverty in the central
area — research work on HIV and AIDS shows that there is a greater
geographical spread within the inner cities, and so we really need to
work seriously with these issues. We need to put pressure on that
purchasing consortium to work, not just with MACHEM — I don't
think MACHEM is the only organisation, with the African Caribbean
mental health project in the area, with housing projects in the area, and
with all the projects that are within central district. I feel it is crucial
that MACHEM make sure that the consortium liaises with all other
projects as well as ourselves. I don't see MACHEM as being the only
organisation. However, I feel our organisation could push and support
to make sure that consultation takes place. However, I think it is also
very difficult from the purchasing consortium's side, because they too
have only just started formulating their structure and policy from last
year to this year. The consortium has planned an open meeting for all
the groups in central Manchester for next Monday and I would like to
reflect after that meeting and in December by which time MACHEM
will have had meetings with the Manchester health consortium to assess
whether we are going to progress or not.

I have just received a document which gives guidelines on purchasers
and providers. We felt that this information was very crucial and the
region will also give these same guidelines to the health authorities,
they will not be able to say that they have nothing to work from. Also
Kais Uddin put in an application for the Central Manchester Health
Authority to the Kings Fund for a grant to pay for a black worker to
look at the implications of black needs when considering contractual
issues: that workers choose to focus on three topics — maternity care,
mental health and sickle cell and thalassaemia trait. That research work
is almost completed, but we are hopeful that it will provide some useful
guidelines on the way forward.

Working with diverse communities

There can be difficulties in working with diverse communities however,
I think it depends on how the committee is made up, who your honorary
officers are — there are dynamics in any group. So far, we have been
fortunate in some ways, although there are issues around of having black
and white people on the group. However, so far, we have been able to
work very well. As the chair, I have to make sure that there are not
too many personality clashes or religious clashes. However, we have not
had many problems but the prospect is always there in my mind. One
of the healthy ways to deal with a situation where you have the full
backing of the officers is to work as a team. I think any committee that
becomes very authoritarian has more difficulties. Our team doesn't have
that failure.

The project never had any feelings about my being a woman or any
sort of gender issue. But, as the group grew and, as the numbers of our
contacts increased, it has occasionally presented a problem. I remember
being at one meeting with a group where the 'FHSA' members present
looked at the men among the MACHEM officers and they were not

making eye contact with myself and they were very much aware of my presence. However, I had made it quite clear to the honorary officers of MACHEM and to other members of the group that, if there was something that I, as chair, have to answer, the group needed to make sure that they put that question back to myself and they would say that in the meeting, 'you want to speak to our chair, not to us'. That also happened in certain situations within the health authority meetings. At the community level, because I have worked for 10 years around the community, I have also experienced gender issues from time to time but I have learned to deal with it. In my previous job in the Race Unit, where I worked with two men on equal status, a lot of people would come in and relate to the male staff and not to myself. But we made a policy that if the enquiry was in my area of work then the person had to come and talk with me whether they liked it or not. I think having that kind of support from my colleagues was very important. There is a problem of sexism sometimes but it is how you deal with it and what support you have from your colleagues.

One's own skills

To be effective as a chair you need to have, or to develop, groupwork skills, organisational skills,

We see ourselves playing a number of roles — advocacy, informing the community, being a grass roots trainer, training people in related services, all sorts of things. Kais Uddin and myself have been involved with the Regional Health Authority working party on services. Another member of MACHEM has been involved in the Regional Health Authority working party on employment and Gilroy Ferguson, the Vice-Chair of MACHEM, has been involved in the mental health aspects.

Points to ponder

▽ The preponderance of professional workers on the original steering group for the project.

▽ The importance of networking at grass roots level to develop awareness and identify local needs.

▽ The different levels of support and training required by grass root projects and their staff.

▽ MACHEM's role as a provider of support and resources to grass roots projects.

▽ The lobbying strategies adopted by MACHEM to obtain representation on selected planning and policy-making groups of the local health authority.

▽ Working with diverse communities.

▽ Implications of 'contacting'.

III Getting and marketing the idea

23 Getting and marketing the idea

In considering each of the foregoing accounts, we might well begin by reflecting on the process whereby these initiatives came into existence. How and where did the idea for the service originate? What prompted the adoption of the idea, and what factors contributed to its development and implementation? To find answers to these questions we have only to consider the accounts themselves.

Directed

Ideas which may provide suitable material for the development of a service-based enterprise can arise in a variety of ways. First, the individual or group associated with the development of a new initiative may be 'directed' in the sense of having their attention drawn to the idea by a third party, who indicates there is a potential or an actual market, or consumer group for a particular service or product, although that third party, for one reason or another, is insufficiently interested, motivated or unable to pursue the idea. Examples of this can be found in the accounts of the supported accommodation project, where the need for a supported accommodation service originally was identified and developed by the Royal Edinburgh Hospital and later passed on by them to the Edinburgh Association of Mental Health, who assumed responsibility for both the leased properties and the tenants. Likewise, the idea for the initial day centre for the elderly at Ghandi Hall arose out of a request for such a service from members of the executive committee of the Indian Association, Manchester who approached local people and encouraged them to 'do something' for the elderly Indian community in the area.

Discover

The individual or group may discover the idea for themselves in the sense of making some connection between a product or service and a particular user group in the community. The link made is a 'discovery' in that such a connection is novel, or at least has never been made previously by those directly involved in providing existing local services. The therapeutic garden comes closest to this notion of discovery in that it brought together the physical condition and the social circumstances of disabled people and the proximity of the training centre for the disabled in a way which was both creative and imaginative.

Association

The idea may come about through close association, either with the service, the client user group, or the agency providing the service, or, possibly a combination of all three. Typically, what happens in this instance is that the individual or the group identify gaps in the existing service provision or the market, or identifies deficiencies in the nature of the existing service provision. An example of the latter might be the provision of a quality care service as against a basic level of service which is currently on offer by some other agency or organisation.

At least five of the accounts reflect the influence of 'association' in the way in which they each proceeded to set up a service to their respective client groups. Both the epilepsy and the dementia accounts demonstrate the workers' ability to spot the gaps and identify ways of appropriately developing services to the benefit of particular user groups. Jane 'saw the potential' of the facilities of the epilepsy information centre early on in her association with that project. Trish too was able to make the link between the need for a short-term (3 to 4 hours) companion sitter service and a full day respite service for carers of people suffering from senile dementia. Rosemary, the worker at the volunteer bureau was also able to identify the emotional needs of some of the bureau's own volunteers and responded by setting up the Buc-Up club to meet those needs. Similarly the Scottish AIDS Monitor Group were also quick to identify trends and future service requirements as the illness spread through wider sectors of the population. Finally, MACHEM provides an example of a project set up to liaise with, support and to lobby on behalf of, ethnic minority groups in their requests for improvements in health service care.

Borrow

The individual or group may arrive at the idea by simply copying or borrowing it from another project which they have worked with or heard about and which has had a measure of success. Both the Durham branch of the Parkinson Society and the Livingston branch of the Scottish Society for Mental Handicapped are examples of the 'borrowing process'. The account of the Ark project which provides housing for adults with learning difficulties also comes close to this example, the Ark project highlighted in the account being one of a number of such projects set up by Ark Housing in the East of Scotland over the past 7 years.

Adapt

The individual or group may arrive at an idea by adapting something which has already been shown to be beneficial as a service, or, which could be beneficial and effective if suitably modified to take account of local circumstances and local needs. The account of the first 'Out-of-the-house' course is illustrative of such an approach using ideas from a project dealing with a quite separate client group and tailoring and developing the ideas to provide a service to a quite different user population. Similarly, the Leominster Mobile Day Centre project development group were familiar with a not too dissimilar mobile services project for the elderly in Hampshire.

However, the physical geographical features of the rural area covered by the Leominster project were such that necessary reductions to the size of the project's mobile vehicle impacted on the nature and range of services provided by the Leominster group.

Translating ideas into practice

However, having identified a potentially marketable idea, the individual or more typically the group, considering translating that idea into some form of a 'not for profit' or 'self-help' service provision may have to confront and resolve the following four sets of questions:

Can we do it?

> Do we have the skills, knowledge, resources, equipment and capital which may be required to convert the idea into an actuality; and if not, can these be acquired, from whom, where, how and when?

Will it sell or be used?

> Who would want the service envisaged? Is there a market for what the group have or seek to offer? Who or what is that market? In what respects does what has to be provided by way of a service differ either qualitatively, quantitatively, commercially (price) or even geographically from those services which presently exist and which are targeted at the same or similar user groups?

Will it pay or who will pay?

> Without some form of income, the long-term viability of any service which makes on-going use of human and material resources is suspect. This question of who will pay is especially critical for the majority of the groups highlighted in these accounts where no financial charge is made against the client or the user group for the service, such as the services provided by the day centres for the dementia sufferers, the epilepsy group and for the frail elderly and/or those experiencing problems with their mental health.

Should we do it?

> Should the group use their energies, time and knowledge to provide services which have been, or should be, provided through the welfare state? Are there social, moral, ideological, economic or political reasons which would question the group's embarking on such an enterprise initiative?

If the group considering embarking on a 'not for profit' or 'self-help' service venture is able to reflect on the last question and still respond in the affirmative, then it is those concerns expressed in the first question — 'Can we do it?', and in the second qestion — 'Will it be used?' — which become central to the group. The question of 'who will pay?' is one which most voluntary groups involved in developing community initiatives postpone to a later stage of their initial planning. Perhaps on the basis that if overmuch attention had been given at the outset to the problem of how a project would be financed, a considerable number of current socially useful voluntary services to the community would never have seen the light of day. Rather, the true believer often travels in hope. As one local activist remarked when describing how a voluntary group, starting with no financial resources, were now in a position after a space of 3 years, to be able to purchase a house at the cost of £150,000 to accommodate former mental hospital patients, 'If you really believe that it can be done and are committed to see it through, then it will happen'.

Although not every initiative has this degree of success, there is often a genuine belief that, if the idea is sound and the group feels that it has the ability to provide the service, and the financial aspects of the service have been identified and considered thoroughly, at the planning stage, the prospect of attracting funding or a package of funds is made more likely.

The nature or type of service being contemplated largely determines the kinds of resources in terms of skills, expertise, labour, equipment and capital costs which will be required both in the short and longer terms. The breakdown of the proposed development of the initiative into stages helps the group identify those resources which are vital to each particular phase or stage of the development process and in what quantity or quality. Not everything which will be required ultimately by the project is necessarily required at the outset of the project and few, if any, voluntary organisations have started up a new initiative on that basis. The time-lag between getting the idea, and converting that idea into an actual service provision, depends on the success of the group in finding solutions to the following sets of issues:

- How shall we get the labour for the project?
- How shall we get the equipment needed for the project?
- How shall we obtain premises or accommodation for the project?
- How will the project be administered?
- How will all of the above be financed?

The solution to each of these potential obstacles rarely is found immediately. Just how protracted the timescale will be is, in part, influenced by such factors as whether the project is an entirely new concept or whether there already exist models and approaches from which the group can benefit, as for example in the case of community business initiatives, or housing associations, to cite illustrations from other areas of community enterprise. In these instances, the timescale is reduced partly because others have shown the way. The availability of external agencies or groups to facilitate the development of the project and the knowledge that these contacts exist and how these can be networked all come into the calculation of how quickly and judiciously any service initiative can get off the ground.

The garden project illustrates the sometimes fortuitous or accidental way in which such networking and information are amassed. That same project also indicates something of the length of time that was involved between getting the idea for the garden project and the twelve month period it took to 'turn the first soil'.

The timescale involved in setting up the new initiative is also dependent on the level of skills and expertise required to operate the service and whether that expertise, if vital, is held by existing members of the group or would require to be located and brought into the project. The services provided to members of the Durham branch of the Parkinson Society and to the mentally handicapped by the Livingston branch of the Scottish Society for Mental Handicap are both illustrative of this point. The requisite level of expertise was held by the groups themselves, the difficulties for both projects lay more with the availability of volunteers rather than with the level of skills required for the tasks.

The matter of whether a group is starting with absolutely no resources or whether there already exists some available capital or the personnel required to investigate and to test out the marketability of the service envisaged by the group is another factor to be considered. In the case of the Leominster mobile day centre the availability of some funds through the auspices of the Rural Development Commission for the development of rural transport facilities acted as a trigger to the project's ability to respond. The Oasis project benefited from the Edinburgh Association of Mental Health having a student on placement who was able to do basic research into the distribution of need in the community, and also from the efforts of a worker in establishing possible levels of support for the project, and for the use which would be made of any potential service.

The timescale involved in getting the initiative under way is also affected by the degree of commitment of the original group members, and whether they are treating the venture as a matter of primary importance, or whether it is being run as a secondary interest. However, the actions of the keyworkers of the Integration Trust demonstrates that commitment alone does not guarantee the quick achievement of a project's objectives.

In certain instances, however, such sustained commitment on the part of project volunteers can be a crucial factor in that project's ability to trade under the umbrella of some larger institution or organisation. Agencies such as L'Arche Homes or Ark housing generally require that local groups demonstrate a commitment on the part of their members to the work of the project, and this commitment is usually measured in terms of the length of time that the group has been in existence and working on the development of that particular service provision. In the case of the setting up of L'Arche Homes, periods of 3 years of preparation are not uncommon.

Finally, the extent to which the service is a top-down or bottom-up initiative will affect the time taken to get the project off the ground. Top-down initiatives typically involve fewer people making key decisions regarding the development of the project which usually means more inform-ation is passed but fewer discussions are held among the members. However, whether a particular project took 2 years or 3 years to develop from the stage of being an idea for a service to becoming an actual service provision is less important than the fact of its success in making that transition.

IV   Making connections

24 The organisation

In making connections between the different accounts, it is possible to detect from the background descriptions how each project, in its own way, had been transformed as it moved from the point of developing the idea to that of developing and producing the actual service and, in so doing, creating the structure or the formal organisation which would make that service possible. Moreover, it is with the creation of the formal organisation that the similarities and the linkages among, what might otherwise appear disparate projects, become apparent. Furthermore, the use of the concept of formal organisation helps to illuminate common themes and concerns contained within the accounts.

Each of the projects depicted in the accounts could be classified as a formal organisation. Each project has: its own goals and objectives; its own separate title or name; a recognised meeting place where the service is managed and/or delivered; different categories of workers or staff each with their own particular roles which have to be performed; and a wide range of activities and functions which have to be carried out if each project is to attempt to reach its respective goals. Moreover, the nature of these goals are such that each of the projects can be further classified as formal organisations of the service type where, ideally, the main beneficiary is the client or user group with whom and on whom its members work is the chief concern (Blau & Scott, 1963).

In order to achieve its objectives, every formal organisation, whether it be service based or commercially focussed, has to devote considerable attention, effort and resources towards ensuring that its own maintenance needs and need for continued survival are met. An organisation which cannot ensure its own continued survival is unlikely to be able to secure the goals for which it has been established. The long-term viability of any organisation is affected by three broad sets of factors. First, the possession of a workforce who are sufficient in number and skill to produce the service or commodity to the required quantity and quality: second, the ability to attract clients or customers for the service or product being offered, again in sufficient numbers as will justify the continued existence of the organisation and the employment of its workforce: third, the acquisition of sufficient income or resources to meet the cost entailed in the production of the service or commodity. These three factors: a sufficient labour force; sufficient clients or customers; and sufficient funding for resources are not always present to the level which the organisation finds healthy for its own survival and maintenance needs. The task of those responsible for the management of the organisation is to try to ensure that any imbalance in one or more of these three factors does not deteriorate to the point where the viability of the organisation as a whole is threatened. Each of these factors: staffing, client numbers and funding for resources were apparent as separate sets of issues and concerns facing, or likely to confront, many of the projects detailed in the accounts.

Staffing the organisation

If we accept the proposition that each of the projects can be regarded as a service organisation whose creation and whose primary objective is to respond to the needs and the requirements of particular client groups, it is reasonable also to assume that those tasks and functions which the organisation must perform in order to produce or to provide that service will be a central consideration when it came to the selection and the recruitment of individuals as workers (McGregor, 1987).

Because the projects are service organisations, whose workers have direct contact and personal relationships with the people who use the service, more than a mere mechanical response is required of the workers when carrying out their respective roles and duties. Indeed, for a number of these projects, the workers *are* the service. Where that is the case, the total character of the person was taken into consideration when deciding the suitability of the applicant or indeed that of an already existing member of staff for the work undertaken (Plumbley, 1989).

Why select?

Selection is a standard feature of organisation life (Bennet, 1981; Cowling & Mailer, 1981). Selection is often the first point of contact where the organisation makes explicit to the recruit what it wants, or, what it expects from its workforce. These service organisations engaged in selection procedures in order to obtain some sense of fit between the individual worker and the demands of the particular project. These demands included the requirement that, within agreed limits set by the project, the worker would be: physically capable of performing the tasks required; be sufficiently mature in outlook, if not necessarily in age, to undertake the tasks allotted; be sufficiently motivated and committed to the needs of the project by agreeing to set aside a period of time for the work; be generally disposed in terms of attitudes and values towards the client user group; give the appearance of being reliable; appear likely to fit in with the other existing workers on the project; appear adaptable to any training demands which may be required to mould the person to the needs of the particular project, and, importantly, be acceptable to the client user population, which in a few instances involved a shared understanding of the language and culture of the user group. However, the selection process itself can also present a project's management with new sets of problems, including whether the project staff, paid or volunteers, are knowledgeable of, or experienced in, selection procedures. In the case of at least eight projects, there was also the added responsibility involved in the selection of paid staff to the project.

We felt that we wanted to involve them (community volunteers) in the selection process so that it was not the same professional group of people who were doing everything again — which meant training. The recruitment and selection panel was a first experience for a lot of the group members and made them realise that they had now become employers. (MACHEM)

In the case of these 21 projects, three different categories of worker were recruited and selected: volunteers, employment trainees, and paid workers. The latter either attached to a particular project or attached to the project's host or sponsoring organisation.

Only five out of the 21 projects relied exclusively on either paid staff, or, volunteers. The remaining projects relied on a combination of workers. One project relied on both volunteers and employment trainees as workers; four projects relied on a combination of volunteers, employment trainees and paid staff; and 11 projects relied on a combination of volunteers and paid staff.

Volunteers

Only two of the 21 projects did not make use of volunteers and, of the 19 which did so, only SAM experienced little difficulty in either attracting or retaining volunteers in sufficient numbers to meet its service requirements. In at least 11 projects the recruitment of volunteers was an on-going concern. Nevertheless, even those projects which experienced difficulty in recruiting and retaining volunteers emphasised the importance of adopting selection procedures in an attempt to ensure only those applicants were accepted who matched in some way the project's philosophy and practices and who expressed a degree of commitment to the service they wished to join. In general, both the character of the individuals as well as the person's physical ability to undertake the work which would be required of them on the project, featured strongly in the different selection procedures adopted by the various projects. For at least two projects, the ability to speak the language of the user groups was an additional critical factor in the selection process.

The actual selection procedures varied according to the nature of the service which each project provided and the tasks demanded of the volunteers within that service. Whilst SAM offers the clearest formal statement of its selection criteria and procedures, each of the projects sought to achieve the best match possible with the requirements of the project, the needs of the users and the type of person who presented herself as a potential volunteer.

The interviewing process itself takes quite a few hours. We want to be sure that the individual would be able to cope with the situations that would arise. We look for the ordinary qualities of warmth, but also someone who is going to be reasonably calm, cool and collected and is going to behave sensibly in a crisis. You need to be wary that they are not being too driven by their own emotional needs. Also, the simple practical consideration, that the volunteers are going to continue long enough to carry out the work for which they have been trained. (SAM)

Employment trainees

In the case of the employment trainees who feature strongly in several accounts and who numbered 38 workers in just five projects, the selection process again set the tone for what was expected of the individual as a prospective worker within each project. However, in at least three out of the five projects, an initial screening had been done by the training agency prior to the candidate coming up for selection by the project.

> Employment trainees are initially selected by ELTA. They send along to us people who express an interest in care work or working with the elderly. They come to see us and then have a further formal interview with the project co-ordinator. The skills we look for, and wish to develop in our trainees, are common sense, patience, listening skills, communication skills, initiative, reliability and trustworthiness. One of the project organisers and myself do the interview fairly thoroughly and select out the people we think might be suitable. There is no use someone coming to us and saying 'I have nothing else to do so I thought I would try this and see if I like it'. That is why we have a fairly in-depth selection procedure, to identify those people who really do have an interest. (Dementia day centre).
>
> If the Training Agency gets someone they think is particularly suitable for this project they contact us. (Epilepsy group)
>
> I interview first to make sure that the person is going to fit in with the team. (Braid House)

Only one project making use of employment trainees adopted a different working principle.

> All of the trainees are long-term unemployed. We take whoever they (training agency) send us, but it has worked. We have 12 trainees altogether. (Garden project)

Possibly the sheer number of workers required by the garden project to prepare the ground and develop the site contributed to that response. However, upon entry to the project the attitudes and the motivation of these employment trainee workers increased in significance for Felix as co-ordinator of the garden project.

Paid staff and key volunteers

When it came to the paid workers and the key volunteers, the ability to determine just how far their attitudes, motives and potential contributions influenced their selection to a particular project was less clear from the accounts. We have to rely on comments which those individuals made about themselves or about a colleague to glean any insight. Considering the paid staff of the dementia day centre, their backgrounds included a qualification in psychology as well as experience with the companion service for dementia sufferers, and work with elderly groups, all of which could reasonably be regarded as factors influencing their selection. Jane, the director with the epilepsy day centre had considerable administrative experience, a professional qualification in the social services and some background knowledge of epilepsy, as an illness. The training officer with SAM had considerable experience and understanding of HIV in the drug-using community, a background in drug counselling and was the author of a training pack on HIV, and AIDS. Gilroy, a trained psychiatric nurse, worked in mental hospitals prior to taking up his post with the Afro-Caribbean mental health project as development worker and later as project co-ordinator. Angela of the Handsworth community care centre had a background of experience in youth and community work, project management experience and experience in working with people with special needs. In the case of the supported accommodation project, several of the paid staff had experience either in housing administration or in hostel work with the homeless.

The key volunteers in many respects selected themselves to their respective project. Felix had his own business, was experienced in management, had considerable voluntary fund-raising experience for the disabled in the community and had also a long-standing interest in and association with the locally based Trinity Training Centre for the disabled and with the August charity fair which acts as sponsor to the garden project. Jean, the key voluntary worker with the Livingston branch of the Scottish Society for Mental Handicap, herself had a handicapped child and had previously set up similar clubs for the mentally handicapped prior to her involvement with the present project. Similarly Joan Wilkinson of the Durham Parkinson's self-help group and Angus and Joan Millar of the Integration Trust each had a relative who fell into the user group category which was serviced by their respective projects.

It seems that the reader must decide if these aspects of the workers' background were likely to weigh in any formal selection to a particular project, or were likely to have influenced self-selection into a particular area of work.

The selection process, unlike simple recruitment procedures, implies the possibility of the rejection of candidates at whichever level they present themselves to the project for consideration and approval. Each project has its own list of criteria which it used as a sort of general grid against which to measure the applicants suitability. On several occasions, the criteria adopted to assess a candidate's suitability, were based on the workers' experiences from other related projects.

> Of course, we have the experience from other day centres that we operate which helps us to know what kinds of staffing is required. (mobile day centre)

However, whilst stressing the fact that each project typically tried to favour and to protect its own interests, requirements, and the needs of its client group when selecting its workforce, more than a mere calculation of the project's interests was evident. There was also a genuine concern for the worth, self-esteem and well-being of the individual volunteer or employment trainee who, having offered themselves as candidates, were unsuccessful or regarded as unsuitable for the service for which they had applied.

> Training Agency sends along, from time to time, perhaps 8–10 people and one of the project organisers and myself do the interview and select out those people that we think are suitable. However, the training

programme we offer here is quite demanding on a number of levels and the calibre is not always up to the requirements of the training. It would not be fair to expose a person with learning difficulties to yet another situation in which they fail, if they started the training for the project and then felt that they could not cope. (Dementia day centre)

If towards the end of the training courses both trainers agree that a trainee is not well suited to buddying, then the trainee is counselled out of the course and other ways in which he or she may assist the organisation as a volunteer are suggested. (SAM)

Training

If members of an organisation are recruited to be used as resources to achieve the goals of the organisation, training might be considered as the method whereby the raw material, in the form of human resources, is shaped into a resource which the organisation can use (Bell, 1989a; Glastonbury, Bradley & Orme, 1987). Training fulfils a number of important objectives for the organisation. Training provides a form of induction which ensures that the members of the organisation: know and understand the nature of demands made upon them; are adequately skilled and prepared for the task they are asked to perform; and are familiar with the procedures adopted for the running of the organisation, including, the rules and regulations, communication channels and lines of command. Training is also a method whereby the organisation prepares its workforce for the present as well as anticipating the demands of the future (Sills, 1989; Bell, 1989b; Davies & Kinlock, 1991). In the case of the various self-help and not-for-profit projects, they too recognised the importance of training and embarked on some form of training programme with their respective workers.

Two complementary sets of objectives entered into the training policies for the different projects. One was that of preparing people to be able to offer or to provide a service to a standard deemed appropriate from the viewpoint of the project's management — a technical objective. The other objective, was that of engaging and committing the worker more completely as an individual in the transactions taking place between the worker, the organisation and the client — a psychological and motivational objective (Silverman, 1970). Only by taking account of the attitudinal and motivational factors present within the individual worker could the projects attempt to protect and enhance the interests and needs of their different client groups and the delivery of any service provision.

Successful applicants go on to take part in a fairly lengthy training course before they begin to work with a client. There are also regular training update sessions held for buddies who have gone through this initial training programme. There are sessions on information concerning HIV and on information handling skills. To ensure that the buddy does work in a way that respects the client's own thoughts, feelings and needs, the course also sets aside a lot of time for self-exploration on the part of the Buddies. Buddies are encouraged to consider their own reactions to the sexual orientation of others, and their feelings and beliefs concerning different groups of clients with whom they may work. (SAM)

If they are suitable, they go through a fairly rigorous programme; visiting different day centres within the community, and working under supervision at both our day centres. The trainee also needs to learn how to adjust to the different needs of different clients. For example, when you do a quiz with a client, you do not stick simply to the quiz book, you make up questions that are sufficiently difficult for some clients, and also questions which they are all capable of answering. If you continually ask people questions which they cannot answer, it is a very disturbing experience for them. You need to go by what you know about each client's general background and their capabilities. (Dementia day centre)

The exact nature of the training and the methods employed by the various projects differed. SAM was unique among the projects in that it had its own paid full-time training officers. The dementia day centres on the other hand, benefited considerably from their links with the Royal Edinburgh Hospital and its medical staff for both the design and the implementation of their external training programmes. The majority of the projects, however, made use of a combination of in-house training provided by key staff at the project topped up with outside speakers who provided more specialist or specialised information, advice or expertise.

Some of these clients when they are on a high, they can really be on a high. You have got to be emotionally stable to take the abuse. So it is for things like that, that we need on-site training. We are trying to put a programme together with the help of the training officer from the social services. (Handsworth Community Care Centre)

In two projects, moreover, that expertise was the distilled experience of the members themselves, which in the case of the Oasis home visit women's support group was the recognition of, and the value given to, the women's own experience as a method of helping others.

The women knew what had been helpful to them and what wasn't in the situation. It is allowing women to convert what has been a negative experience in their lives into a tool which they can use to help others. (Oasis)

In several of the projects which relied on having paid staff, opportunities which would allow workers to address some of their own particular training needs were less in evidence, either because of inadequate funding or because the workers were not always free to avail themselves of any training opportunities outwith the project.

There is always something new coming round. There are always new statutory regulations to think about, benefit changes and welfare needs. There is a lot of training that the support workers can do to benefit clients enormously. Counselling, stress management, dealing with your own anxiety and here we find it where we can and if we can't find it we do a bit of in-house training. However, if you are working part-time it is hard to make sufficient time available for training. (Supported accommodation project)
     One of the things that I have missed, in fact, is regular on-going training. What we are doing is — we've got a group workers' group

which meets. That's the volunteers and the workers who work with any of the groups. We are trying to get a day's workshop for that group to explore its own function and the group processes going on within that. We also want to do some work on group work skills. (AMWEL)

Work demands

Both selection and training may be thought of as something which prepares the worker for the real demands which are likely to be made once the individual becomes a fully active member of the organisation. Each of the projects had its own sets of requirements in terms of the tasks and the demands which were made upon the workforce. These demands could be broken down into three broad categories: fixed routine demands; extended routine demands; and non-routine demands (Brech, 1983). Routine demands are those demands which were contained in the job remit agreed between the volunteer or the paid worker and the management of the project. Routine tasks for the various projects typically would include the general planning, organisation, administration and preparation needed to be carried out prior to any activity or event taking place at the level of management; the execution of the activities themselves such as the crafts, games and procedures used within some projects to stimulate and to engage the interest and the participation of the clients; the worker's involvement in any socialising activities taking place as part of the service; the collection or escort duties which may be required, and, in over half the projects, the preparation of meals and snacks for the clients. Each of these tasks could be anticipated, and every member of the project would have a fixed agreed number of these tasks as her personal responsibility and role within the project.

Over and above these routine demands were the demands to perform routine tasks whose only limits were those of time and energy of the worker. In several projects where there were several workers — paid or unpaid, there had been tacit agreement between the worker and the managers of the projects that there would be some degree of flexibility in terms of how the worker would be used and an informal understanding that the worker would take on more than had initially been agreed, or would normally be expected, of someone in that role.

> We have two drivers who are drivers/handymen but, to be quite honest, they are drivers/care assistants because we need to use them during the day to provide extra assistance for the handicapped members who use the day centre. (Braid House)
>
> How we work is actually helping residents to take responsibility for the house. So it is basically rolling up your sleeves and living together, rather than staff standing there and saying This is what you must do. (Ark housing)

On other occasions, however, the extension of the worker's role was less consciously recognised or formally acknowledged and the worker often only became aware of the change in her work retrospectively.

> One thing leads to another here. Once you say you will help you will not be given much option of getting back out again. Myra, our

driver/secretary, came in to give a hand one day and has been here ever since. (SSMH youth club)

Moreover, the demands made upon the staff, or demands which staff may have placed upon themselves, often came close to being excessive. Typically, the worker's role demands had become over-extended either because there was no one else available to take on the work or as a result of a sense of commitment and compassion for the clients, or, typically a combination of both these things.

> For the first year there was really just myself and my part-time clerical assistant. By the end of the first year we had around a dozen users coming to the adult day centre as well as eight families attending the children's centre. We found that we could not possibly continue running both centres on the basis of one and a half members of staff. We also undertake a number of home visits in order to assess the need of the individual. Because of the work of the adult day centres, a lot of home visits have had to take place in the evening and sometimes, especially, in the first year, we were working 16 hours a day.(Epilepsy group)
>   Casework was one of the biggest gaps in the service that we offered. No one had been specifically appointed to undertake the casework role and people have been coming to the centre for more than a year now, seeking help and self-help workers have had to take on most of that casework. (Afro-Caribbean mental health project)
>   All the people who work at the day centre do so without any payment.
>   But it is all getting too much; they are not getting any younger — they are mostly old people. I have worked from 9 in the morning until sometimes late at night. My wife says I am now working more than before my retirement.
>   Now I feel we need a paid worker. The treasurer is 75, Mr Mamtora is 74 and I am 72. . . . For if something happens to us, then what will happen? — It will vanish. (Ghandi Hall day centre)

Over and above these routine and extended routine demands were the non-routine demands of the work of the different projects: demands which occurred with much less frequency for the worker but which confronted and challenged the worker's sensibilities and personal self-image to a more marked degree (Moore, 1977). Examples of such non-routine demands were toileting the clients and attending to other aspects of their personal hygiene which many people in the community would have found difficult.

> We would expect the volunteers to be able to wipe the dirty noses of some of the smaller children, but that is just the wee ones. But we would not expect volunteers to be asked to do that straight away. There are two club members who use nappies and, although it is very rare that they need to be changed, Jean has been the one who gets the job of changing the dirty nappies. (SSHM youth club)
>   Some volunteers feel that the type of work which is done here is difficult and, although we are inclined to say that we do not want to use a volunteer to take an old person to the toilet or to wash someone down or change them, we cannot guarantee that this will not happen. If there is an emergency or, we have an 'accident' then we might have

to ask them to do that. Certainly some volunteers find that the work is hard going and the older volunteer particularly finds lifting or assisting too heavy. (Braid House)

> Everyone at our day centre is primed to expect the occasional accident. I don't think we have anyone at the moment who is terribly incontinent. We have the odd accident and Kirsty was on the phone the day before yesterday to say that we had this horrendous mess and that could she go and buy rubber gloves. That sort of thing is coped with. If someone is very incontinent then the chances are that the relatives will provide pads and so forth which can be changed here. (Dementia project)

Sometimes, however, the demand was less of a physical and more of a verbal or emotional nature which required a degree of acceptance on the part of the individual worker.

> There are sometimes occasions when someone is experiencing a lot of anger and part of that anger is expressed towards the buddy and that can be difficult. People can take on the difficulties which their clients are experiencing and so there is a need for support and supervision. (SAM)

Supervision and support

Because of the often heavy or intense demands made by the work upon the worker, a number of the projects spoke of the need for some form of support for those workers who were at the front line of providing the service to the client. In several projects such as SAM, the dementia day centres, the epilepsy day centres and MACHEM, supervision sessions were formally established features of the back-up service offered to the workers.

> I think it is important that all the staff feel that they have the support and backing of whoever is in charge of their particular bit. There's a good system of support for all the members of staff. We have support meetings with the co-ordinator of the project and we ourselves have regular support meetings for the trainees in which they have the opportunity to speak about any problem or dissatisfaction they may have. If there is a matter which the person feels cannot be raised in the group, then she could meet with the organiser on a one-to-one basis. (Dementia project)

Much of the support and supervision related to matters affecting the routine task responsibilities of the workers. However, in a number of other instances, the support offered and received by volunteers or paid staff was not related directly or necessarily to matters of task performance or service delivery. Rather, the support provided recognised the legitimacy of the emotional expression of the needs of the workers, whether or not the trigger or cause for that emotional expression was related to situations or events which had arisen within the project, or, had occurred in some other area of the workers' private lives.

> The staff are a very close-knit group in the day centre, because of the type of work we do. There is a dedication to their work and they are

often asked to do more than what I feel would be asked of them in other centres. I think the girls are so committed because there is such close team work within the building. If there is a problem with a member of staff, it affects us all and that is something we have discovered very much this year. We have had a lot of problems affecting staff this year. If there is illness in someone's family or if there is a death, then it affects everyone and brings us together. However, it also places some additional stress on us all and on myself as the one with overall responsibility. (Braid House)

We are in here every day and we all pitch in to help. Sometimes we even cry on one another's shoulders.(SSMH Youth Club)

Staff turnover

A problem confronting any formal organisation is the provision of sufficient incentives to motivate individuals to participate and to remain active members of the organisation (March & Simon, 1967). Members of an organisation are recruited to be used as resources to achieve the goals of the organisation (Graham, 1987). However, as Selznick (1949) and others have demonstrated, men and women bring into the organisation other private purposes of their own. They react not simply as resources, but as 'wholes'. Individuals bring to the organisation their own needs and expectations, and their ability to achieve these personal goals within the organisation are important inducements which constitute a basis for continued participation. These observations apply as much to volunteers as they do to the paid workers of the organisations.

The work contract or the initial agreement between the worker and the organisation marks the beginning of an ongoing exchange relationship between the two parties and not its conclusion. This is due to the fact that although the individual, in joining the organisation, is initially prepared to accept whatever tasks are assigned to her, she knows very little of what the work will actually entail and will not be fully aware of the demands until she is in post (March & Simon, 1967). What is acceptable prior to entry becomes subject to revision by both sides after the entry has taken place. Moreover, the worker's pursuit of these private goals or personal needs, is an on-going feature of organisation life. At the outset, the individual has only a limited knowledge of the possibilities which may exist for meeting or for furthering her own personal needs and interests through engagement in the work. Conversely, the worker may feel her initial expectations regarding what the work might offer have not been realised. In the event of the person's hopes or expectations not being met, there is a greater likelihood of leaving the organisation if she feels herself unable to alter her situation and, or, if she believes better prospects are available to her elsewhere.

An assumption behind much of the theory of organisations is that there is a reserve of untapped energy in the individual which is potentially available to be harnessed by the organisation if it can produce the right set of inducements. However, some considerable empirical evidence of the behaviour of groups and individuals in organisations would appear to indicate that the workers are concerned less with the contributions they are expected to make to the organisation and more with retaining or increasing those rewards or benefits which are important to themselves as individuals. These inducements may range from material concerns such as earning money or furthering the individual's career; to more aesthetic aspirations such as the desire for approval, acceptance and self-actualisation (Litterer, 1967). The stance which the individual adopts and the decision she will make with respect to the exchange will tend to be in terms of her own sets of interests and concerns rather than the requirements of the organisation (Rubenstein & Haberstroh, 1960).

Volunteers

For more than half the projects an on-going and central concern was the problem of both recruiting and retaining volunteers to a level that would guarantee the day-to-day operations of the different services. Moreover, this difficulty throws into relief the sets of assumptions which underpin the thinking and the official policy on the subject of care in the community. Much of that thinking rests on the belief that there is an untapped pool of people in the community who are prepared to give freely of themselves, their time and their energies to provide a degree of support to others who, because of their physical or emotional condition or circumstances, left unaided would be unable to maintain or to regain a life in the community (Wall, 1988). The assumption of a large untapped volunteer force appears to ignore a number of possible limitations to such expectations. First, the assumption ignores the possibility that, though there may indeed be a pool of persons generally prepared and willing to offer some form of community support to others, they are not necessarily motivated or prepared to offer that support for the periods of time which may be required to make the service operable at a level which meets the needs of the client. Secondly, it ignores the probability that some categories of individuals most in need of community support, because of stigma or myths associated with their condition or state, have a negative public image and as a result are unattractive to the volunteer (Jordan, 1987). In a society which has traditionally marginalised the elderly, the mentally ill, the physical and mental handicapped, and the drug user and has reflected this in the formal welfare and social service provision, it should come as no surprise that volunteers to these groups are but a fraction of the volunteers who have been mobilised into work with groups who are generally regarded as more socially useful members of the society such as, for example, the able-bodied youth of today (Scottish Standing Conference of Voluntary Youth Organisations, 1991). Thirdly, the assumption ignores the possibility that, even where volunteers initially offer their services to particular individuals or groups, the volunteers may discover on entering into the support-giving relationship that the physical or emotional demands made upon themselves are greater than they are able or prepared to sustain for any period of time.

More than half of those projects which made use of volunteers, and which required the use of their services on a regular basis experienced problems both with recruiting volunteers in sufficient numbers and with retaining that support at the levels which would guarantee the long-term viability of the services provided through the different projects. In most instances, the limits set to the demands which any project could place on the volunteers were related to: demands made on the time required of the volunteer; demands made on the emotional or physical energies of the volunteer; and demands which created conflict for the volunteer's other role obligations such as those of parent, wife, partner, student, etc (March & Simon, 1967).

> You get commitment from volunteers when they are here, but you cannot look upon a volunteer as being the same as an employee. We have a pool of 12 volunteers, five of whom are really reliable. The others will come when it is suitable as they have other commitments of their own. Some days there will not be a single volunteer and on other days there could be as many as three or four volunteers.(Epilepsy Project)
>
> At the moment we have 11 volunteers who come on different days. Some come 2 days a week and some just 1 day. It is difficult to get them and sometimes we find that when they come in they find the work is too difficult or too heavy for them. The older volunteer particularly finds the lifting or assisting too heavy. (Braid House)
>
> I think initially five people volunteered and dropped out one by one which I think illustrates the concerns people have about using volunteers on a project that is so important and needs a lot of commitment. (Dementia project)
>
> On average, we get about six volunteers attending the evening clubs and between two or three attending some Saturday morning clubs. If it happens that not enough volunteers turn up, we just do it ourselves. (SSMH youth club)

Moreover, even in those instances where the demands placed on the volunteers were less intense and onerous, the difficulty of attracting sustained volunteer commitment was still apparent. A case in point is that of the Parkinson self-help group which only meets on a monthly basis and which has street collections three times a year.

> A lot of our fund-raising is generally on a Saturday so relatives can sometimes spare us an hour for our fund-raising efforts. There again, we are short of street collectors because of the nature of our illness. Most patients, themselves, cannot help us. Their carers are unable to come because they are already caring for someone who has Parkinson's disease so we have to rely on their family members to come and support us. We have about seven or eight collectors, between us we work for about 4 or 5 hours with very little break, trying to catch the shoppers before they spend their money. (Parkinson's Society: Durham)

In those projects totally reliant on the services of volunteers, it was left to the regular and key volunteers to take up the additional strain of providing the service. However, a number of these individuals were, themselves, not without their own personal share of family and other commitments outwith the project, and, when illness or bereavement entered their personal lives, the burden of that caring increased. In the case of the project for the mental handicapped, the clubs closed down for an additional second week following the Christmas and New Year holiday period as a result of the combination of heavy demands made on the energies and time of the key women volunteers in the period leading up to and including, the festivities for the clubs, and the occurrence of family illnesses among these women.

We just felt washed out, so we have closed the clubs for a second week.

Even when making that statement, the three women were at the club premises tidying up; attending to correspondence and administration; and making all the preparations for the opening of the club to the members. However, the question must surely remain as to how long such commitment can be sustained. After periods of service to the clubs which range from 6–12 years, are there limits to continued participation at the present levels?

The long-term prospects are not too good as far as we can see. I don't know what would happen if all three of us were to say, 'Right, that's it. We have had enough!'. I don't think that the clubs would continue. But there is a limit to what we can do. There is a lot of work involved. We are all here 5 days a week, either for the clubs, or attending meetings, and there is a problem in fitting in our own social lives as well. (SSMH Youth Club)

Employment trainees

Employment training schemes have come under considerable criticism from a number of quarters. General concerns expressed have been that the training is often of a very low quality; is another method of exploiting the unemployed because any financial incentive is limited to the entitlement to welfare benefits; is a political stratagem to keep the unemployment figures artificially low; and/or is unrelated to the needs of the local economy. From the viewpoint of the host organisation, concerns often expressed are that trainees are not especially motivated; are unreliable; and/or are out of the work habit. Certainly a number of these different concerns were evident in the viewpoints expressed by the management of those projects which made use of employment trainees either to establish or to provide a service to the client or user group. Five projects made use of a total of 38 employment trainees and, although the experience was mixed, the overall assessment of the contribution of the employment trainees to the project was very favourable. Only one project had, on balance, a less than positive experience with this category of worker.

Generally, we have not found the use of employment training all that successful. Even although I interview them first to ensure that the person is going to fit in with the team, I would say that there is not the commitment to the work from the people who are coming from employment training. We have had employment trainees, but have found that they are very unreliable. We have had trainees who have lasted 2 days. They are not really being paid and we have only had one girl who was successful and she is now employed with us. (Braid House)

However, three other projects were much more enthusiastic to the use of employment trainees and of the benefits which their contributions had made to the clients and to the projects.

The trainees have basically got to do the same type of tasks as the staff who are here on a permanent basis. At the present time we have five employment trainees at the adult day centre. To be absolutely honest, without the trainee workers I would find it very, very difficult to run the project. I mean the project would still continue, don't misunderstand me, but, it would be more limited. (Epilepsy project)

We had a bit of difficulty finding enough volunteers to staff the projects and were actually approached by the training agencies of the employment training scheme.

I have mixed feeling, I am not terribly in favour of the employment training programmes because I think they are exploited a lot in industry and elsewhere. However, I feel that we can offer a bit of training to these people if that is where their interest lies. That is why we have a fairly in-depth selection procedure, to identify the people who really do have an interest. They have proved to be very good. We have had two or three people who have dropped out for one reason or another, but overall, a very good reliable staff. They are placed with us for a maximum of a year and we have, in fact, been able to offer a couple of them some part-time work with the companion service. So it is working nicely. (Dementia project)

In the case of the community garden, Felix the key volunteer worker with the project was acutely aware of the general concerns surrounding the use of employment trainees and consciously built into his contract" with the employment trainees a recognition of their condition and their needs as well as the requirements of the project.

Under the old community programme schemes workers got paid between £65–80 per week. When the government changed to employment training, the pay was reduced to what they would get as dole money plus £10 for travel expenses. That is what these people working here are getting. All the trainees are long-term unemployed. We take whoever they send us. We have 12 trainees altogether. One of the bonuses for them, and us, is that at least seven trainees have gone from the project into permanent jobs.

I only work my lads 30 hours which is the minimum laid down in the contract because I feel that the money they are paid is so cheapskate. Although it's surprising because some of these lads are given a job to do and will work on after the 3 o'clock knocking off time, just to finish the job.

You've got to show the trainees that you are going to teach them something, so a programme is laid on for them. I also try to consider the needs of the individual as well.

Felix also recognised that, in order to increase the workers' commitment to the project, it was important to try to establish some personal links or association between the workers and the labouring tasks needing to be done to get the project to the stage where the disabled themselves could become actively involved in the garden's development. Felix did this by bringing the workers and the disabled clients together in a natural, informal setting which allowed opportunities for the trainees to make the connections themselves between their work and the needs which would be met for the disabled people in the community.

I also saw it as very much part of my job to get the trainees interested in what they were doing. One of the things I instigated with the trainees was a cup of tea or coffee down at the Trinity Centre before we came up here to work on the garden. Most of the disabled make for the canteen for a drink and a blether. I suggested they start off at the Trinity Centre because I wanted to give the trainees an opportunity to see who they were making the garden for and it worked well.

None the less, the garden project which was particularly successful with its employment trainee staff still had a staff turnover of 60% in the 18-month period that the project had been in operation.

However good the project's experience with the employment trainees, there are inherent difficulties in the use of such workers for any project wishing to offer a regular service that also requires considerable face-to-face work and relationship forming with particular client groups. The first source of tension lies in the fact that, even when the interest and the commitment of the employment trainees is not at issue, there are limits to the time which the employment trainees can remain with any project. The longest period of time which people can continue in employment training is 1 year.

However, we get employment trainees and get them trained and then they go away onto something else, so there is a big turnover with trainees. A year with a project like this is not long enough.(Epilepsy Project).

The difficulty, however, is that the workers may not arrive on the project at the start of their year's training period, but more likely, may be several months into their training experience. Secondly, in some projects which made use of employment trainees, there was an expectation, indeed a requirement, that they perform the same types of tasks as those of other paid workers on the project. The fact that others on the project were being paid for the same work and also had a relative degree of job security whilst the employment trainees received only benefits for their efforts could be expected to have given rise to a sense of relative deprivation for the employment trainees. Unless incentives were built into the exchange by the project for the employment trainees, the attractiveness of the workers situation would inevitably be reduced. Thirdly, people on employment training have previously been registered as seeking full-time employment. If such opportunity for full-time work should arise, as happened with several projects, the employment trainee worker will leave. She/he will do so because paid work and full-time employment will satisfy a number of their own personal needs which preceded any involvement with a particular project. Paid employment feeds positively into the person's self-image as a fully participating member of society by providing an important source of status in the community. Paid work also allows the individual to purchase goods and services at a level which is not possible on unemployment or welfare benefit and so satisfy personal needs of their own or of their dependents. The availability of paid work outwith the project therefore constitutes a permanent influence which acts to draw the worker out of the project unless the project itself can offer employment to the worker. This occurrence was relatively rare on the projects. Only one full-time and two-part time jobs arose out of any of the projects using employment trainees. The fourth inherent difficulty in using employment trainees is that the turnover in staff gives rise to the need for on-going training programmes to initiate newcomers to the project. The fact that some former employment trainees may be able to go on to paid work is a positive aspect of the use of employment trainees. What is less positive is that having invested heavily in the training of their employment trainee, staff demonstrated the benefits of that new-found expertise to the quality of service offered to user groups and established the project's need to use such staff on a more or less continuous basis. Few projects were able to offer trainees any real prospect of paid employment with the projects.

Paid Staff

The turnover situation with paid workers, whether full- or part-time, posed fewer difficulties for the various projects. However, in several projects, it was evident that a number of staff had intentions of remaining with the project for periods of 1 or 2 years, and, whilst this gave the project greater stability than was the case with either volunteers or employment trainees, it nevertheless posed its own set of problems for what are relatively small projects. The departure of one member of staff from a team of two or three staff members could have considerable impact on the project as a whole. Part of their reason for moving on appeared to be linked to career development and the fact that the nature of the funding, typically being limited in terms of time, undermined the worker's sense of job security with the project.

Conclusion

Issues related to staff or staffing constitute central concerns for every organisation, including service organisations. Key staffing issues are those of recruitment, selection, training, work performance, worker motivation and staff turnover. Each of these factors, either separately or collectively, has been the subject of much research and debate. At the operational level, the literature on organisations is full of empirical illustrations of organisations' various attempts at confronting these aspects of organisation life. Certainly, each of the projects, when viewed as service organisations, could be seen to have been confronted by, and to have addressed, all of the above staffing issues. Every project: engaged in the recruitment and selection of staff; undertook some form of staff training which would familiarise the worker with the demands of the services provided through the project; tried to achieve a match between the abilities, aptitudes and attitudes of the worker with the needs of the clients served by the project; and dealt with issues associated with staff turnover.

In the case of service organisations generally, the problems of training, work performance, motivation and staff turnover have been addressed by building into the structure of the organisation a formal role and associated set of responsibilities for the supervision and the support of staff. By dealing with each of these factors through the mechanisms of supervision and support, the service organisation seeks to improve its ability to achieve its formal goals and objectives and, in the process, protect or enhance its own maintenance and survival needs as an institution (Ross & Bilson, 1989; Bamford, 1982; Glastonbury, 1987).

Staff support and supervision can be regarded as internal mechanisms used by the projects to help resolve problems associated with either the work performance, or, the motivation of the worker, or both. Staff supervision and support are, at one and the same time, instruments of quality control as well as genuine attempts on the part of the organisation to assist development and growth in the level of the worker's effectiveness.

A simple sequential model of the process undertaken with respect to staff by the various projects is contained in Fig. 24.1.

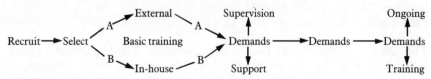

Figure 24.1

The organisation first of all seeks to attract and recruit its workforce. It then engages in the selection of the candidates who either undergo basic training prior to working directly with the clients (Route A), or are recruited, selected and undergo direct on-the-job training within the project with the client user group(s) (Route B). Supervision which is internal to the organisation and is on-going, monitors workers performance in their roles. Staff support is also internal and on-going but serves a quite separate function and purpose. Both supervision and support are important means whereby the organisation tries to bring about improved workers performance and commitment thereby attempting to meet the needs of the organisation, the client user groups and the needs and interests of the workers themselves. On-going training is that additional training required in order to update the workers in new techniques and developments associated with the work undertaken by the project, or to assist the workers to respond more effectively and appropriately to any change of circumstances at the level of the clients. An example of the latter might be a project's ability to adapt the service to meet either improvements or deteriorations in the user group's mental or physical health.

The reality of the situation for a number of projects was much more complex. Figure 24.1 portrays a situation of general stability within the workforce. However, only SAM appeared to have the stability of staffing which would allow the project to proceed in a sequential manner and in such a way as to permit the project to build upon the skills already established through earlier training programmes and from the supervision and support which staff had already experienced. For a number of other projects, especially the four day centres and the gardening project, staff turnover meant that the work situation was much more fluid and the key workers to the project were required to revert to basic training practices for each new intake of worker(s). Adding to the dynamic of the situation was the fact that the project staff rarely joined or left the project simultaneously. This factor placed an additional burden on to the key worker(s) who were then faced with the problem of balancing the different training, supervision and support needs required by workers who had different levels of expertise and experience with the project. For those projects most heavily reliant on the use of volunteers and employment trainees, staff turnover therefore represented a drain on the resources to the projects.

People enter an organisation whether as volunteers, employment trainees or paid members of staff for needs and interests of their own and leave the organisation for very much the same sets of reasons. Each of the projects had achieved some measure of success in coping with the different sets of issues related to staff. However, none of the projects had completely resolved such issues and some projects, by their very nature, appeared more vulnerable than others in this respect.

If staffing is a key concern for any organisation, so too is the subject of users of the projects' services. Without users or clients in sufficient quantities to take up the services on offer, the need for, and therefore the survival of, the organisation is threatened. However, in the case of service organisations, the issue is not simply a question of the numbers of users. It is also very much a question of the extent to which the ideals and values underpinning the services to particular client groups are upheld and reflected in how the services are actually delivered.

25   The projects' users

There are at least two broad categories of beneficiaries to any services provided through care in the community. The first and obvious category is that of the carer and/or the relative who is being cared for, or worked with — the direct users of the services. The second broad category is that of indirect users and beneficiaries of the services, the social work and medical staff and the various statutory and voluntary agencies who also share involvement with the same client populations (Richardson, 1988). These indirect users of the services provided by care in the community benefit from (a) having their own work with clients buttressed and strengthened by the existence of such services and (b) from being released from the full burden of care by handing over to, or sharing part of that responsibility for the welfare of either the carer or the client with, a third party. The other less immediately obvious beneficiary is the wider community itself. The community as a whole benefits from the existence of additional resources within the community for its members; from an image of itself as a caring community; and also benefits from any financial savings on the cost of community-based services as against residential services funded either locally or through state taxation. Because each of the accounts deals primarily with services directed towards specific client groups, the discussion will centre principally on the client users. However, where appropriate, reference will be made to the indirect users of the services in order to obtain a picture of their views of, and responses to, the needs of the clients within the community. Moreover, reference to indirect users of the services may also offer insights into the differing sets of interests held by the various partners to the caring. Because the observations made are based on a total of only 21 projects, the problems of over-generalising from the accounts are obvious. None the less, it may be possible to identify recurrent themes and issues which also exist within other, similar projects.

The client user groups

In only one-third of the projects was it realistic to speak of there being two direct beneficiaries and users — the carer and the client. These were the seven day centre projects which offered respite care for carers in the community. The majority of the projects, including the day centres, had, as their prime beneficiary, the person for whom the service had been designed, namely the clients. These clients, however, were as different as the projects were varied and are incapable of being reduced to one common dimension, even if such a reduction were desirable. For example, the ages of the clients ranged from young to old. In one project alone, the members ranged in age from 6 years to 76 years. Clients also exhibited different types and different degrees of vulnerability, which called for community support. Physical and mental handicap; physical and mental illnesses; educational, learning and emotional difficulties; all indicate something of the diversity of vulnerability among the user population. The gender of the user group serviced by particular projects also varied. Although the majority of projects had mixed sex groupings, four projects were women-only self-help support groups and there was also one single sex male Muslim day centre project. Five of the projects made explicit reference to a service provision directed exclusively to black or ethnic members of the community (Ellice-Williams, 1988), although, it was possible that members of ethnic communities were, in fact, recipients of some of the other services detailed in the accounts.

The nature of the disability or vulnerability of the clients, their ages, sex or even their ethnicity can often become overriding categories which people use in order to label individuals in some way (Moore, 1977). Labels, however, reveal little of the persons to whom such labels have been applied. Moreover, sometimes these labels can be used to package, shape and limit the response which society will make to, for example, the elderly; the physically handicapped; people with learning difficulties; people who are or have been mentally ill (Jordan, 1987; Jowell & Ritchie, 1988). But, clients are not packages to be stamped and shipped willy nilly between referees and agencies. Clients are not one-dimensional, they are wholes. To think exclusively in terms of the labels or the infirmities is to lose sight of the essence which is the individual.

Fortunately, each of the projects described above demonstrated their belief in the principle of human worth as was evident in their use of the referral system; the criteria used in the selection procedures adopted for intake to the project; and the attention given to the activities and the personal relationships which would constitute the service provided to the different client groups. Furthermore, these projects did not choose to ignore, or to dismiss, the client's vulnerabilities, but, rather took these into account along with whatever else they knew or could learn about the client in terms of the person's likes, dislikes, hopes, fears, ambitions, culture, language, religion, etc to arrive at a view of the person in the round and to deliver a service which had that whole person in mind.

Recruitment

A concern for any service organisation is that of attracting sufficient clients or users, since, without people who are willing and prepared to make use of the service, the organisation will fail. That is as true of service organisations as it is of organisations in the commercial or industrial sectors. Each of the projects adopted fairly standard methods of client recruitment (Human Resource Potential Project, 1973). Most projects used, or had used, leafleting, public notices in local churches, health clinics, general practice waiting rooms, community centres and local press releases (Banks, 1988). Representatives from the projects had also canvassed personally specific agencies which might reasonably be viewed as access points to targetted user groups in attempts to both inform these agencies of the existence of the projects and their services and also to obtain contacts or referrals. All of these would have been regarded in the commercial world as routine marketing procedures. The extent to which any project relied on one or more of these methods of recruitment was influenced by:

- the amount of funds available for publicising the services;
- how long the project had been in existence and the degree to which it had already established a regular user group for its services;
- the visibility or public profile of the project;
- the existence of networks and linkages with other voluntary and statutory agencies in the community;
- and finally, the number of users actually required to make the project viable.

A comparison of two, not dissimilar, projects on the single dimension of professional networking, however, shows something of the varied experiences when enlisting the support of outside professional bodies.

> Over 100 women have been in contact with and supported by Oasis. Of these women 70% have been referred by statutory and voluntary agencies and the remainder by personal recommendation of Oasis members and as the result of publicity. The majority, however, are referred by health visitors, GPs, children centre staff, hospital social workers and the Royal Edinburgh Hospital. (Oasis)

> About 40 are involved in groups at the moment. We find our main source of referrals is the people referring themselves. There are several areas we have targeted to work with in the coming year (1991). One is to try to get more direct contact with the GPs whom we feel would be absolutely key to this. (AMWEL)

Referrals

Clients were referred to the different projects via a variety of routes which could be grouped together under four broad headings: self-referrals; medical referrals; social work referrals; and a final residual category. The breakdown of the different sources of referrals which were specified in the accounts shown in Table 25.1.

Table 25.1

	Source of referral		
Self	Health	Social work	Other
17	28	13	4

*Note these figures relate to the number of times a referring agency was mentioned in the accounts, and do not indicate the actual number of referrals coming from any one of these sources.

At least two important points can be drawn from the above figures. The first is the predominance of health referrals to the different projects, a point which should not be lost sight of when considering the subject of support funding to these same projects.

The second is that two-thirds of all referrals mentioned in the accounts are from secondary sources. That finding squares with the comments made by the worker of Ark Housing who stated:

> Mostly residents have come here because somebody else has recognised that they needed to come here. (Ark housing)

Referrals of clients to the projects were influenced by three broad sets of factors. First, *knowledge* of the existence of the project; knowledge of the extent to which the services would appear to fit in with or meet the needs of the client; and knowledge too of the track record of the project in successfully addressing the needs of existing clients.

> We have got a lot of interest from hospitals as more and more from the first out-of-the-house course returned to the day units and fed back how well they had done on the course. What has happened is that on the third out-of-the-house course, referrals were coming from both the wards and the day unit and they too returned with tales of the support which they had obtained from the course. (Out-of-the-house course)

The second factor influencing referrals to the project was that of *motivation* on the part of the referee and the extent to which the agency or the individual was concerned to increase the community support for clients for whom they had an on-going responsibility.

> More and more people are beginning to acknowledge that this kind of community provision with its integration of people referred from the wards, day units, GPs or from the social work department is really helpful rather than separating and stigmatising these individuals. (Oasis)

Or the motivation may have been a desire to share the burden of caring with some third party. That latter decision was not necessarily motivated by self-interest, but perhaps by a genuine recognition of the limits to the time, energy, expertise and resources available to the individual to deal with the client's needs and the value to the client of bringing in external support.

> The kinds of people that we have time to spend with are people who come to them (GPs) in their 5 minute slot but who need a lot more time to talk. (AMWEL)

The third influence is that of *alternatives* open to the referee when trying to find suitable support services for the client within the community. In the majority of cases, these referrals appear to have been appropriate in as much as the referee had identified what was on offer through a particular project and the client group(s) targeted by that project. Nevertheless, there were occasions when a referral was considered inappropriate by the project and appeared to have been guided more by a sense of gaps in the existing provision rather than an attempt to match the client's needs to that of the service.

> I think there has been a tendency to refer women to Oasis knowing how stretched resources were and wanting to offer the women something and that could result in a referral to Oasis. That is an on-going piece of negotiation work being undertaken mutually between Oasis and the referring agency in deciding which individuals would be suitable for

Oasis and which persons would not be suitable for Oasis. Where the referral is perhaps questionable, in that the person has a lot of problems and the referring agency is not intending to keep in touch with the individual, we would suggest somewhere else. Basically, we are concerned that the referees do not regard Oasis as purely a place for people with severe mental health problems. (Oasis)

We also have a lot of people referred to us who have epilepsy as a result of mental handicap. However, their epilepsy is the least of their problems, but, try telling that to some of the other agencies who refer them our way. When they get someone who has a lot of handicaps, they will say, 'Oh, but they have epilepsy, so it is your problem'. They see epilepsy as the *problem*, but in most cases epilepsy is not the key problem. (Epilepsy project)

I refuse to have a referral from the health authority or social services without a worker. If you are in hospital and you know your social worker, you feel safer. If you are just given the bus fare to come to the centre, it is not nice. (Handsworth Community Care Centre)

Though every project requires users to take up its services and so protect its continued existence, that viability was not bought at the expense of the services provided to the client. Clearly evident in each of these comments is the sense in which the project sought to safeguard the integrity of the services to the client. Moreover, these concerns with maintaining sets of standards for the service on offer was equally apparent in the manner in which the different projects established their selection procedures which governed access to the services.

Selection

If selection of staff was a standard feature of organisational life for each of the projects, so too was the selection of clients. Over half of those projects providing a direct service to the client adopted some formal method for vetting and selecting their users and at least seven projects had established formal selection panels when deciding client intake. The fact that over half of the projects engaged in formal selection procedures raises the question as to why this was so, since selection by its very nature also implies rejection of some individuals who, for whatever reason, had sought the services of the project as a way of meeting their needs. Moreover, any service organisation whose primary interest is the welfare of the clients, and who turns clients away, requires to offer some explanation for its actions.

Why select?

There are a number of reasons why a service organisation might decide to operate formal selection procedures, some of which could be described as negative or positive selection procedures depending on what was the primary concern, the needs of the clients or those of the organisation. Negative selection is that where the main purpose of the selection criteria is to protect or to enhance the project as an organisation. A project may engage in negative selection in order to ensure that the clients it attracts, and for whom it assumes some responsibility will be the *least troublesome*.

Certainly, that could not be said of the epilepsy project or the Handsworth Community Care Centre where :

> We have taken people here whom the Adult Training Centres could not cope with because of their epilepsy, or, because they have behavioural problems.
>
> In 80% of all cases medication can control epilepsy, but the centre is geared to those people who are not controlled. These are the people who have the problem. (Epilepsy project)
>
> We are open-door at the moment and I don't think that we are going to change that policy. The main reasons that the centre started in 1983 was for people who got turned away from the usual day centres; those were the ones that we take in. They were usually people who have behavioural problems — we seek to be more understanding. So we try not to turn away people. I can only think of one person where we had to do that. We would do that if somebody was particularly disruptive and was upsetting other clients who use the centre, but so far, as I said, there has only been one instance of that in the 7 years that I have been here. (Handsworth Community Care Centre)

Or, they could select those people as clients who would provide the quickest and *greatest throughput* and so demonstrate statistically to the wider public, especially their funders, how many people had used the provision. However, if selection were simply a matter of playing the numbers game, neither Oasis nor Braid House would provide useful models of such an approach; indeed, the reverse was true of both projects.

> Unlike the hospital setting we don't discharge a case. Women can come and go in Oasis — it's open ended. Oasis has always been a quality service and we have always resisted saying to women, 'You can only come on a Wednesday or a Thursday or whenever'. There are no restrictions, yet. (Oasis)
>
> One suggestion was that we should look at our clientele and say, 'Right, you've been coming here for a certain length of time. We have provided you with the service and we think now is the time you stopped coming along and made room for someone else coming in'. But, I don't agree with that view at all. That is a model which the day hospitals use. But, when they put the old people out, they do not provide an on-going support and you get deterioration. That is what would happen again, but, we are a social provision. We cannot just say to old people — go home. (Braid House)

Another negative reason for the establishment of formal selection procedures might be to determine the clients' ability to pay — the *profit motive*. Fortunately, none of the 20 projects contained in the accounts which provided services directly to clients introduced that consideration into their deliberations. All of these projects were not-for-profit or self-help organisations and as such, in most instances, there were no charges made against clients for the services offered other than that for snacks or meals which clients may require. The exceptions to this approach were the housing projects where costs of paying staff were built into the service cost to the client. Again, however, the not-for-profit element kept these charges to a minimum.

Looking at selection of clients as a positive strategy, one designed to protect the welfare, needs and interests of the client or user group, a number of positive motives were evident in the accounts. A project may engage in selection procedures in order to establish, together with the client, whether the service provided was likely to *meet* with the *expectations* or *needs* of the client. This was the case with the Buc-Up club and the out-of-the-house course.

> If I get a person coming through the door who wants to register as a volunteer but who I feel is not quite ready for the Buc-Up club, I would try to encourage the person to go to the mental health centre for help and go so far as saying 'I will phone them for you and make an appointment' that has worked at times in the past and people have gone onto there and sometimes we might find that we will get them back again, but at a time when they are more able to cope with what we do. (The Buc-Up club)
>
> We spent as much time as possible speaking to each potential group member to explain the aims and possible content of the course and to ascertain that it was the sort of course that they wanted; what they felt they wanted out of the course; and that their expectations were realistic. (Out-of-the-house course)

The project may select because it offers a *specialist service* which is geared toward a particular user group. That was the situation with the Council For Mosques Muslim day centre which was an all-male facility and with the dementia day centre project where clients for the latter project were accepted only where there was a formal medical diagnosis of dementia. Or, selection may be used as a *protective mechanism* by a project, excluding individuals whose presence on the project would disadvantage or adversely effect those clients whom the project sought to support or to serve.

> The women we targeted for the out-of-the-house course were likely, in addition to being traditional non-participants in education, to be lacking in both confidence and self-esteem, some perhaps experienced feelings of isolation and depression.
>
> Course information was deliberately *not* being made freely available in libraries and community centres as we did not wish to attract additional course users. (Out-of-the-house course)

The *limitation of the resources* available to the project was another legitimate reason for applying some form of selection and constituted one of the most frequent reasons behind a number of project decisions. Common resource problems were the limited size of the accommodation, insufficient staffing, or inadequate transport to the project. To take on more clients without augmenting the resources of the project would be to dilute the service already on offer.

> We cannot expand with the staff numbers we have. It is not a case of saying just because we are good-natured we will take this extra person or push the walls back a bit to accommodate more people. We now have 50 frail elderly a day. We also have a waiting list of 60. (Braid House)
>
> However, there are certain problems with the accommodation in Marionville which means that the clients would also have to be fairly

> mobile. Look around. We do not have the facilities here for people who are in wheelchairs or who have severe physical disabilities, or, for people who cannot get into the minibus. (Dementia project)

Positive selection in some projects was also related to the *quality* of the *service* provided and was directly linked to the needs of the client group. In some instances, in order positively to address the needs of certain individuals, the numbers which might otherwise have been in operation by the project were revised downwards. This was particularly true in the case of the adult epilepsy project.

> We have 22 here every day except for Tuesday. On that day we do not bring in so many as we bring in people who are quite profoundly handicapped. Tuesday is a games day. This is to encourage them to use their limbs and increase their mobility. It is about helping them to communicate and we do that by going for a one-to-one ratio. (Adult epilepsy project)

Selection, especially within the day centre provisions, also took on the form of a *priority system*. Because of restrictions on access to the services brought about by limits of staff, accommodation, transport or funding a number of the projects had established waiting lists. These waiting lists in turn sometimes give rise to a form of rationing of the service in which the selection of clients played a key role.

Finally selection, especially when formalised by a panel system, was a device whereby there was a guarantee of *fair play* for those potential users on the waiting list. The selection panel ensured that individuals were offered a place within the project on the basis of need, rather than on personal influence or the whim of the worker attached to the project, thereby adding to the credibility of the service within the local community.

Apparent in all of the positive sets of reasons listed for selection of clients is the emphasis made on the needs, interests and well-being of the clients themselves, rather than on any self-interests of the project as an organisation. In this respect, these projects reflected the service ideal which underpins the philosophy of care in the community.

The services

It is not uncommon among certain professional bodies when making reference to the types of clients referred to in the accounts to speak or to write of them as either cases or causes, rather than as people (Robertson & Osborne, 1985). Social work, for example, often defines clients as cases and groups of clients as the worker's caseload. As cases, the clients have differing success in attracting the support of the professional departments. Many social work departments have established their own priority system for identifying eligible users and some, like the frail elderly, have traditionally come low on that priority list.

> Social work with the elderly has tended to be relegated to the lower end of client priority. (Challis & Davies, 1986)

However, those same categories of users who are generally targeted for care in the community are even less well represented in the thinking of community education (Baldock, 1983). When the subject of community care is raised among the community education profession, it sometimes appears that it is a matter which is more to be avoided or waged against, rather than embraced and developed (Shaw & Player, 1990). At best, community care is regarded as a cause, reflecting a set of issues which require to be addressed, more at a political level than at the level of service provision or of stimulating and facilitating local initiatives (Findlay, 1989). Happily for the clients, others: lay people and some in the voluntary sector, have identified the challenge; made some response, and shown the community several possible directions. Certainly, in the accounts contained here, clients were not referred to as either cases or causes but as people with needs. Moreover the assessment of these needs reflected a view of the person in the round rather than of a 'case' or an 'issue'.

Obviously these observations do not depict the work of every social worker or every community worker. What they do comment upon is the general attitudinal response which would appear to typify these services and which inevitably affects and constrains the workers. The reader will be provided with examples of both responses later on in the text.

The services provided through the different projects span a continuum of needs which ranged from physical and recreational needs; social and socialisation needs; emotional and psychological needs; educational needs; religious needs; to self-actualisation needs. Each of the projects addressed a number of these needs simultaneously, while at the same time attending to the presenting needs expressed by the client or by the referees. Therefore the descriptions of the projects abound with examples of each category of need and the responses made, here are some illustrative comments:

Physical/Recreational

Tuesday is a games day, this is to encourage them to use their limbs and increase their mobility. It is about helping them to communicate and we do that by going for a one-to-one ratio. (Epilepsy project)

Socialisation

Some of our members just like to sit and talk with their friends; some play darts, some do computer games, some paint, some do dancing downstairs. They just mainly do their own thing. We are not here to teach them. We are here to let them enjoy themselves. (SSMH youth club)

Emotional/Psychological

I think as well as maintaining the physical and mental abilities which the clients still possess, the day centres are also providing a safe environment where dementia sufferers can come in and feel secure and happy. Every day in life they are out in the real world, so to speak, and every day they are coming up against things which they cannot do any more. They cannot remember how to use money, or, how to cook meals, or, how to put their clothes on properly, or, the shops do not look familiar, or, they do not recognise where they are. But when they are here, everything is gauged to dementia sufferers. They are never put in the position where they are unable to cope. (Dementia day centre)

Educational

I was thinking about the kinds of things which disabled people could get involved in which were new, which had not been tried before — at least here — and where they could learn to do new things. The garden was going to be something to stretch the disabled.

There is also a scheme afoot to have the disabled record on to the computer all the different varieties of plants, their colour, texture, scent and season, in order that the disabled can plan ahead the best combination of plant life for all the garden users throughout the year. In this respect, the garden has broadened the curriculum and learning experiences offered to the disabled which was the intention underpinning the initial idea for the garden project. (Garden project)

Religious

We also have a prayers room for the prayer times for members of the day centre. (Muslim day centre)

We also have some temples here in the day centre so that people can go and pray. It is important to them that they are able to keep up their devotions and we are able to offer that here at the centre. (Ghandi Hall day centre)

Self actualisation

We are really trying to make people as independent as possible within the setting (a community home). We have had people coming whom we were told would never be able to handle money, yet one person has been decorating her own room, goes out and buys records, goes to the post office, buys clothes and yet has only been here a year and a half. (Ark housing)

Over and above the ability of these projects to respond to the different sets of needs which clients had as individuals, irrespective of their particular vulnerability, there were two additional features of the services which gave them a special quality. The first was the sensitivity which can be seen from the accounts where project workers were able to discern the different levels of individual need among a group of clients whom a casual observer of the service might have regarded as a homogeneous user group. Moreover, having identified these layers of needs, workers attempted to tailor services which took account of that variability.

With the drop-in group the idea is that they do not have to commit themselves to coming every week and they can come when they feel like it. It is much more a social group and that works much better. We had a core of people who were needing that but, within the group, there were people wanting to work on something specific, so we separated out the needs basically. (AMWEL)

The second qualitative aspect to the services is a realisation and acceptance of the fact that whatever hopes may have been held in some quarters about community care giving rise to self-help and independence (Wilson, 1988) there were a number of individuals for whom continued support was an ongoing requirement. This continuing support, however, presented some projects with potential tensions in their relationships with referring organisations and funders. These tensions were, none the less, resolved in favour of the needs of the existing client groups.

> All the members of the Buc-Up club are volunteers of the bureau but, having said that, they do not have to do any voluntary work if they do not wish to (or feel unable). There are a few people who will only ever come to the Buc-Up club and never actually get around to doing anything other than that — and that is also fine. (Buc-Up club)

> For people with mental health problems, it is not always a case of feeling better, it is a case of needing long-term support. So we needed to find a way which was not putting pressure on people and saying, 'You are not getting any better and we need to get new people in this group so that we can tell our funders that we are doing a good job'. (AMWEL)

> The initial idea was to go out into an area and set up a mental health resource in that area and help it to become self-sufficient and move on to another area. However, after 2 years of Oasis being established, it became apparent this was not possible. The nature of mental health is such that groups will always have a high level of vulnerability. Care must be taken not to pass too much responsibility to key activists to the detriment of their own mental health, or to the detriment of the group. Such a group needs a group worker attached to it. (Oasis)

Client choice

'You cannot resource choice'. This was a remark made by a senior social work official in conversation at a conference relating to community care. What that worker very much had in mind at the time were the financial implications which would be involved in attempting to tailor services to the varieties and levels of need within the community (Issues, 1988; Biggs, 1988). That was a management view of choice. For the clients, however, the choice of support within the community has a very personal and direct meaning, and concerns the quality of their lives.

Assuming that the clients have been fortunate enough to be given the opportunity to accept or reject an offer of support from a community-based project, that opportunity in itself can give rise to a number of personal apprehensions on the part of the clients, more especially perhaps, if these same clients are already experiencing a degree of vulnerability in their lives.

The thought of entering into a new situation, whether that be a one-to-one relationship such as the buddies system, or, as a member of a group at a centre, confronts the individual with personal questions, reservations and doubts. 'Will I be able to do or to manage whatever is expected of me in the new relationship or the new situation'? 'Will I be accepted and fit in with the other members of the Centre or project'? 'Will I be able to exercise some degree of personal control over both myself and the situation which I am about to consider entering'? 'Will the move help me in my situation or make it worse'? 'In what ways might it improve my situation'? 'What do I want from this move'? 'How realistic are my hopes and/or expectations about meeting my needs as a result of entering into this new relationship, or, joining the project'? 'How justified are my fears and anxieties about the move, or, the decision I am being asked to make'?

These are but a few of the possible sets of questions which any individual capable of making a conscious decision might reasonably consider when attempting to arrive at a choice which could have direct impact on their sense of personal well-being. Choice, therefore, not only offers opportunities for altering the person's situation, but, making the choice, taking the decision and following that decision through into action is not always easy. This difficulty of making choices was perhaps heightened further for those clients who were directly approached by the project or who were referred to the project by a third party. These clients required specialist assistance and support in making up their minds on whether or not to take up any offer of support of a place within a project.

To make an informed choice requires that the client or the carer has information. Not just factual information which may be contained on a factsheet or a booklet on the project (Bamford, 1989), but, affective information which takes account of how the client feels about the situation based, in part, on her experience of her contacts with the project's representatives; her initial experience of the project itself; and the state of the client's emotions at the time. Choices are very rarely made on purely rational ground. Rather choice involves an element of subjectivity. Individuals do not simply calculate their decisions when making important choices, they anticipate and feel the implications of that choice for themselves. The person's anticipated hopes and fears regarding the consequences of any choice are as 'real' to the individual as any factual information which they may have on the matter. The worker, therefore, needs to recognise and respect these emotions and feelings in the client in order to help the client arrive at a decision which will overcome these concerns. Several projects consequently went about the business of attempting to alleviate any initial fear and anxiety among new clients by providing clients with opportunities to talk through their concerns and also to help clients arrive at a realistic understanding of likely benefits which may come from their association with the project.

> Many of the women were unable to join a group situation immediately, due to the lack of confidence or the nature of their illness. These women were visited in their homes in liaising with the referring agency, by the worker at the time, or by a volunteer from the project who discussed with the women the ideas behind Oasis and how she could possibly benefit from it. Arrangements would then be made for another member of the Oasis group to accompany her to the centre. In some other cases, however, long-term support in the home was necessary.(Oasis)

> They are invited to come and see the premises, meet with myself as the project worker, and have coffee with one or two other potential members. In this way, we felt able to dispel as many of the external barriers to attendance as possible. Everyone would have met the two workers who were organising and running the course and they would have met at least one person intending to join the course as well having

found their way to and become familiar with the centre. (Out-of-the-house course)

On that first visit we usually offer an invitation to visit the day centre. If someone refuses to accept, we cannot force them. However, we may go back at some later date and try to encourage them to visit the day centre, although that is not always possible. (Dementia project)

In each of these comments the worker is demonstrating sensitivity to the client's uncertainty and reservations and was allowing space in which the client could make the choice with which she felt most comfortable.

On other occasions, however, a decision may have already been taken on behalf of the client. None the less, the projects would still typically seek to obtain the agreement of the individual client to any previous arrangement entered into or contemplated on the client's behalf.

David knows what we are talking about but he does the ostrich on us . . . he cannot possibly fully appreciate what it is we are attempting to do. What we are trying to do is almost ease David and the others into the situation of independence long before they require to be there. It is trying to pre-empt the trauma; by being around to support the transitions. (Integration Trust)

Mostly residents come here because somebody else has recognised that they needed to come here. The individual would come and see the house and would have the ultimate choice to come in or not. Once people were in we would try to impress on them that the choice to stay is theirs. Everyone has a front door key and can virtually walk out of the door and not come back. (Ark housing)

This last statement illustrates an important point about having made a choice, namely that the decision on the part of the client to enter into a relationship with the project did not mark the end of their ability to continue to exercise choice in the situation (Eaton, 1988). The respect given by the projects to the dignity of the individual and the client's right to be self-determining featured throughout the period of contact.

The process of matching up a buddy with a client and the nature of the buddy in relationship is very much determined by the needs and wishes of the client. Once the people are matched, 'buddying' goes on for as long as the person wants it to continue. (SAM)

If somebody wants to leave, that has to be their choice, not ours. Even if we feel that somebody was not ready to move but was saying 'I want to move', we would check all that out and help with the actual move itself; obviously in co-operation with the social work department or whoever. Three of those we moved on actually identified that they wanted to move on. They wanted to be more independent. Some because they reached a stage where they did not like living with another nine people. (Ark housing)

Benefits

It is very easy when considering the term benefits to fall into the trap of viewing benefits in financial, material or even numerical terms. It was a fact that the clients benefited financially from having a service which either was free or provided at cost by the project. However, it was equally the case that the community also benefited from the existence within the community of such provision. There were the financial benefits derived from the fact that clients were either being taken out of hospital care, therefore saving a cost against the health service, or were retained within the community when otherwise they might be candidates for residential provision.

> Many of the elderly attending Braid House day centre would be acceptable candidates for residential care and old people's homes or something similar if there were adequate places available for them.(Braid House)

Equally as important as these financial or material considerations for both the projects and for their clients were the social and psychological benefits which arose out of the client's involvement with the project's services. For the carers, the services offered an important break from the routine and the burden of caring for a relative however much loved. The social and psychological space created by the service allowed carers to attend to personal or household matters in the knowledge that the relative was in safe-keeping, which was important for the carers' own sense of well-being and equilibrium.

> The carers are delighted with the service offered. They enjoy having a day's break from caring and they can relax to do things of their own interest knowing that their relative is in safe hands. Often carers have no contact with home-helps, support groups, day hospitals etc and we may be the only service that they receive. Carers feel that they can talk to us about problems, or ask us where to go for help if they are not coping with their home circumstances. Many of them feel that this support is invaluable. (Dementia project)

For the clients themselves, the social and psychological benefits which arose out of their contact and involvement with the projects were also significant.

> David's real interest in life is people and he gets great happiness and joy from going out and meeting people. Institutionalisation just finishes him and to envisage institutionalisation as an inevitable future for David is not only not appealing but is totally unacceptable . . . what happens when the care network finishes? Given David's handicaps, and others like him, the immediate response from the system would be to put him in an institution because he needs feeding, etc. However, that would move David from the community that he knows and would place him somewhere he is a stranger. I feel very strongly that people like David, Jean and Dorothy belong in the community. When I take David out, he knows more people that I do. In fact, his social network is huge compared to mine. We should be working to retain that for David, Dorothy, Jean and others like them.(Integration Trust)
>
> When I visited old people in their homes, many people were not aware of the facilities that are available from the social services. They were not aware of the social security benefits they are entitled to and they were not getting these. So I asked them at the department of social security and they were very kind. They send us an officer every

Thursday to give us welfare benefits advice. We have a retired teacher
who acts as an interpreter on these days because many of our clients only
speak Gujarati, they do not understand English, especially the ladies.
We also have some local doctors visit the day centre to talk to the elderly
in their own language. Gujarati doctors will sometimes come, Punjabi
doctors will sometimes come and sometimes Bengali doctors come and
talk about illnesses that effect the elderly and how to prevent these.
(Ghandi Hall day centre)

Compared with the hospital I think we are offering a lot. I have
visited the hospital where these people are sitting looking at each other
and that is not something which happens here. These people are given a
lot of attention on a one-to-one basis, taken out for walks and taken out
into the community. I would say that we are enhancing their quality of
life 100% by attending the adult day centre. (Adult epilepsy project)

Others, such as the frail elderly who were housebound, or the younger,
isolated women experiencing some form of emotional stress, were given
support and opportunities to make contacts with other people in a secure
environment. The effects of their vulnerability were acknowledged and
responded to in a manner which, while sympathetic, did not leave the
individuals stranded in their condition, but rather attempted to strengthen
and harness those resources within the person which would enable them to
relate to themselves and to other people in more liberating ways. That was
true even where the benefit to the clients was initially confined to offering
support which would help them on their return into the community.

Members in crisis situations are visited by fellow members. An immediate
response by Oasis on return from hospital, together with understanding
of the problem of home management and family relationships, is
recognised by group members as an effective way of sustaining recovery.
(Oasis)

For other client groups, the benefits from the support lay in helping clients
to retain or hold on to their sense of who and what they were and their place
within the community.

Although there is no cure, you can perhaps slow down the progression
of the illness. If people are isolated and do not take part in any social
activity, they not only get depressed and lonely, but, their memories
will go even faster. Coming here not only keeps them happy in terms
of socialisation, but the activities also jog their memories. (Dementia
project)

There are other day centres, but black people feel more free with
this centre and the activities we provide. They can come in here and
shout and nobody will arrest them because of the old stereotypes that
black people are aggressive, they talk loud and they play music loud.
They can actually do that here and don't feel that someone is watching
them. Language and culture and ideas can be expressed — they feel
safer here. (Handsworth Community Care Centre)

For yet a number of other clients, the benefits derived from involvement
with the project were less a matter of 'holding on', than of moving on,
moving on to new ways of being, acting and thinking.

About 30% of the people who come now are from the original group, though by now we have gone through the process of building up their own self-esteem or they are taking on a more supportive role with other members. They have done this by telling their story so that any new Oasis members can learn what can be achieved within the group, before finally leaving and moving on. (Oasis)

When you think back to how the person appeared on the first day they walked through the door and then look at the improvements that have occured in the person you see the benefits that have taken place. We have one lady who started in the Buc-Up club and who has now gone on to employment training in a job situation — it is really wonderful to see people do that. They come in lacking in confidence and go out at the end feeling more confident. (Buc-Up club)

However, not all clients had to disengage themselves from a project in order to experience a degree of self-actualisation. With at least one project that element of self-actualisation on the part of the clients was a central objective. In a situation where a number of aspects of people's conditions were outwith their control, the project offered the clients support in seeking to influence the response made by others to their situation in ways which more closely met with the clients' own concerns and wishes.

It is important that people know there is someone there offering a helping relationship which is under their (clients') control. But it is a very special relationship where people know that they are calling the shots. Part of the training on information handling is concerned with how volunteers can assist their clients to gain skills in planning and putting questions about their condition and treatment to doctors and other health care professionals. (SAM)

Clients' attempts to understand more fully their situation and to shape the community's response to that situation represent not just self-actualising behaviour, but, through their activity, a means of regaining or retaining self-esteem and social worth.

Whilst all of the above benefits were extremely important to the clients' favourable perceptions of themselves as individuals, there remains a final important ingredient of the relationship which clients had with a number of the projects — that was the sense of involvement and fun. These benefits, as much as any of the others, gave the projects their very human quality and spirit.

Our aim is to stimulate, to get people going, to make them feel uplifted, to come out for the day perhaps feeling down, but to return home on the bus in a fit of laughter since they have had such a good day and enjoyed the care and companionship which we offer. (Braid House)

They had a great time this summer, we went all over, as far as Dunoon, to Portobello, the Safari Park, North Berwick, the fire station, the bus station, we went swimming, to the airport — we had them all over and we had a fantastic time. The volunteers enjoyed it as much as the weans did. (SSMH youth club)

Conclusions

Blau suggests that a service organisation is one where officially the main beneficiary of the service is the client or user group with whom, and on whom, its members work is the chief concern. Explicit in that suggestion is the view that the needs and the interests of the clients and not those of the organisation, take centre stage in the deliberations and the decisions made by the organisation with respect to any services offered. Unfortunately, the real situation is that not every service organisation holds equally to these aims or objectives with respect to the clients. The professional statutory services of social work, health and education provide instances where service organisations have displaced client needs in favour of professional or organisational enhancement and survival. Staying true to a concern with the interests and the welfare of clients is not an automatic response, but is hemmed in by other sets of organisational concerns, only incidentally linked with client welfare. These service organisations, therefore, were impressive in the emphasis placed on the needs of the clients and the ways in which the resources of the projects were used to meet those needs. Hard decisions, whether regarding the selection of clients or the numbers served by the individual projects were made in a manner which showed respect for the dignity of the applicant as well as the integrity of the services to the existing users. Clients were not sold short or made to 'come last'. The thought and the attention given to the nature of the service provision and the subsequent benefits which were provided to the users as a result of such planning and commitment are clearly reflected in the various accounts. Moreover, what these accounts illustrate is that the promotion and the sustainment of clients' self-esteem are matters which have to be fought for, with, and on behalf of, certain groups of people who have traditionally been marginalised within our society. Sadly perhaps, part of that fight for the retention and the promotion of services such as those detailed in the accounts may involve categories of workers and agencies who, sharing a common interest for a particular client group, appear to adopt a different, narrower understanding of what constitutes care within the community. A number of these projects were faced with referees and funding bodies who held competing and possibly conflicting sets of understandings and expectations of the work undertaken on behalf of certain groups of clients. One can already discern from a number of comments made by staff that the aims and objectives set by the projects for the clients may be displaced at some not too distant future date by the influence of the indirect users of the projects' services. But, to influence any shift in emphasis away from the needs of the clients to some other set of interests, most likely coming from the direction of the projects' funding bodies, would be detrimental for both the clients and for the community.

26 Funding and resources

All but one (MACHEM) of the 21 projects had originally been set up as, or subsequently developed into, a direct service provision which catered for particular client groups, one characteristic of that spread of clientele being the number of individual users who had or were experiencing difficulties with either their physical or mental health. Although the projects, themselves, did not set out to treat medical health problems, they nevertheless took these aspects of the clients' situations very much into account when it came to planning the services and selecting the clients to the projects. MACHEM, the single project which did not provide a direct service to clients, was, however, involved in supporting projects and staff who were engaged in direct service delivery and also lobbied on behalf of such service provision with the local health authorities.

Each of the projects featured in the accounts can be grouped according to whether or not there is an identifiable health dimension to its service provision. By doing so, we obtain the breakdown shown in Table 26.1.

Table 26.1

Health focus			
Physical health & physical disability[a]	Mental health or disability[b]	Physical and mental health or disability[c]	Non-health focus[d]

[a]Hatch, 1980; [b]Fenwick, 1988; [c]Brown, 1975; [d]Bessel, 1989.

This connection between the projects and the factors of either physical or mental health or disability mirrors the information obtained earlier on the named sources of referral to the various projects. Health sector workers were the largest single group of referees, accounting for almost half (45.16%) of the total of those listed as the indirect users of the projects' services. However, when these findings are set alongside information on those bodies who contribute the main source of funding to the various projects, a different picture emerges.

Four broad categories of main support funding to the projects can be identified from the accounts. These are health, social services, joint funding and a general 'other' category. The health category refers to those projects which obtained their main source of funding directly from, and as the result of, an application to the relevant health authority or health board. Similarly, the category of social services relates to those projects which obtained funds, again following on from a direct grant-support application, from the social services, or, in the case of the Scottish projects, from the respective social work departments. Joint funding was typically provided by both health and social services/social work, albeit not necessarily in equal proportions, to fund particular projects where both these bodies recognised a shared interest and assumed a common responsibility to provide a degree of financial support. The final 'other' category refers to those projects where the main source of funding came via Trust funds, charitable organisation, government agencies (other than health or social services/social work), local businesses, individual philanthropy, local fund-raising events and, or, typically some combination of these sources.

Table 26.2 shows that, whilst the health sector staff constitutes the most frequently mentioned source of client referral to the various projects (45.16%), the position of the health authorities as the main source of funding to the projects was in the reverse direction.

Table 26.2

Main named sources of referral[a]		Main sources of project funding	
Health	45.16%	Health	19.04%
Self	27.4%	Social services	28.5%
Social work	20.96%	Joint funding	19.4%
Other	6.45%	Other	33.3%

[a]Some projects named more than one source of referral.

Furthermore, even if one takes account of any funding contribution made by the various health authorities under the category of joint funding to projects, the position of the health category, relative to that of the other principal funding sources, remains unaffected. For example, if one made the assumption that the health share of any joint funding arrangement was in the order of 50% of the joint funding total, given the figure of 19.04% for projects which were joint funded, health authorities would then be credited with 9.52% or half that total figure. However, in adopting such a stance one would also have to credit the remaining half portion, again 9.52%, to the other principal partner in the joint funding arrangement, namely the social services/social work. If this half portion (9.52%) for the joint funding contribution was then added to the figures for both health and social services respectively, an overall increase in the level of support funding to projects by these two bodies is obtained. However, even with the recognition and addition of that involvement, the health category continues to come at the bottom of the league of funders in the case of these projects as a whole (Table 26.3).

Table 26.3

Main sources of project funding		
Combined social services funding	38%	(28.5% + 9.52% Joint funding)
'Other'	33.3%	
Combined health funding	28.56%	(19.04% + 9.52% Joint funding)

Social work features as the single main funder to the projects with approximately 38% of the projects benefiting from that financial support, but only just ahead of those projects (33.3%) which were funded primarily through voluntary rather than statutory sources. However, all but one of these 'other' category projects had previously made unsuccessful attempts to either social services or to local health authorities for main support funding of their respective projects.

Only one project, the garden project, preferred to generate its own funds and took a conscious decision to avoid making approaches to any statutory body for financial assistance. However, the garden project, along with a number of other projects detailed in the accounts, benefited from cash-in-kind services from other government and non-government agencies, that cash-in-kind support representing a hidden or indirect source of funding to each project.

Funding difficulties

Funding, or rather the problems associated with obtaining funding, stood out as the single most recurrent set of concerns expressed by staff from the various projects. Although not every project worker shared the same degree of concern, there were four sets of funding issues identified by the various projects. Some of these difficulties had occurred early on in the life of a particular project and had been resolved only to be replaced with other funding issues as the projects developed or became more established within the community.

The first funding difficulty identified by staff from several projects was that of attracting, or perhaps more pointedly, extracting financial support from a source which had been targeted as a legitimate potential sponsor for the projects' activities. A legitimate sponsor was the relevant government agency, health board or national voluntary body which had a particular responsibility for the kinds of people served by the projects as well as a general responsibility for the promotion of health or social welfare within the community

> We did manage to get something from the health board — £1000. I kicked up such a fuss about having no staffing in the children's centre and at one stage we thought we were going to have to withdraw the service completely simply because the staff we had could not cope with any more and the health board gave us £1000 towards the salary of an additional worker. (Epilepsy project)
> We have no financial support from the health board or social work department for either of the day centres. That is not to say we will not be asking for it, but, at the moment we have no input into that at all. We actually approached the social work department in our funding application 2 years ago and said this is a need that had been identified and that we were prepared and able to go ahead and provide a service and would they like to give us additional funding to do this? They said 'no' at that time. (Dementia day centre)
> The capital funding and the revenue funding were two different aspects. Help the Aged were prepared to help us with fund-raising, on condition that we identified revenue funding for us to continue.

> We could, through the Rural Development Commission, get 3 years' revenue funding or a proportion of revenue funding. After that, it would cease. So we had to have a commitment from the social services department, and that was the hardest thing. On the capital side, we had to raise something like £40,000. We were lucky in that we got some of it from the Rural Development Commission and the rest Help the Aged managed to get through two or three major trusts. In fact, we had all the capital funding identified by January/February 1990. But still no commitment from the local health authority. This went on and on and on. In fact, by about July 1990 we really thought that the project would have to be shelved. (Mobile day centre)

However, there was also a sense in which projects appeared to be required not simply to make the case for funding for a service but actually to mount the provision and demonstrate the need for the service before financial backing from statutory bodies was forthcoming. Even then, extracting funding from certain quarters was not necessarily a simple matter. Moreover, difficulties did not cease with the initial offer to support the project or even the actual acquisition of support funding since there was no guarantee that such funding would continue on into the future. In the case of several projects, the difficulties of obtaining continued funding were further complicated by the fact that their respective main funding bodies were themselves experiencing financial problems with their own budgets (Bessel, 1989).

> I do not think there will be a problem getting funding for next year (1991). I think the problem will come the year after. The health board have no money. (AMWEL)
> The joint funding which we received was from the three health authorities and the social services. However, once the initial offer of funding was agreed there was a cash problem with joint finance which meant that all bids that had previously been granted and were continuing had to be reviewed. The joint finance committee cycle started in September 1989. They met MACHEM and the lay members and all of us had to do a lot of work and lobbying from September 1989 right up to January 1990 when a final decision was made as to which projects had succeeded in being given the grant. (MACHEM)

A second set of issues concerning funding was the sense in which projects felt constrained by the terms upon which the funding was made available (Meller, 1985; Wicks, 1987; Hatch, 1980). The principal difficulties were the 'strings' or the restrictions which particular types of funding placed on the project's ability to recruit certain kinds of staff. This was particularly the case with funding obtained through the unemployed voluntary action fund (UVAF). Although this source of funding has a number of very positive features, there is a requirement that any project supported by UVAF will be staffed largely with volunteers. However, in the case of those projects which experienced difficulty in recruiting sufficient volunteers to staff the project, the terms under which UVAF funding was given placed restrictions on the project's ability to compensate for any shortfall in volunteers by the use of a paid workforce.

The funding we received was given on the premise that we would use volunteer staff. No one was prepared to actually pay staff, they will pay the organiser's salary and an administrator's part-time salary, but no one wants to pay for day care staff. (Dementia day centre)

Funding came from the unemployed voluntary action fund. Wherever our funding has come from influences how the project is worked and because that was the first place to offer funding for the project, the use of volunteers had to be emphasized. (Oasis)

A third difficulty arose out of the now common practice of a project going for a package of funding: that is funding which is made up from contributions from different sources. This particular problem was not peculiar to the projects detailed in the accounts (Brown, 1975). However, the fact that problems associated with funding packages are not uncommon does not negate the difficulties which such funding arrangements can create. One difficulty was that the joint funding arrangements were not always sufficient for the project's financial requirements.

More money is needed, that is the bottom line. We never get our full budget of course from the health board and social work joint funding and we are always trying to raise funds elsewhere. (Dementia project)

The funding for the volunteer bureau, however, is always very difficult — that is a sore point. It gets more difficult as time goes by. We managed to get a donation from joint funding which is health and social services and that covers about one-third of our running costs. We have to fund-raise in order to raise the other two-thirds we require, and that involves writing to local businesses, to industry, writing to charitable Trusts and applying to various agencies for grants. That is a constant thing that we have to do in order to survive. (The Buc-Up club)

Another problem arising out of any joint funding set of arrangements can be that of attempting to balance the sometimes competing sets of interests held by the different parties to the funding package (Lgiu, 1990).

One of the issues which was around, and still continues to be around, is the whole nature of joint work involving, in this case, the three different bureaucracies of the health board, education department and social work. Each has its own financial arrangements and its own way of managing its budgets and somehow our management committee has to marry these together. There is also the issue of just dealing with these different bureaucracies in an administrative way as well as dealing with their different expectations and priorities. (Out-of-the-house course)

Every year we have to satisfy the different criteria and different interests of the joint funding bodies. You are assessed as to where the money has gone and this is possibly where the numbers game comes in. For instance, in the case of clients who are referred to us for the sitting service and the dial-a-ride scheme, I have to keep a record of where that client came from, whether it be a social worker, or a health visitor referral, and at the end of the year submit the numbers and try to ensure that both the health and social services are getting their fair share. (The Buc-Up club)

Though not specifically identified by any of the projects detailed in the accounts, the potential for conflicting and not simply competing expectations and priorities being held by the different parties to any joint funding arrangements are self-evident. Moreover, to the extent that there is any serious divergence between the interests of the funders on the one hand and the aims of the project on the other, the influence exerted by the funding bodies could have the effect of displacing the project's own goals and services to their clients in favour of the interests of the funders (Bamford, 1989; Leat, Testa & Unell, 1986).

> For example, sometimes it seems that there is less emphasis placed on preventing people in the community from having to go through the whole mental health spiral. Sometimes it seems that the health board would prefer us to work with people they consider to be sick. Social work services too have their expectations of us and somehow we have got to balance all these different expectations of the different agencies. (Out-of-the-house project)
>
> There is also a possible difference of viewpoint about how the service should be offered. One suggestion is that we should look at our clientele and say, 'Right, you have been coming for a long time. We have provided you with this service and we think now it is time you stopped coming along and make room for someone coming in'. I do not agree with that view at all, that is the model that some day centres use. But when you put the old people out and do not provide an on-going support, very quickly there will be a deterioration. (Braid House)

Six projects referred to the fact that there were potential tensions between themselves and their main funding body concerning the nature, volume and the throughput of users of the projects' services. The fact that six projects independently raised the matter as a potential issue would appear to suggest that their concerns had some substance. The statutory bodies were generally viewed by these projects as wishing to record more clients being given access to the services provided. However, this did not imply any additional financial support to enable projects to extend their service provision, but rather appeared simply a concern to make what little there was available, go further. Moreover, to the extent that some projects may at some future date enter into a contractual relationship with their main funding body, the latter's ability to influence the volume and throughput of clients is likely to increase rather than decrease.

In addition, such contractual arrangements could also be expected to affect the way in which the project conducts its relationships with both its direct as well as its indirect users (Fenwick, 1988).

> There is talk about our being contracted out by social work. In terms of the actual service which we offer our day centre users, I do not think there would be any change in policy. However, it would mean that the management committee would need to start looking at what we are doing in a more businesslike manner if we were to be contracted out by social work. (Braid House)
>
> I know that we are hitting a recession and that it is a very bad time to get grants. But we are determined, as are the workers, to search for more funding. We have had offers from the health authority to do specific tasks with them and they are willing to offer us contracts. However,

we feel that they need to write out clearly the contract specifications of what they require from us. So I feel that contracts will be one of the areas that we will get into in the future. But we need the health authority to declare that we, as a project, can also be pro-active. We would also have to consider the knock-on effects of any contracting work that we might undertake on behalf of the health authorities with respect to our level of joint finance funding. If we were to attract funding through contracting, this could have an affect on the money given to the project to cover the workers' salaries. This is a problem at the moment with every grant-funding body. The minute they realise that the project is generating income, because they are all short of money, they claw back. (MACHEM)

The fourth and final set of difficulties emerging from the accounts relates to the limits imposed by the duration of the project's funding (Whiteley, 1989). For those projects who are unable to generate their entire funding (the majority), the continuity of funding to the project was an on-going concern. Short-term funding created the obvious drawbacks to the projects' ability to plan ahead for the services and also sapped at the workers' sense of job security within the projects (Brotchie, 1989). Moreover, that latter aspect itself contributed to the turnover rate for staff who sought a more stable, if not a more permanent, work situation (Butcher, 1986).

We were on a yearly basis. That meant that jobs were not certain from one year to the next. (Supported accommodation project)

We had one-off small grants like slippage grants from social services, which run out this year. So we have lost one member of staff who was paid out of those funds. (Handsworth Community Care Centre)

However, the conditions set by somewhat longer-term funding can also give rise to sets of problems for any project. The movement into a three-year cycle of funding may not be without its own peculiar shortcomings.

Today the Oasis project has changed significantly in that it is now mainstream funded through joint funding for a 3-year period, which is great in that we know the project is secure and we can plan ahead. However, we are locked into what we are required to do on the basis of last year's grant, which means there is no room for further growth. (Oasis)

If a project's entry into a 3-year cycle of funding could give rise to certain dilemmas, these dilemmas were replaced by other difficulties when the project reached the end of that three year funding period. When a project reached the end of its period of funding, the continuity of the work became uncertain. The uncertainty surrounding the project's future was not necessarily related to the quality of the work undertaken by the project, or to any significant reduction or change in the level of need for the services provided through the project to the local community. The key factors were often political and financial.

In terms of costs, we are looking at a gross care budget of about £88,000 of which figure the youngsters, with their severe disability premium plus their independent living fund money are providing somewhere around 50% of the running costs. However, the question of 'Who is going to pick up the tab to keep the project running?' is a problem. If the community care thing had gone through as it was supposed to do in 1991, when it was imagined that all sorts of money would go to the social services, the situation may have been clearer, but it did not happen that way. I now doubt if this is going to happen in 1993 — who knows? (Integration Trust)

We have already been warned that the hospital endowment funding was for 3 years. This is the third year and we do not know whether that will be forthcoming. We can only see our prospects in terms of funding, and, I suppose, our funding in terms of how relevant our role is seen to be. If it can be said that there is somebody else doing the job which is not costing them anything, we will probably be on sticky ground. (AMWEL)

That last remark was one which echoed comments made by staff from other projects where there was also a sense of being in competition with other agencies. However, what was of interest here was the fact that these 'competitors' did not necessarily exist yet. Rather, it was the spectre of such a development which gave rise to the concern. Moreover, the fears expressed were not with respect to any possible duplication of work or of projects chasing after the same few clients. Every project except MACHEM, the buddy network and the garden project had waiting lists for their services. Indeed the companion service had a waiting list of a hundred. The spectre of competition then, for a few projects, was related to the access to what are regarded as the limited funds obtainable from statutory bodies which could ensure the continuity of the project. Such concerns, if based on fact, would appear to indicate serious shortcomings in the Government's own funding arrangements with respect to the financing of community care.

If statutory bodies are, themselves, unable to provide the respite and support services required for the kinds of people served by these projects and are, for whatever reason, unable or unwilling to financially support projects which are prepared and competent to provide such services, then the future of some clients would appear to be made potentially worse by the encouragement of any move towards care in the community (Killeen, 1989).

While private commercial enterprise initiatives may respond by providing domiciliary care or residential care, there remain gaps in those services required by people whose needs are not commercially marketable and will therefore fail to attract a commercial response. Moreover, if community care is to respond seriously to the needs and well-being of groups of individuals who have traditionally been overlooked, then reliance on either commercial interests or private philanthropy, especially during periods of economic recession, are not a secure base on which to found such services.

Cash-in-kind

Cash-in-kind resources are those amenities or services which stand in the place of money which are given freely to the projects, or given in exchange for certain reciprocal services provided to the community, or, to the trading partners in the relationship. These resources are resources which the projects themselves would otherwise have had to purchase and therefore, constitute a saving to the projects. Three main types of cash-in-kind resources or services were mentioned by workers from at least 13 of the 21 projects. These resources were — accommodation, staff and transport.

Accommodation was provided either free, or, at a peppercorn rent from several sources, the local authority, from a development corporation or from a religious or community group to 'house' 11 (52.4%) of the projects. The acquisition of these facilities represented a considerable saving to these projects who, without such resources, would have found their continued existence difficult if not impossible.

> Funding is still the most important factor. In some ways we have been quite fortunate to have been given the space for the project in this building, so that has helped us. Also having a reasonable rent, security and everything that goes with the premises has also been helpful. (MACHEM)
> In addition to these funds for staff and running costs the health authority for Central Manchester — which is now a trust, also contributed in direct ways by giving us the use of a room at the centre to accommodate the project at a minimum cost and also provide some support. (Afro-Caribbean mental health project)

Moreover, in several instances, the properties acquired had been specially renovated, adapted or decorated for the project's use. The cost of such alterations and improvements again being borne by departments of the local authorities rather than by the projects themselves.

> I was asked by Livingston Development Corporation if we would like these premises which was a five-apartment house. I went and had a look and said 'yes please'. Livingston Development Corporation did a lot of alterations to the property before we moved in including small structural changes to the kitchen and cupboards and to doors. (SSMH youth club)
> I telephoned the District Council and asked if they had anything at all that might be suitable for use as a day centre that we might lease from them. I must say the District Council were superb. They said that there was a little bit of money if any redecoration was needed. I telephoned and said we could do with a bit of gloss paint and when I went back again, they had actually redecorated completely with woodchip paper and paint. (Dementia day centre)
> This building is owned by the Indian Religious Pastoral Trust. Until now, the Pastoral Trust have said that as we are under the umbrella of the Indian Association we did not have to pay any rent. (Ghandi Hall day centre)

Even though projects which made use of such accommodation were very grateful to the assistance provided through the housing department of the different local authorities or provided by local religious bodies or community groups, in several instances, the nature of the accommodation placed restrictions on the use which might be made of the properties.

> We need to move because there is no privacy. We have only got the big hall and two small rooms. Since 1983 the project has expanded. What it started as originally was a drop-in centre, but we have outgrown that and

have become more of a day social service. We plan, when we move, to open in the evenings and some weekends. This is what the clients have actually asked for. At the evenings and bank holidays that is the time when they feel lonely and bored. We are not allowed to open at these times at the church. (Handsworth Community Care Centre)

It is unfortunate that we cannot accept people with severe physical disabilities. As you can see the dining/activities room is quite small and we could not fit a wheelchair in there. That is also the problem with the toilets. (Dementia day centre)

Even where structural alterations were possible, the absence of sufficient personal funds to make improvements and/or the inability to enlist financial assistance from other bodies to carry out such work, again meant that the needs of particular client groups could not be met within the project.

We have been based here now for 8 years although even these premises are not entirely suitable. The fire regulations put a limit on the number of members which we can take and we are already at that maximum number. There are also problems about wheelchair access. We just cannot get them in. We do not have a ramp, although we are trying to have one built. However, the social work department is unable to help with the cost of that because they say that is not within their remit. You see, these premises are not a private house, but a club, and social work funding only covers private dwellings. (SSMH youth club)

Apart from any structural limitations imposed by the nature of the properties which prevented or severely restricted access to wheelchair users, several projects had reached the legal limits to the numbers which could be accommodated with safety within their respective premises. All of these projects had waiting lists for their services and this, in turn, gave rise to concern on the part of a number of project staff.

We have reached our maximum intake and have a waiting list. It is very sad when you cannot offer a person a place until another person goes into long-term care. Although we can refer people to other day centres, most of these are also fairly full. (Braid House)

We would like to grow to meet new demand, but it is very difficult to get funding. There is a need for more flats and we gauge that by the number of applications we receive. (Supported accommodation project)

Though accommodation in a number of projects represented an important cash-in-kind funding resource, for other projects, the nature of that provision typically had failed to continue to match the levels of demand which the community were making on th e projects. Often a victim of their own success in identifying and responding to the needs of client groups in the community and, unable to generate funding to purchase their own premises, the projects were thrown back on to the local authorities for larger or more suitable accommodation. However, the likelihood of such requests being met were constrained by the finances available to the local authorities themselves.

Staff

The amount of funding and the conditions surrounding its use were such as to place quite severe limitations on the ability of several projects to establish the paid full-time or part-time posts for the number of workers actually required to make the project viable. To compensate for any deficiency in paid staff, a general expectation held by some funders was that volunteers would undertake much of the work of any particular project. Such expectations regarding the availability and quantity of volunteers to staff projects to the required levels, however, were not met. In several instances, an alternative source of labour supply was needed. In the case of the garden project, the two dementia day centres and the epilepsy project, the shortfall in the number of volunteers and paid staff required to cope with the volume of work generated by each project was compensated for by the use of employment trainees. These employment trainees represented the first cash-in-kind input to several projects. These employment trainees, referred to the projects by the training agency, had their monies paid through the Department of Employment for any work undertaken by them on the project and therefore constituted an obvious and important indirect source of project funding. The use of employment trainees by the projects, however, also represented a reciprocal four-way exchange. The training agency obtained placements which offered high standards of supervised training for their trainees; the employment trainees were able to choose and to pursue the type of training experience which most closely met their own training requirements; the projects gained from the acquisition of additional staff to the project; and the Government and community as a whole benefited from the new sets of skills and work experiences of the trainees which might increase the trainees' future paid employment prospects and thereby reduce the financial burden on the state.

The second area in which staff represented a hidden source of income to the projects were those occasions where the services of professional staff from other agencies were recruited for project activities. In those projects where a specialised staff training programme was considered necessary for establishing and maintaining appropriate standards of client care, the ability to have such training programmes designed, mounted and provided free by agencies related to the projects represented an important form of indirect financing. The charges for such training, which might otherwise have had to be found by the project itself were absorbed by the external training body. The training programmes provided by the health personnel to the dementia projects, the companion service and by social services to the Handsworth Community Care Centre were illustrative of this type of cash-in-kind support. Again, however, this was a reciprocal arrangement. The ability of the projects to provide respite care and support to clients and carers in the community helped reduce the impact of demands for support and respite services on formal statutory agencies.

A third area where staff could be regarded as a cash-in-kind contribution to the project has more recently emerged. The significance of this type of contribution lies in the fact that whereas previously, staff borrowed or obtained from another public body would have been viewed as a supplementary resource to the project. The contribution of staff could now come to replace concrete funding hitherto received by the projects from certain agencies.

> The Health Board have continued to fund their side though there are rumours around that the Regional Health Board's financial straits might mean that future contributions will be limited to staffing rather than staffing and finance. At the moment the community psychiatric nurse works with us which is in addition to health board funding. (Oasis)
>
> The health board have no money, they are not putting any money into the project though they are hoping to work co-operatively. I think they are hoping, for instance, that hospital staff will do sessions at the project so that won't cost them money. (AMWEL)

Obviously, there are limits to which staff can be exchanged in this manner. The nature of the project and the types of work being undertaken can place constraints on the transferability of skills and expertise from one area to another. The hours and times at which the service operates could also be seen as posing potential barriers to any automatic attempts to switch from concrete payment of funds to the provision of seconded staff to the projects.

Transport

Transport in which to convey clients to and from the projects was provided to at least five projects and this again represented hidden additional financial benefits to these projects, saving them the need to find funding to meet these particular transport costs. Three of the projects had been given a new or secondhand bus which the projects augmented by transport services made available through a separate agency.

> The actual arranging of transport has nothing to do with ourselves. The people from Gogarburn Hospital come by minibus, others come to the centre via social work transport and other users come by public transport. (Epilepsy group)

However, the problem of a project's dependence on transport from any external source was highlighted when the continuance of the facility appeared to have come under review.

> We are now bringing people from Central, North and South Manchester, Stretford, Trafford, Stockport, and Gatley, because there are no other Indian Day Centres for old people — so they are coming from all those areas. The three minibuses are all community transport. They gave us the use of the minibuses free, but we pay for the drivers. However, one organisation has told us that, because of the number of clients applying to them for the use of the transport, they have had to cancel our use of their minibus from this July. (Ghandi Hall)
>
> We also have access to two buses from the social work department for the clubs so that there are three buses in all coming here. Two social work drivers drive the social work buses and social work covers the hiring cost of their buses. However, there is a possibility that we may be going to lose some of the social work transport which we get every week. We

were told that we might be cut back to having transport for the club from social work once a fortnight instead of every week as happens at the moment. (SSMH youth club)

Clearly, if there were to be a reduction of that magnitude in the transport provision to these projects, the social, leisure and recreation services made available through the clubs to the mentally handicapped and to the Indian elderly in the areas would be greatly depleted. Moreover, any such depletion would have occurred in areas where social, alternative leisure and recreational facilities for mentally handicapped people and Indian elderly were largely absent. As the organiser for the youth clubs for the mentally handicapped remarked,

Without the clubs, the kids would be sitting at home watching TV.

Other funding

Over and above these primary sources of direct and indirect funding, a number of projects also sought to attract funding by a variety of other means (Leat, 1986). These attempts, however, met with varying degrees of success. The most commonly used methods were enlisting financial support from philanthropic individuals, commercial companies and charitable trusts, and of course a variety of small local fund-raising events. Only two projects — The community garden project and the Parkinson branch project — relied exclusively on these sources of finance. The ability of both projects to do so was greatly affected by the nature of the service provided and the fact that neither employed paid staff. For a number of other projects, the funds attracted by such fund-raising activities were never viewed as a realistic alternative method of funding the projects' activities.

Our only source of funding comes from social work other than a few small donations from fund-raising activities. We have a Christmas fair for fund-raising and 'shake the can' in the summer as well as selling the crafts we make at the centre at the local galas. (Epilepsy project)

We also have a charitable financial element to our funding but that is peripheral. It provides a little jam on our workday bread. (Braid House)

Conclusion

A major concern challenging any organisation is that of generating or attracting funds in sufficient quantities as will enable an organisation to meet its financial obligations with respect to wages for staff, and the purchase of resources required to mount and deliver any service provision or products (Troup, 1989). For 15 of the 21 projects, funding assumed a prominent position in the sets of issues which each project had to resolve. Projects differed in terms of the levels of funding required to guarantee the delivery of the services, and also in terms of the types of difficulties connected with either attracting or retaining that funding.

Four distinct funding difficulties were evident from the accounts. These were:

- getting the initial funding;
- coping with the strings or conditions associated with any funding arrangements;
- balancing competing and possibly conflicting sets of interests and priorities between joint funders to the project, or between those agencies and the project itself;
- the time limits attached to any funding provision.

These problems associated with project funding, though not new to service organisations operating in the voluntary sector, may none the less be critical for those voluntary groups attempting to break new ground and become established as a resource or service to people in the community. Moreover, for those projects with only one or two workers, the time devoted to pursuing such funding distracts and detracts from the actual service delivery which is also limited by constraints of time.

Cash-in-kind benefits to some projects, including accommodation, staff and transport, were obviously important sets of hidden income to the projects. Apparent from the accounts of such benefits is the general sense of goodwill and support from particular sectors of the broader professional community. That goodwill, in some instances, was forthcoming, in part, because of the reciprocal direct or indirect benefits which were provided through the projects to its partners in the exchange relationship, as, for example, in the case of employment trainees. However, these exchanges rarely implied that the projects then had extra financial resources to devote to other areas of the projects' work. On the contrary, the existence of such cash-in-kind inputs indicated the projects' inability to provide these services directly for themselves through their own financial budget. Any taken for granted reliance on cash-in-kind benefits to the projects was itself conditional on the continuing generosity and support of these other agencies. Changes in the circumstances of the latter could result in a curtailment of the resources provided which had, for each project, become an important part of the foundation on which the services were established.

V Conclusion

27 The organisation and its environment

When we considered the staffing and funding arrangements of the projects and the clients for whom the services were offered, it was all too clear that none of the projects, as organisations, were socially isolated. They were not insulated from influences and contacts with the wider community within which they were located. However, no project or organisation relates to every facet of its social and physical environment, only those aspects of the environment which are significant for its own functioning and maintenance needs. Of particular importance in this respect are those organisations, groups and individuals who supply the projects with resources, or who constitute the project's consumers or client groups. In the case of these projects, a number of points of contact and relationships were prominent. The user groups were of particular significance, since the ethos and *raison d'être* of the projects were derived from perceived needs and expectations of the users themselves. In addition, key workers in the projects were often involved in establishing working relationships with professional staff in related agencies, including other voluntary agencies and units set up by central and local government agencies as part of the network of services for the users concerned. Many of the projects also had formal dealings with government departments or bodies, often in connection with funding arrangements, entailing the maintenance of effective working relationships with a range of officials. Finally, in each case, the social, political and economic dimensions of the environment in which these projects operated coloured all of these relationships in some way or other.

The projects catered for a range of clients and, as we have suggested, benefited as a consequence both direct users of services and those carers on whom the users might otherwise depend. The labels which might attach to the users involved in these projects, including physical and mental handicap, physical and mental illness, educational disadvantage, learning and emotional difficulties, are convenient, but incomplete ways of characterising the services on offer and the needs which they seek to address. It is important not to allow these labels to obscure our understanding of the individual characteristics of those who seek support within the community. Indeed, the agencies and workers associated with the projects described revealed very clearly their sensitivity to the varied, personal and sometimes unique needs and aspirations of users, as well as emphasising the projects' commitment to meeting these needs.

It is, perhaps, worth noting that, in some instances, the projects we have reviewed sought to involve family and community members concerned in their care of users. In some cases, users' families are invited to participate in discussions about plans for the projects themselves and for their own family members. Much of the ethos of community care, as is revealed in these accounts, entails committed staff and volunteers trying to secure an improved quality of life for users of their services. They are then sometimes faced with conflicts of interest and loyalty — even if these may not be immediately apparent or dealt with. The rights of users to privacy and confidentiality sometimes lies uneasily along side the expectations of family and community carers with whom project staff want to cooperate and collaborate. The principles which inform practice at this particular interface may not be clearly understood or articulated. None the less, tensions may emerge — and this may be particularly true in projects whose initiation and continuation embodied self-help by carers and users, but will also be revealed in the work of agencies dependent on paid and volunteer staff.

The emergence of training and enterprise councils and other government-sponsored enterprise bodies each charged with establishing their own, local priorities, has posed particular problems for some agencies traditionally linked with community initiatives. The Handsworth project, like others, has experienced the effects of charges of this kind in the way training for the unemployed is managed. There seems to be an inexorable shift from care work to more commercial areas including retail, administrative and tourist occupations in some areas.

Inter-agency relationships

Central to implementation of policy on community care is the development and management of a network of relationships. Users, carers, health, social work and social service staff responsible for assessing needs and preparing care 'packages', and staff in agencies responsible for the delivery of services, have to be able to collaborate effectively. However, the ethos of collaboration and co-operation in which, as one agency worker argued, they were not 'vying with each other' may be harder to sustain within a climate tinged by a competitive edge of market economics. The strength of interagency relationships, and interprofessional collaboration which the projects seek to promote, may well have an important role to play in preserving welfare in the market place.

The experiences of community care which we have incorporated reveal a number of ways in which interagency relationships were sustained. Some of the projects found it helpful when key agencies, like social service and social work departments, identified specific liaison workers with whom the project staff could relate directly. Arrangements of this kind can help to establish close links between agencies and, as a consequence, promote better understanding. However, in some cases, key workers in the projects were having to relate to local authority and health staff at a local level and also negotiate with senior management. Wide disparities in the statuses of those with whom project staff had to maintain links could, so easily, engender unease and distrust. Furthermore, project staff sometimes were having to maintain relationships with a number of different outlets of the same agency, particularly different offices of the local authority departments. The maintenance of effective working relationships can, as a consequence, be time-consuming. None the less, identified points of contact can be more productive and constructive than haphazard arrangements which might otherwise occur.

A number of projects established liaison meetings of varying degrees of formality. As one of the project accounts indicates, a liaison meeting allows workers to meet to 'discuss what is best for each . . .'. As a consequence 'we have a constant contact with professionals'. A number of projects also have formalised liaison arrangements as a result of representation on management committees and the like. While, on the one hand, representation of this kind allows local authorities and government agencies to monitor the work being undertaken and, as a consequence, provides one of the strands of accountability which goes with financial support, on the other hand, they can be the arena in which more effective interagency relationships can be developed.

Given that workers in local authority and central government agencies are often involved in seeking services which are provided by the projects described here, the individual contact between project staff and specific professionals involved in the care of users, may be quite variable. Social workers may slip away after a client has been introduced to a unit or, medical staff may be unwilling or unable to go outside catchment areas. Follow-up in circumstances of this kind may depend more on the initiative of project staff than the spontaneous efforts of those in the statutory agencies. However, in some instances, local authority and health board staff may be required to make a formal commitment to contribute to the package of care being prepared. The supported accommodation project, in its well-established use of client contracts, seeks to ensure that agency staff are both clear about the requirements which are placed on them and the obligations which ensue.

In some cases, special relationships are established between projects and particular agencies or workers. As one project worker noted, the local children's hospital had given them a lot of support, as had doctors from the local health centre who were prepared to assist if a serious health problem occurred. It also appeared that the community development worker had done particularly good work for the three projects in the Livingston area, helping to address a variety of difficulties including repairs to premises, publicity work and general support. Indeed, a worker in one of the projects concerned noted that 'never once, since we opened in 1987, have we asked a professional to come who has refused us'. This reflects an experience of another project worker who noted that 'people are very willing to co-operate if you are prepared to ask them'. However, as another project worker noted, 'in supporting and making referrals to OASIS, professionals are placing trust in professionally untrained people to enhance their input, not undermine it. . .'.

We have also seen how the initiative taken by one organisation can act as a catalyst for new partnerships amongst voluntary agencies and between voluntary agencies and the statutory services. The introduction of the mobile day centre in Leominster has begun to bring together services for rural communities in innovative and effective ways. Of course, collaboration of that kind comes out of effort and time. It owes itself to some willingness to risk and a commitment to review and clarify boundaries; an examination of the expertise of agencies leading to productive partnership or co-operation.

Maybe the economics of the market do not have to diminish goodwill amongst voluntary agencies.

As we have suggested earlier, the relationship between voluntary agencies, including the projects which have been described here, and the public bodies which fund, in part or whole, some of the work being undertaken, can be tense. Considerable uncertainty surrounds the work of many of the projects since commitments to their funding may be subject to annual renewal. Apart from the implications such funding arrangements have for forward planning, the dependency which comes from financial accountability can be used both constructively and destructively. It can be destructive in diverting development energies of workers into inordinate concern with negotiating and obtaining a more secure financial base. Alternatively, since developments undertaken by voluntary agency projects can break new ground, they can become a feather in the cap of the supporting central or local government agencies. It is possible for imaginative project workers to harness the drive for innovation and achievement while, at the same time, demonstrating a commitment to value for money which inescapably features in this sphere of community care. As one worker noted, projects need to become more 'businesslike' but without sacrificing the very characteristics of voluntary initiatives which form their strengths.

The environment for progress

It would be absurd for us to ignore the potential for conflict in ideology between many of the projects and their workers — whose commitment to a more collectivist view of social service provision enshrines much of the ethos of the welfare state in the UK — and government commitment to the development of a market economy of some kind in community care. In this respect, we could identify alternative strands to the development of individual care; one strand which we choose to call the individual and the other strand individualism (Table 27.1).

Table 27.1

Individual	Individualism
Self-help	Self-advancement
Self-worth	Material worth

As the projects we have described so readily demonstrate, it is possible to conceive of service development which enhances the self-help elements characteristic of the development foreseen by the Government, whilst maintaining a commitment to the worth of individuals. Contrast that with the individualism which derives from a more materialistic view of personal worth where achievement is a goal, even at the expense of others. It would be too easy to see success solely in relation to the acquisition of material resources.

Self-help embodies much which reflects a sense of collective worth. It expresses both the worth of others and of self. Collective action through shared concern, sometimes set against the indifference or fear of the wider community, serves as a reaffirmation of the value of human experience and the intrinsic worth of people. This it does irrespective of disablement or weakness; regardless, in fact, because of the pain and distress people encounter.

By recognising and reaffirming the rights of individual users/clients, and championing their cause, self-help groups can enhance the self-esteem of themselves. Furthermore, through their collective and mutually supportive actions, they confirm the entitlement of all members of society, themselves included, to general acceptance and recognition.

In providing services which seek to enhance self-esteem, and by recognising the significance of participation in social life within communities, self-help projects underline the community dimension of community care. Moreover, by calling on the resources and assistance of other bodies, including professional groups, government agencies and local authorities, the truly collective nature of the wide community's responsibility and relationship with disadvantaged groups is demonstrated and endorsed.

Conversely, self-help when viewed against the values which underpin the economic and commercial world, particularly over the last decade, can too easily be translated into self-advancement. Helping yourself in the pursuit of economic advantage, acquiring the rewards, resources and advantages of society, regardless of the welfare or well-being of others in the community.

A too ready and mechanical application of commercial models can have far-reaching effects. Quantity and efficiency, a distancing of the work force and users, could so easily influence the ethos and work of social service agencies, at the expense of concern and recognition of the user.

It would be naive to suggest that materialism and greed were the preserve of one political party or political system. Capitalist and socialist societies have each given rise to a preoccupation with materialism. The worst excesses of individualism could so easily become a scramble for a share of resources, accentuating the competitive dimension which already exists as voluntary and self-help groups lobby and plead for resources to survive, let alone expand, in their communities.

If the Government is about choice, then let us as a society and as communities not simply share out the care, but take up actively our share of that caring; providing the resources that projects such as those highlighted in the accounts here require to sustain real care in the community.

We are all too well aware that the physical environment of the world is under threat, and has been for some considerable time. The threat emerges, in part, from the actions and values of industrial and commercial enterprise. While the present generation seek to make good the more obvious scars of past industrial development — landscaping in order to disguise industrial dereliction — the continuing pursuit of economic and industrial achievement leaves exposed to pollution new areas of the natural environment. Would it not also be true that our current culture, in relation to moral and ethical values, is being debased, corrupted and threatened through similar processes. Much of the strength of the voluntary effort, which is described in this work, derives from attempts by individuals and groups in society to retain and promote more liberal and humane values, thereby keeping faith with a view about the intrinsic worth of people. That, after all, is what civilization ought to be about; recognising the worth of people. That is demonstrated in the commitment, ingenuity and concern which these projects encapsulate — serving the marginalised by looking at them as complete beings. Responding to them in ways which put their needs first, rather than serving the maintenance of the institutions through which services are offered. Society cannot afford to sacrifice those values which these developments reflect. Would it be too alarmist to suggest that the voluntary sector may be the last refuge for values of this kind? Having said that, perhaps some projects would prefer to run down with their integrity intact rather than survive with funding arrangements, efficiency targets and productivity figures which compromise the values on which they were originally built.

There is, then, an inevitable double-edged accountability which has to exist between funded voluntary agencies and government agencies. While it is appropriate for projects to be held accountable for any monies they receive, it is also imperative that funding agencies, whether they be local or central government, are in turn held accountable to the users, carers and society as a whole for the promotion and provision of the services they require and deserve.

The experiences of the people involved in the projects we studied have led us to identify some suggestions which may be helpful to other workers and people considering new developments in community care. The collection of suggestions is not exhaustive, nor does it provide answers to all the questions you may have. However, it may help you in the formulation of plans and the implementation of new community care initiatives.

Setting out

Any new enterprise depends, to some extent, on the character of the people involved. This would suggest that an assessment of the individuals concerned ought to lie at the heart of initial planning. Ask yourself and others with whom you seek to collaborate, the following questions.

- Are you in good health?
- Can you cope with stress and hard work?
- What is the nature of your experience of the running of a project/activity of this kind?
- Do you have experience of managing/organising?
- How will the undertaking affect other significant people in your life, and are they supportive?

Assessing the idea

The ideas which you might have for any new development ought to be given as full an appraisal as time and resources allow. It may not always be possible to assess your idea accurately, but you ought to be as rigorous as circumstances allow.

Demand

First, try to ascertain the extent to which there is a demand for the service you envisage. You may have to set some limits on your appraisal. For example, how wide a geographical area could be covered and how much otherwise unrecognised demand will emerge once knowledge of your project becomes widely available.

Feasibility

Secondly, assuming there is demand, you should try to gauge the extent to which your early plans match the nature of the demand. Some adjustments may have to be made to tailor the project activities more closely to the requirements of users, carers and other services with whom you may become allied.

Advice

Thirdly, you should secure advice from other, well-informed people. The introduction of a competitive edge which the air of community care generates for some projects can, so easily, lead to an environment in which there is mistrust and secrecy; agencies seeing themselves in competition with others for funding and support. None the less, by being secretive, you may find yourself denied the support, advice and collaboration which is there for you to tap into. In reality, you're more likely to get helpful advice from others in your field, than find your ideas stolen or your plans blocked.

Planning

Your resources for planning may be very scarce. Indeed, the time required is very likely to be voluntary effort, free time or time 'stolen' from other work commitments. However, assuming that you have a particular service in mind, it is probably wise to set targets related to the number of people to be served, likely levels of volunteer recruitment, and financial outlays which are demonstrably manageable. Grand schemes are likely to test the credulity of funding agencies, better to go for the achievable than for the unachievable — whatever the ideas might be.

An integral part of planning is research. Searching for, and evaluating, premises, for example, has to be done thoroughly. The facilities of the local area, including transport, car parking, planning and fire regulations, and the like should all be checked out against the type of client envisaged.

Most significant is the research into the population to be served, including users and carers. You may have to research questions such as:

- Where is the existing user population?
- How many potential users are already identifiable?
- Is demand likely to increase or decrease due to population changes, housing development or other factors?
- How much of the service cost is likely to be met by users?
- Are other facilities available which cater for the needs identified?
- In what respect is your provision necessary?

Management and staffing

Projects which rely entirely on volunteer effort have particular problems to overcome; not least because a ready supply of volunteers one year may not be there the next. Population shifts, changes in the pattern of employment locally, the attractions of other volunteer outlets, can all affect the size and character of the volunteer pool. A service which is dependent on a small group of volunteers may also be vulnerable to sickness, personal crises and interpersonal tensions. Even the most committed enthusiasts can become tired and drained.

Appropriate selection, training and support for staff is, of course, essential. Projects which are able to support paid staff can enjoy special benefits, including professional or administrative expertise. Unfortunately, funding secured from outside bodies may be rendered vulnerable by changes in policy of central and local government agencies. We found a number of projects which had been able to utilise funding connected with youth training and employment training initiatives. However, these have been areas of government policy where several changes have occurred in the recent past, with priorities, terms of reference and funding arrangements being changed. These have led to some agencies having to re-appraise their services and, in some cases, curtail them entirely.

Costing

Any new care initiative will cost money. It is important that a realistic costing is made of the plans prepared, thereby avoiding the difficulties which come from underfunding. There are many elements of a costing exercise and we have identified some of them here.

- Accommodation costs
- Gas, electricity and other service costs
- Personal and property insurance
- Furniture and equipment
- Telephone — installation and charges
- Travel expenses of paid/volunteer staff
- Salary, national insurance and allied expenditure
- Transport of clients

Planning and review

Assuming that a new project is successfully launched and funded and given the particular emphasis on the evaluation and monitoring which is an integral part of community care strategies and linked with the role of local authorities, it is important to maintain a process of continuous review. In a sense, there needs to be a planning cycle in which aims and objectives and service plans are given careful and honest re-appraisal. It may well be that the process itself has a number of phases, including the following.

- An idea is conceived.
- The idea is assessed in relation to demand, feasibility and advice.
- A service plan is prepared.

- The skills and resources, including people, required are identified and assessed.
- An organisational context is developed in depth.
- The funding, staffing, training and programming of the project is completed.
- Service is monitored and evaluated — users, carers and workers are fully involved.
- Existing plans are reviewed and amended as required.

Like any enterprise, community care services operated by voluntary agencies do not enjoy a natural right to continue. Services which are not responsive to change are placing themselves in danger of becoming redundant. However, projects which are alive and incorporate a continuing commitment to self-evaluation and review will be in a much stronger position to respond to changes in demand, heightened expectations of service quality and new sources of funding and outlets for development. Of course, cost and the quantity of service provided must not be the only criteria against which community care initiatives are judged. A commitment to quality and the embodiment of a sense of purpose which is about collaboration, the empowerment of users and carers and a commitment to the worth of individuals will always be the yardstick against which services of this kind can be judged. It is all too painfully evident from the experiences described here, that many of the groups in society for whom these service developments have occurred, are disadvantaged groups. They are often disadvantaged by the very nature of their personal circumstances or by their physical or mental health. In addition, many suffer from the network of discrimination which is all too common in this society. As the project accounts indicate, personal difficulties of users can be compounded by discrimination in relation to age, gender, disability, ethnic origin, class and sexual orientation. There is a continuing thread throughout the project accounts of workers' and users' efforts to confront prejudice, stereotyping and ignorance. We hope that this work goes some way towards addressing these issues too.

Bibliography

Chapter 1

Beardshaw, V. and Towell, D. (1990) *Assessment and Case Management Implications for the Implementation of 'Caring for People'*.

DHSS (1989) *Caring for People: Community Care in the Next Decade and Beyond*, HMSO.

Finch, J. (1989) *Family Obligations and Social Change*, Polity Press.

Griffiths, Sir R. (1988) *Community Care: An Agenda for Action*, HMSO.

Pancoast, D.L. and Collins, A.H. (1976) *Natural Helping Networks*, Sage.

Twigg, J., Atkin, K. and Perring, C. (1990) *Carers and Services: A Review of Research*, HMSO.

Chapter 17

Phillips, A. (1988) *Charitable Status*, Interchange Books.

Chapter 24

Bamford, T. (1982) *Managing Social Work*, p. 20, London: Tavistock Publications.

Bell, L. (1989a) 'Putting the System in Place', *Insight for Managers in the Community*, p. 17 (30 Aug.).

Bell, L. (1989b) 'Planning the Right Route', *Insight for Managers in the Community*, p. 25 (16 Aug.).

Bennet, R. (1981) *Managing Personnel and Performance: An Alternative Approach*, p. 8, Business Books.

Blau, P.N. and Scott, R.W. (1963) *Formal Organisations*, p. 51, Routledge Kegan & Paul.

Brech, E.F.C. (1983) *The Principles and Practice of Management*, 3rd edn., p. 574, Longman.

Cowling, A.G. and Mailer, C.J.B. (1981) *Managing Human Resources*, p. 8, London: Edward Arnold Publishers Ltd.

Davies, H. and Kinlock, H. (1991) 'Improving Social Work Practice Teaching: Steps Towards the Goal', *Social Work Education*, 10 (2) pp. 24–25.

Glastonbury, B., Bradley, R. and Orme, J. (1987) *Managing People in the Personal Social Services*, pp. 91–96, John Wiley & Sons.

Graham, H.T. (1987) *Human Resources Management*, 5th edn., p. 124, M & E Handbooks.

Jordan, W. (1987) *Rethinking Welfare*, p. 205, Basil Blackwell Ltd.

Litterer, J.A. (1967) *The Analysis of Organisations*, pp. 26–29, John Wiley & Sons.

McGregor, D. (1987) *The Human Side of Enterprise*, p. 55, The Penguin Business Library.

March, J.G. and Simon, H.A. (1967) *Organisations*, pp. 83–93, John Wiley & Sons.

March, J.G. and Simon, H.A. (1967) *Organisations*, p. 90, John Wiley & Sons.

March, J.G. and Simon, H.A. (1967) *Organisations*, p. 97, John Wiley & Sons.

Moore, S. (1977) *Working for Free*, p. 35, London: Pan.

Plumbley, P. (1989) *Recruitment and Selection*, p. 8, Institute of Personnel Management.

Ross, S. and Bilson, A. (1989) *Social Work Management and Practice System Principles*, pp. 79–80, London: Jessica Kingsley.

Rubenstein, A.A. and Haberstroh, J. (1960) *Some Theories of Organisation*, The Dorcey Press, Inc.

Scottish Standing Conference of Voluntary Youth Organisations (1991) *Half a Million*, p. 15, Edinburgh: SSCVYO.

Selznick, P. (1949) *T.V.A. and the Grass Roots*, p. 74, Barcley: University of California Press.

Sills, P. (1989) 'A Need for Progress on Training', *Insight for Managers in the Community*, p. 11 (16 Aug.).

Silverman, D. (1970) *The Theory of Organisations*, pp. 81–84, Heinemann Educational Books Ltd.

Wall, A. (1988) 'Good for Whose Health?' *Insight for Managers in the Community*, p. 16 (22 Apr.).

Chapter 25

Baldock, P. (1933) 'Community Development and Community Care', *Community Development Journal*, **18** (3), p. 231.

Bamford, T. (1989) 'Where will the Specialists Go?' *Insight for Managers in the Community*, p. 22 (7 Feb.).

Banks. P. (1988) 'Cutting the Cloth to Suit the Client', *Social Work Today*, p. 14 (19 May).

Biggs, S. (1988) 'Quality of Care and the Growth of Private Welfare for Old People', *Critical Social Policy*, p. 78.

Challis, D. and Davies, B. (1986) *Case Management in Community Care*, p. 5, Gower Publishing Co. Ltd.

Eaton, L. (1988) 'A Taste of Life in the Community', *Social Work Today*, p. 7 (10 Nov.).

Ellice-Williams, R. (1988) 'Community Care: The Invisible Vanguard', *Social Work Today*, p. 21 (9 June).

Findlay, J. (1989) *The Changing Direction of Community Work*, p. 16, Clydeside Network.

Human Resource Potential Project (1973) *Voluntary Help Organisers Training Course*, p. 9, University of Surrey.

Issues (1988) 'Positive Choice — A Key to Good Residential Care', *Insight for Managers in the Community*, p. 8 (22 Apr.).

Jordan, W. (1987) *Rethinking Welfare*, p. 68, Basil Blackwell Ltd.

Jowell, T. and Ritchie, J. (1988) 'Listening to Their Needs', *Social Work Today*, p. 18 (26 May).

Moore, S. *Working for Free*, p. 18, London: Pan.

Richardson, K. (1988) 'Building a Community Network of Care', *Social Work Today*, p. 14 (17 Nov.).

Robertson, A. and Osborne, A. (1985) *Planning to Care*, p. 9, Aldershot: Gower.

Shaw, M. and Player, J. (1990) 'Care in the Community', *Concept*, 1 (1), pp. 6–8 (Autumn), Moral House Publication.

Wilson, J. (1988) 'When to Let Go', *Community Care*, p. 34 (26 May).

Chapter 26

Bamford, T. (1989) 'Where will the Specialists Go?' *Insight for Managers in the Community*, p. 22 (7 Feb.).

Bessel, R. (1989) 'Reading Between the Lines', *Insight for Managers in the Community*, (16 Aug.).

Brotchie, J. (1989) 'Demonstrating Needs', *Community Care*, p. 18 (2 Mar.).

Brown, R.G.S. (1975) *The Management of Welfare*, p. 128, Fontana Public Administration.

Butcher, H. (1986) 'The Community Practice Approach to Local Public Service Provision — An Analysis of Recent Developments', *Community Development Journal*, 21 (2), p. 107.

Fenwick, J. (1988) 'Mental Handicap: Evaluating Respite Care;, *Social Work Today*, p. 12, (9 Nov.).

Hatch, S. (1980) *Outside the State*, p. 130, London: Croom Helm.

Killeen, J. (1989) 'Caring for People with Dementia', *Inter-change* No. 38, p. 5 (Dec.), Glasgow Council for Voluntary Service.

Leat, D., Testa, S. and Unell, J. (1986) *A Price Worth Paying?*, p. 8, Policy Studies Institute (PSI).

Lgiu — Special Briefing (1990) *Caring for People — the Government's Plans for Care in the Community*, p. 5, Local Government Information Unit Special Briefing No. 32 (Jan.).

Meller, H.W. (1985) *The Role of Voluntary Organisations and Social Welfare*, p. 138, London: Croom Helm.

Troup, G. (1989) 'Under Pressure', *Annual Report*, p. 2, Edinburgh Council for the Single Homeless.

Wall, A. 'Good for Whose Health?' *Insight for Managers in the Community*, p. 16 (22 Apr.).

Whiteley, P. (1989) 'Concern Over Allowances', *Insight*, p. 11 (13 Sept.).

Wicks, M. (1987) *A Future for All*, p. 224, Penguin Books.

Appendix 1 Making connections: list of contacts

The Garden Project

Felix Lynch   New Trinity Centre, 7A Loaning Road,
Edinburgh EH7 6JE (Telephone: 031 661 1212)

Youth Club, Livingston

Jean Hain   Scottish Society for the Mentally
Handicapped, Livingston Branch, 16 Larchbank,
Livingston EH54 6ED (Telephone: Livingston
39209)

Oasis

Be Morris   Edinburgh Association for Mental Health,
40 Shandwick Place, Edinburgh EH2 4RT
(Telephone: 031 225 8508)

Out-of-the-House Project

Lami Mulvey   Craigentinny Health Project, Craigentinny
Community Centre, Loaning Road, Edinburgh
(Telephone: 031 659 6044)

Livingston and District Epilepsy Group

Jane Aitken   The Adult Centre, 118 Kennilworth Rise,
Dedridge, Livingston EH54 6JL (Telephone:
Livingston 418183)

The Dementia Day Centres

Trish Combe   31 Guthrie Street, Edinburgh, EH1 1JG
(Telephone: 031 225 1829)

Braid House Day Centre

Sheila Laughlan   Labrador Avenue, Howden, Livingston
                             EH54 6BU (Telephone: Livingston 30615)

Scottish Aids Monitor

Administration (Telephone: 031 557 3885)

Ark Housing

Marion Malcolm   Ark Housing Project, Market Street,
                             Musselburgh

Supported Accommodation Project

Fiona Meikle   Edinburgh Association for Mental Health,
                             Shandwick Place, Edinburgh.

AMWEL (Association for Mental Welfare)

Joy Harris   AMWEL, Association for Mental Welfare, 14
                             Church Street, East Lothian

Council for Mosques

Mr Akhtar   Elderly Day Centre, 126 Ryan Street, Bradford 5

Ghandi Hall

Dr B C Das   Indian Association, Ghandi Hall, Elderly
                             Day Centre, Brunswick Road, Withington,
                             Manchester M20 9QD

Buc-Up Club

Rosemary Raine-Howe   Newton Aycliffe Volunteer Bureau, 4 Beveridge
                      Walkway, Newton Aycliffe, Co Durham,
                      DL5 4DP

Afro-Caribbean Mental Health Project

Reeya Lal   c/o Moss Side Health Centre, Monton Street,
                             Moss Side, Manchester, M14 4GP

Integration Trust

                             How Cans, Front Street, Esh, Co. Durham,
                             DH7 9QS.

Handsworth Community Care

Angela Powell   Handsworth Community Care, c/o Methodist
                              Church, Villa Road, Handsworth, Birmingham

Leominster Mobile Day Centre

Magda Praill   Age Concern, Community Centre, School Road,
Geraldine Duncan   Leominster, Herefordshire HR6 8NJ

Appendix 2   The 6 Ks questionnaire for workers in community care initiatives

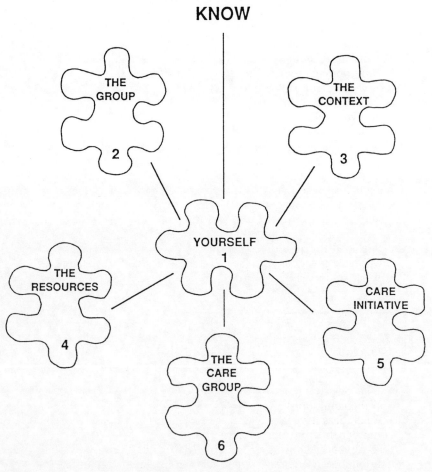

KNOW

THE
GROUP
2

THE
CONTEXT
3

YOURSELF
1

THE
RESOURCES
4

CARE
INITIATIVE
5

THE
CARE
GROUP
6

Figure A3.1   The 6Ks questionnaire for workers in community care initiatives

We refrain from prescribing but suggest an alternative. Before committing yourself to a community care initiative, and during the process of development, ask yourself these questions. They have all been derived from the accounts in the earlier part of the book and from the comments and advice offered us by others associated with the development of community care initiatives. We believe that they will help you to appraise your work as you progress through the stages of development.

Know yourself

○ What is your own motivation/reason(s) for wishing to become involved with care project/initiative?
○ How do you cope with *working with adults* — male and female?
○ What views have you got of the targeted client group's *capacities* and future?
○ What is your view on the *concept of 'community care'*? Is it compatible with working with a local or interested group towards developing a community care service?
○ Have you an *opportunistic approach to life*?
○ How have you shown this so far?
○ Can you spare the *time*?
○ Are you willing to give many hours a week to the group in the early period of the project's development and later at times of crisis?
○ Would you feel comfortable as a *catalyst* within a group *or* are you more comfortable as an *enabler*?
○ What special skills would you bring to the initiative/project? e.g. people skills, practical know-how, expertise, management/organisational skills, fund-raising skills, etc.
○ Do you know *when to quit*? What might lead you to leave the group?
○ *Team support* — if already employed by a statutory or voluntary body.
○ Is your team/colleague(s) ready to allow you the time and resources you will need for a commitment to community care development?
○ What resources does your department/agency offer?

Know the group

○ What ideas have you got for *identifying* the need for particular service in the community?
○ What ideas have you got for *contacting* the individuals who would receive and benefit from the service?
○ Have you had any *approaches* from individuals or groups which indicate an interest in the development of a community care initiative?
○ How *experienced* is the group in functioning as a group?

- Socially?
- As a committee?
- As decision-makers?
- As administrators?
- As deliverers of care services?

○ What *training needs* would the members have as they move towards providing the service or care?

- Skills for producing the service or the caring?
- Skills for selecting an organiser?
- Skills for monitoring the service delivery?
- Skills for and understanding of funding arrangements, budgeting, and financial accountability?

○ How would you seek to enable the group to acquire these skills?
○ Is the *pace of development* too fast, just right, or too slow for the group?
○ In the light of this assessment, what do you plan to do?

Involvement

○ How many people regularly participate in the process of the development of the care initiative or the actual delivery of the service? In what capacities? Does this need thinking about?
○ What have you done to involve women, ethnic groups, clients, carers and in what capacities?
○ What are the constraints on volunteers, employment trainees, other staff in terms of time, family commitments, social obligations and personal needs, etc.
○ Does the service provided place limits on what are acceptable demands on staff, e.g. age, physical strength, health, etc.
○ How heavy are the burdens placed on a few activists?
○ How do you plan to widen volunteer group membership?
○ How do you plan to *sustain* group commitment?

- In the early stages?
- During the development of care initiative?
- Once the service has begun?

○ How would you respond to the emotional and physical demands which may be placed on the project's workers (volunteers, employment trainees, paid staff)?
○ Is the group *dependent* on you? For what?
○ What steps are you taking to handle this dependency?
○ How is individual or group staff support on the project provided? Informally or formally? By yourself or someone else?
○ Has the project outgrown the group in terms of the sets of skills, developments, management, demand? How can that be resolved?
○ What attention is given to the needs, values, development of individual workers on the project (volunteers, trainees, paid staff)?

Know the context

○ Does the context know you, either personally or professionally?
○ What is the *image* of social work/community work/education/health services in your locality?
○ What is expected of these agencies and their staff?
○ What is expected of you?
○ What do you know about the local community in terms of:
  • the *population structure*: its age and sex composition?
  • the *local culture* and the pattern of interaction among the local people?
  • the *range of social problems* and issues facing the local community and its capacity to respond to these sets of problems. What was the past/present experience of other local volunteers, activists, professional agencies in responding to local needs?
  • the *significance of community care* as an issue for the local community in the context of its other sets of interests. How would you find out?
  • the social and work related *skills and expertise* of the local residents
  • the local *care opportunities*, trends and developments. Do you know how to go about finding out?
  • the *local authority interests and policies* with respect to education, housing, unemployment, mental illness, physical handicap, mental handicap, frail elderly etc?

○ What, for example, is your knowledge of the interest and policies of the social work, community education, housing and planning department for your local authority? What do you know of the interests and policies of the local health boards?
○ The broader *economic and social factors* operating in the area in terms of employment/unemployment, changes in delivery of health services, housing, etc?
○ What do you know of the interests or policies of large voluntary organisations with respect to developing initiatives in community care?
○ Have you carried out a *social needs audit* for your area? What does it reveal?
○ If you already have a group with a community care project in mind, can the skills, expertise and knowledge required be found in the local area or would they have to be found outwith the community? Where could these be found and how long would the project be dependent on such input?

Know the resources

Networking

○ Which local *councillors* are interested in community care initiatives? Do you know them?

○ Have you relevant contacts in the *social work, community education, housing* and *planning* departments or *health officials*?

○ What are their opinions of community care initiatives and the nature of your group's involvement?

○ Do you know the main *interest* groups?:

  • the *professional* groups? health, social work, education, etc.
  • the other providers of leisure and training?

○ *What contacts have you with social workers, health workers, community workers and with the schools?* What form of partnerships could be established?

○ How might you work with other voluntary agencies and groups? For example, national and local voluntary councils and organisations.

○ Have you any contacts with *local employers*?

○ Are they interested in helping you? What help would you seek to enlist?

○ What *political* interests in your area would affect the community care initiative you have in mind?

○ What are the *community's knowledge* and expectations of the community care initiative?

○ What plans have you got for dealing with any problems in these areas?

Funding

○ What do you know about sources of *funding*?

○ What do you know about the shortcomings of different sources of funding?

○ Who or what will you *consult* to extend your knowledge?

○ Have you contingency plans if funding runs short?

○ If you are considering 'contracting' what are the implications for the clients, carers, paid and voluntary staff, numbers, throughput, quality, standards and approaches to the work?

Know about community care initatives

○ Have you kept an eye out for *local opportunities* — gaps in services, provision or amenities?

○ What do you know about *types* of community care initiatives? For example, private — commercial care; not-for-profit organisations; community businesses care initiatives; self help initiatives; joint-funded care initiatives?

   • If not much, how will you find out?

○ What have you done to generate *interest* in developing community care initiatives?

○ What sorts of *activities* do you envisage as useful starting points? Why?

○ What factors determine that number? — accommodation, volunteers, staff, equipment, transport, running costs.

○ What *premises* are required and how can they be obtained?

   • Are they suitable?
   • What prospects are there if you have to move on?

○ What training requirements are essential for providing appropriate standard of quality care?

○ What *agencies* in your area act as support units for local care initiatives?

○ How do you expect to use them for the group?

○ How will you define '*success*' for the project or care initiative?

○ How far does this match the expectations of the group?

○ How will you address the question of obtaining a match?

○ What size of group do you intend to service?

○ What is *your familiarity* with management responsibilities and techniques?

○ In what ways do you intend to extend your knowledge?

○ What will be *your role* when the delivery of the service or the project begins?

○ What will be your role:

   • with regard to the project director/organiser?
   • with regard to the management committee?
   • with regard to the project staff?

○ What *monitoring system* are you planning to establish? How will it operate?

○ How do you intend to deal with any excessive demands on the projects services? — waiting lists, rationing attendance or receipt of the service(s) on offer.

○ Does the project go for throughput (i.e. greatest number in shortest period) or client need?

○ How will that be decided? By whom? When?

○ How will the service be marketed to clients/carers, funders, sponsors, volunteers, workers and training agencies?

Know your client group

○ What do you know about your client/user group in terms of their

emotional, physical, educational, developmental, social and recreational needs?
○ How important is such information for any service/care which you intend to offer/provide?
○ How/where can that information be found?
○ Are any related services/statutory agencies useful in this respect?
○ How do you plan to involve the client/carer in the setting of the service provision and the organisation and running of the service?
○ How is choice expressed by clients/carers within the project?
○ What are the benefits you seek for the clients/ carers from the initiative?
○ How do you intend to plan for such benefits to come about as a result of the clients/carers involvement with the project or care initiative?
○ Do you know who you will select or exclude from the project and the basis on which any selection of clients would take place?
○ How far does your project respect the rights and dignity of the clients/carers?
○ Is it important to establish such safeguards for the clients as confidentiality, screening, selection, training of staff, volunteers, complaints and appeals procedures?
○ How will the service safeguard the client's vulnerability without restricting the client's need for personal development, continued growth and the exercise of self-determination?

Conclusion

This is an intimidating list. If you have managed to get to the end, take heart you clearly have perseverance, an essential quality for work in this field. You are not expected to be able to *answer* all these questions, but you do need to realise that each of them has created a problem for at least one of the project workers or support workers who have already been involved in this type of community development. They are therefore well worth your consideration.